THE UNLUCKY VIKING

A SAGA OF SEALING & SHIPWRECKS IN THE SOUTHERN OCEAN

Cathrine Harboe-Ree AM, Anders Harboe-Ree's granddaughter, is an Adjunct Research Associate with the School of Philosophical, Historical and International Studies at Monash University. From 2003 to 2016 she was the University Librarian at Monash, and before that was a Director at the State Library of Victoria.

CATHRINE HARBOE-REE

THE UNLUCKY VIKING

A SAGA OF SEALING & SHIPWRECKS IN THE SOUTHERN OCEAN

A∫P

© Cathrine Harboe-Ree 2023

First published 2023 by
Australian Scholarly Publishing Pty Ltd
7 Lt Lothian St North
North Melbourne, Victoria 3051

tel: 61 3 93296963
enquiry@scholarly.info / www.scholarly.com

ISBN: 978-1-922952-73-8

Cover image: Detail of an illustration by W.G. Wood in an article about the loss of the ship *Cathrine*, *New York Times*, 15 December 1907, p. 51.
Cover design: Lucia Sankovic, Amelia Walker

CONTENTS

The answer to your query as to what people go to seek in that country, and why they fare thither through such great perils is to be sought in man's three-fold nature.

One motive is fame and rivalry, for it is the nature of man to seek places where great dangers may be met, and thus to win fame.

A second motive is curiosity, for it is also in man's nature to wish to see and experience things that he has heard about, and thus to learn whether the facts are as told or not.

The third is a desire for gain; for men seek wealth wherever they have heard that gain is to be gotten, though, on the other hand, there may be great dangers too.

The King's Mirror[*]

---

[*] *The King's Mirror*, 1917, p. 142.

PREFACE

Two paintings hang on a wall of my study in the house where I live in central Victoria, Australia. One, by the Norwegian artist John Paulsen, is a portrait of my paternal grandfather, Anders Harboe-Ree,[*] as an elderly man. Pipe in mouth, he is looking downwards in what appears to be quiet reflection. The other is a very detailed watercolour of a large steamship lying half out of the water, a wreck beached in a cove with distinctive black cliffs rising behind it and rockhopper penguins in the foreground drawing the viewer's eye. Some small timber buildings can be seen on a grassy rise above the rocky shore, to the left of the ship. Painted in the lower right-hand corner the words *Solglimt Bay, Marion Island, 1908. AHR* can just be made out.

Not long before my father's death in Australia in 1989 he received from a nephew living in the Faroe Islands the diary his father – my grandfather – had created in 1906 and 1907,[†] when as a 24- and 25-year-old he was making his first voyage as a ship's captain. The ship, of which he was master and part-owner, was a small two-masted schooner named *Cathrine*,[‡ §] and the voyage was a sealing expedition to the subantarctic

---

[*] Anders was variously referred to, by himself and others, as Anders Ree, Harboe Ree and Harboe-Ree. I use Harboe-Ree, which was what Anders used for most of his life. I refer to him throughout as 'Anders' unless there is a reason to use a more complete or different version of his name.

[†] Part of Denmark, the Faroe Islands lie in the North Atlantic Ocean between Norway, Iceland and Scotland.

[‡] *Cathrine* was always referred to as a schooner, however, using English classification, she was a brigantine, that is, two-masted, fully rigged on the foremast and fore-and-aft rigged on the mizzen.

[§] I was named *Cathrine* after a great-aunt, my grandfather's older sister (Cathrine Thorbjørnsen, née Ree). The ship *Cathrine* already had this name, with its unusual spelling, when my grandfather became its captain and part-owner. At the time it was more common than not for new owners to rename their ships when they took possession of them, so it is possible that my grandfather sought to keep the name because of his fondness for his sister. It is

islands in the Southern Ocean.[*] The diary is not just a record of the weather conditions, the distance covered each day and details about life on board for the fourteen men on the ship, it is also a beautiful artefact, with many watercolours and pen and ink drawings, as well as poems and other creative writing.[†] Largely because I share a name with the ship, but also because of my interest in history, when my father was dying he gave me the diary and other notebooks of my grandfather's and told me that the ship *Cathrine* had been wrecked in the subantarctic on the voyage that generated the diary. He also gave me the painting from Solglimt Bay that he had had in his possession for some time, and told me that my grandfather had painted it after *Cathrine* had been wrecked.

In the years following my father's death my mother and I spent many enthralling hours translating and editing the diary and other material. In parallel with this undertaking, I set about trying to learn more about the shipwreck. Almost immediately I discovered that the ship in the painting from Solglimt Bay was not *Cathrine* at all, but was instead a ship named *Solglimt*, and in this way I learnt that my grandfather had been wrecked not once but twice in the subantarctic: first with *Cathrine* in 1906 on Possession Island, which is one of the islands in the Crozet Islands group, and then with *Solglimt* in 1908 on Marion Island, which is the main island of the group named Prince Edward Islands. It seems that my father had no knowledge of the *Solglimt* wreck. Because he was himself a sailor, it is surprising that he did not realise as soon as he had both the painting and the diary in his possession that the painting, which was of a large

---

possible, therefore, that there is a link between my name and the ship's, but it is also just as possible that there is not.

[*] The name used throughout this book – the Southern Ocean – was not formally adopted until 2000, however it was often referred to by this name prior to that. *Cathrine*'s voyage was to the section of the Southern Ocean south of the Indian Ocean. For the history of the names associated with the Southern Ocean see McCann (2018).

[†] The diary has been lodged with the Vestfold Museum in Norway, and a digital version of it is available through the National Archives of Norway: https://media.digitalarkivet.no/en/view/117212/1.

steamship, could not have been of *Cathrine*, which was a small sailing ship. His failure to appreciate the significance of what he was looking at can be explained in part by the fact that he was not well by the time he received the diary, but it is also clear that my father knew nothing of the second extraordinary event in his own father's life. I was soon to discover that nobody else in the family I was able to consult knew about it either, and nor did they know about most of the other exceptional events I uncovered in my research.

This book is the result of a voyage of my own, a voyage of discovery that has proceeded in fits and starts over three decades. The catalyst was the coincidence of my name being the same as a ship's, but the life I began to uncover was so interesting and dramatic that, like many a person bitten by the history bug, I have been happily sailing in the waters of a time over 100 years ago, albeit from the safety of my desk, exploring pursuits such as sailing, sealing and whaling that had previously been completely foreign to me, imagining what it must have taken to survive two shipwrecks and be a castaway on desolate subantarctic islands, and trying to gain some sort of understanding of a man I was related to but did not know.

You would think that being wrecked twice in the subantarctic was enough excitement for any one man, but my grandfather was a risk-taker and excitement was a feature of his working life. In addition to discovering that there were two shipwrecks, not one, I also discovered that my grandfather became famous for embarking on, and surviving, a daring and perilous rescue mission after the first shipwreck, setting off from the Crozet Islands in a 5.8-metre whaleboat with two of *Cathrine*'s crew members in an attempt to sail 7,300 kilometres across the wild Southern Ocean to reach Australia and thereby get help for the remaining eleven shipwrecked men.* For this he was hailed as a hero and a Viking.

His ambition and entrepreneurial drive were not crushed by the two shipwrecks, despite the toll they must have taken on him, and towards

---

* This is the distance from the Crozet Islands to Melbourne, which for some reason was the target destination, despite Fremantle being over 1,700 kilometres closer.

the end of the First World War he was a pioneer in the use of ocean-going concrete-hulled ships. This endeavour also ended in disaster, albeit of a less thrilling kind, namely, bankruptcy.

For the greater part of his working life – from 1925 to 1939 – my grandfather was a whaler in the oceans surrounding the Antarctic, working on the ships that transformed pelagic, or open sea, whaling.

In 1925 there was a further remarkable episode in his life, a scandalous affair involving the smuggling of liquor into Norway during the Prohibition.

In something of a counterpoint to the excitement and rigours of his working life, my grandfather was also a skilled and productive artist, specialising in woodcarving and creating hundreds of distinctive items throughout his life, particularly in retirement.

What follows, then, is the story, or saga, of my grandfather, Anders Harboe-Ree, an adventurous, uncommonly unlucky modern-day Viking.

CHAPTER 1

SAILING WITH VIKINGS

My mother once told me
She'd buy me a longship,
A handsome-oared vessel
To go sailing with Vikings:
To stand at the stern-post
And steer a fine warship
Then head back for harbour
And hew down some foemen.

Egil's Saga[*]

On 23 August 1906, in beautiful late-summer weather, a small ship named *Cathrine* motored out of the Oslofjord. The ship was bound for the distant Southern Ocean on a sealing expedition and was expected to be away for up to two and a half years. On board were fourteen men, all Norwegians. On the morning of their departure, they had been woken at three o'clock by the sound of rain and the discovery that there were no hops on board for making bread on the long voyage.[†] This delayed their departure, as did the realisation that they were about to set off without a Bismer scale.[‡] With both of these essential items procured in nearby Husøy and Tønsberg,[§] necessitating two separate trips to shore by rowboat, they

---

[*] Magnusson, 2016, p. 9. This is Magnusson's translation of a poem from chapter 20 of *Egil's Saga*.

[†] Hops was used in breadmaking to make yeast.

[‡] A Bismer scale is a weighing device.

[§] Tønsberg, which is on the western side of the Oslofjord and 60 kilometres

were finally ready to leave. The expedition leader's wife and daughter said their farewells and left the ship, marking the beginning of many months of life without female company. With the sun now shining and a light breeze blowing, the anchor was hauled in and they were on their way: 'the whole blue ocean with adventures and experiences before [them] and [their] dear country' receding behind them.[*]

Although this was a modest expedition, it was an adventure for the men on board, only two of whom had any familiarity with the Southern Ocean. One of these was the expedition leader, Henrik Johan Bull,[†] who had acquired the ship, established a company to manage it and raised the funds needed for the voyage. At 61, Bull was embarking on a very risky expedition for anybody, let alone a man his age. He was, however, an Antarctic pioneer and a man of unusual drive who knew from experience something of the risks he would be facing. Although he was Norwegian, he had been working as a businessman in Melbourne in the late 1880s, where he had attempted to mount a commercial and scientific Antarctic expedition. He did not succeed there but, when he returned to Norway, he was able to persuade the famous 84-year-old whaling entrepreneur Svend Foyn,[‡] his uncle by marriage, to finance an expedition to the south. This resulted in the 1893–95 voyage of the ship *Antarctic*,[§] with Bull as the expedition leader and another Norwegian, Leonard Kristensen, as the ship's master. Although this was intended to be both a commercial and a scientific expedition, it was not a commercial success. Nonetheless, it resulted in the first modern landing on the Antarctic mainland and is credited with triggering both Norwegian commercial activity in the Southern Ocean

---

   south of Oslo, was a major national and global whaling centre.

[*] Unless otherwise stated, quotations in this chapter are drawn from Anders Harboe-Ree's diary.

[†] Henrik Johan Bull (1844–1930) is almost always referred to as H.J. Bull.

[‡] Svend Foyn (1809–1894), who introduced the modern harpoon cannon and other innovations, is credited with bringing whaling into the modern era.

[§] Bull, 1896.

and the 'heroic age' of Antarctic exploration,[*][†] in both of which Norway went on to play such an important role.[‡] Bull is also acknowledged in Australia as being one of the small group of men, Ferdinand von Mueller included, who generated the early interest in the southern continent that led eventually to Australia's significant presence there.[§]

While the *Cathrine* expedition was primarily commercial, Bull was aware of the strong scientific interest in the Southern Ocean and Antarctica, and he included in the complement of men the naturalist Johan Koren,[¶] who was the other man on board who had previously ventured to the far south. Although only 27 when he joined the crew of *Cathrine*, Koren was a seasoned Arctic and Antarctic explorer. As a boy he had become passionate about natural history and, when he was 16, he signed on as a sailor on the first of the heroic age Antarctic expeditions, the 1897–99 *Belgica* expedition, which was a purely scientific voyage. The leader was a former Belgian navy officer, Adrien de Gerlache, while the second officer was the Norwegian explorer Roald Amundsen who, in 1911, famously led the first team of men to reach the South Pole in a race against Englishman Robert Falcon Scott. *Belgica* spent over a year south of the Antarctic Circle and was trapped in the ice for an entire winter. While on board *Belgica*, Koren became an assistant to the scientists and spent countless hours dissecting and preserving wildlife. In the years following that voyage, Koren had been exploring Arctic regions and collecting fauna and flora specimens for museums and universities, work he was to continue on the *Cathrine* expedition.

---

* While not fully substantiated, the first actual landing on the Antarctic mainland probably took place in February 1821, when crew from the American sealer *Cecilia*, captained by John Davis, are believed to have gone ashore in what is now Hughes Bay. See Pearson, Zarankin and Salerno, 2020.

† The 'heroic age' of Antarctic exploration, so named, describes the two decades from the final years of the nineteenth century to the Second World War, a period of intense national and individual exploration of the southern continent.

‡ Drivenes and Jølle, 2006, p. 8.

§ McConville, 2007, pp. 143–153, and McConville, 2022, pp. 137–157.

¶ Evjenth, 1938, and other sources.

Cathrine's captain was Anders Harboe-Ree, master for the first time at 24 years of age and part-owner of the ship. Anders was born on 20 October 1881 on a farm called Store Ree, in Stange, which is in the rich farming district of Hedmark in Norway.[*] Store Ree had been owned by his family for hundreds of years, perhaps since the Viking Age, and was a prosperous farm, large by Norwegian standards, of 166 cultivated acres with a further 716 acres of forest and summer pastures. Anders was the third of seven children, and the second son, of Anders Henriksen Stor-Ree and Emma Harboe.

It was unusual for children born in Hedmark to gravitate to the sea. The older brother of Anders, Henrik Waldemar, became a farmer. He took over responsibility of Stor Ree from his mother when he reached maturity, because Anders senior had died in 1898. His younger brother, Birger, also became a farmer briefly, before turning to a military career, and his youngest brother Lorentz became an architect.

Anders was a physically active and restless child. As a boy he was sent to boarding school in Kristiania,[†] where, by his own account, he soon became something of a troublemaker. He was drawn to the sea at a very young age and, despite there being no records of how old he was when he first signed on to a ship, there are unconfirmed accounts of him being as young as 10 or 12.[‡] Nevertheless, he was certainly at sea by the time he was 15. Like a true Viking, he loved the sea, and he was attracted early on to the dangerous but exhilarating world of whaling and sealing, which at that time was largely based in Iceland. Anders referred to this attraction as 'getting blood on the tooth'.[§] He gained his master's certificate in June 1901 from the Kristiania

---

[*] Hedmark was an inland county in Norway until 1 January 2020 when it was merged with another county to form the new county Innlandet. Innlandet is the only county in Norway to have no coastline.

[†] From 1624 to 1877 Oslo was named Christiania. From 1877 to 1925 it was Kristiania, after which the older name Oslo was adopted.

[‡] *The Argus*, 14 February 1907, p. 7, and other sources referring to Anders having been at sea since childhood.

[§] This is a literal translation. It could also have been translated as 'a taste for blood', or 'bloodlust'.

Seamen's School at the age of 19, graduating sixth in a class of sixteen.[*] When on shore in Norway, Anders was a keen skiing competitor.[†]

Little is known of the other eleven men on *Cathrine*, except that all were sailors from the Tønsberg district and most had experienced whaling and/or sealing in the hunting grounds north of Norway. The senior crew members were B.E. Rode,[‡] first mate, David Hansen, second mate, and Thorvald Johansen, bosun. The carpenter was Anton Kristian Pedersen. The roles of steward and cook changed during the course of the voyage. In the beginning Hjalmar Kristiansen was the steward, but the initial cook, Julius Sundset, was also listed as steward/cook, and seaman Hans Lysacker eventually took over these roles. This shuffling of positions signalled difficulties over the course of the voyage, and Anders' views about this bubbled over into public comment about stewards and cooks in the months to come. Of the remaining crew, Lauritz Sorensen was an able seaman, Hans Christian Antonsen was a seaman, Emanuel Thiis was described as 'one of the boys forward' and the one in charge of the engine and, in the records relating to the voyage, the only references to the last of the fourteen crew members, Hjalmar Jensen, are to his name and youth. Some of these crew members went on to play a major role in the adventurous voyage as it unfolded, while others were barely mentioned in the diary Anders wrote or in any of the published accounts or newspaper articles.

The most popular crew member, and certainly the one with the least onerous duties, was Anders' dog, Beef, who was a lively and entertaining companion throughout the voyage and while the men were hunting at the Crozet Islands. Not surprisingly, he became an even greater focus of attention and affection when they were marooned on Possession Island. His

---

[*] *Morgenbladet*, Saturday 13 July 1901, p. 2.

[†] Nowadays we think of skiing as a long-standing, quintessential Norwegian sport, but early in the twentieth century it was still in its infancy. One of its primary advocates was the Norwegian explorer Fridtjof Nansen. Anders' interest in the sport suggests his interest in innovation and its association with Norwegian nationalism.

[‡] Names mentioned here and elsewhere are as complete as possible from the records.

fond master liked to say that his dog was a wonder, the wonder starting at the time of his birth when he was supposed to be a Newfoundland pup but instead proved to be a small mixed-breed dog of indeterminate parentage. His legs appeared to be too short for the length of his body and he had asymmetrical patches of colour on his face. What he lacked in size, bearing and breeding, however, he seemed to have compensated for in intelligence and spirit. Anders had not been sure that it was a good idea to take Beef on this long and potentially dangerous voyage and had considered asking his sister Cathrine to look after the dog, but she was expecting her first child and Anders thought that Beef would be an unnecessary addition to her responsibilities.

Cathrine was a small vessel of 127 tons. She was 29.5 metres long and 7.2 metres wide, and was built in Fanø, Denmark, in 1871 for J.N. Christensen, who christened her *Cathrine*. She changed hands several times and was acquired by Bull from its owner A. Brechlin Andersen & Co of Tønsberg in 1906, by which time she was already equipped for whaling and had been operating in the bottlenose whale fields north of Norway. Bull established a new company, named Cathrine, which was based in Kristiania and managed by his son, Ole Olsen Bull, who was a trader, and another relative, Cornelius Bull, a shipbroker. Capital for the expedition of 36,000 Norwegian kroner (about A$400,000 today) was raised through the sale of thirty-six shares of 1,000 kroner each (A$11,000).* Anders was described as a 'large shareholder' in a newspaper article, but the extent of his holding is unknown. Under the auspices of her

* To provide some indication, albeit flawed, of the value of amounts in the book, they have been converted to a 2022 Australian dollar (AUD) value as follows: Norwegian kroner (NOK): Norges Bank Price Calculator, https://www.norges-bank.no/en/topics/Statistics/Price-calculator-/, accessed 23 January 2023; British pounds (GBP): Bank of England Inflation Calculator, https://www.bankofengland.co.uk/monetary-policy/inflation/inflation-calculator, accessed 23 January 2023; Pre-decimal Australian pound: Reserve Bank of Australia's inflation indicator, https://www.rba.gov.au/calculator/annualPreDecimal.html, accessed 23 January 2023; The exchange rate was taken from Google Finance, https://www.google.com/finance/quote/on 23 January 2023. The estimated amounts have been rounded.

new company, *Cathrine* was additionally fitted out in Norway for a longer expedition to the southern hemisphere. The most important change was the addition of a 20-horsepower auxiliary diesel engine that was intended to provide assistance when there was no wind, or when there were strong headwinds.[*] Bull and Anders planned to be away from Norway for up to two and a half years, hunting in the Southern Ocean then selling the oil and skins from their catch in Melbourne or Buenos Aires. They intended to focus their hunting on the subantarctic islands located in the Southern Ocean, especially the Kerguelen or McDonald islands.[†] The purpose of the expedition to these remote and largely unknown islands was to hunt for seals, especially southern elephant and Antarctic fur seals (*Mirounga leonina* and *Arctocephalus gazella*, respectively), although the ship was also fully equipped for whaling.

In 1906, whaling and seal hunting by Norwegians in the southern hemisphere was in its infancy. These activities had been important industries for Norway in the northern hemisphere for many decades, however, by the early 1900s a collapse in the price of whale oil, in combination with technical advances, led entrepreneurial and adventurous men to turn their attention towards a number of other hunting grounds, including the Southern Ocean, which had not seen whaling or sealing at scale for fifty years or more due in the main to over-hunting by whalers and sealers from North America, Britain, New Zealand and Australia earlier in the nineteenth century. This period with little whaling and sealing activity had allowed stocks of animals to build up, which meant that more efficient hunting could be undertaken in these waters in comparison with other areas. Coincidentally, laws that prohibited whaling and sealing off the coast of Norway came into force in 1904, and some have argued that this

---

[*] Sources: Norwegian newspapers *Norges Sjøfartstidende* and *Kysten*, and the Norwegian Historical Shipping Association, https://www.skipet.no/skip/skipsforlis/1906-1/view, p. 23, accessed 23 January 2023.

[†] Bull may well have considered McDonald Islands as a possible sealing site, but in fact the first landing there did not occur until 1971, and that was by helicopter due to the island's extremely rugged coast.

also encouraged expeditions to seek new hunting fields, including in the south, but this claim is disputed.[*]

Regardless of the factors leading up to it, in the early years of the twentieth century Norwegians were starting to exploit the Southern Ocean for its commercial potential. By 1904 the pioneering Norwegian whaler Carl Anton Larsen had established the whaling station Grytviken at the head of King Edward Cove in South Georgia, and he shipped the first cargo of whale oil produced in the Antarctic to Buenos Aires in February 1905. Interest in Norway in the Southern Ocean accelerated rapidly, in part fuelled by national pride, especially since Norway gained its hard-won independence from Sweden in June 1905. While whaling was the primary interest in the Southern Ocean, sealing was an integral part of hunting in the Southern Ocean and the Antarctic from the outset.

To a modern reader the killing of seals and whales in order to extract their oil seems repulsive, but in the nineteenth and early twentieth centuries this oil played a critical role in many aspects of life. It was used for the manufacture of soap, linoleum and paint, for lubrication, for lighting, in the tanning and textile industries, for tempering steel and for many other purposes. In the mid-nineteenth century, whale and seal oil were being replaced for lubrication and lighting purposes by vegetable oils, and the industry was thought to be in terminal decline. The invention of hydrogenation in 1905 made whale and seal oil central to the production of margarine and soap, and consequently revived the fortunes of the industry.[†] Whale oil was also extremely important in the manufacture of nitro-glycerine for explosives in both world wars, and whale liver oil was a major source of vitamin D through to the 1960s.[‡] Whale and seal products were also used for clothing – seal pelts were in demand in the fur trade for the creation of clothes, especially coats, and whalebone was used in women's garments.

---

[*] Tønnessen and Johnsen, 1982, p. 75.

[†] Ibid., p. 11.

[‡] Encyclopedia Britannica, https://www.britannica.com/technology/whale-oil, accessed 23 January 2023.

The *Cathrine* expedition, with its crew of fourteen on board, was one of the first to set sail to the Southern Ocean from Norway, and so was in the vanguard of several decades of dominant Norwegian sealing and whaling in that part of the world. *Cathrine* was a small ship to be tackling such an undertaking so far from home, however she was typical of the boats from North America that had first plundered the seal populations on the subantarctic islands in the nineteenth century, and that were still to be found there, albeit in much lower numbers. For all of these sealers the waters and islands were very risky, frequently catastrophically so, and the beaches of these islands are littered with wreckage from largely unidentified vessels. At the time *Cathrine* made her voyage in 1906, charting of the islands was still incomplete, and they were to all intents and purposes new lands. That is certainly how Anders viewed his destination: new lands with the lure of riches and promise of adventure.

It took three months for *Cathrine* to reach the Crozet Islands. Although the Kerguelen Islands were the primary destination for the expedition, Bull and Anders decided to investigate the Crozet Islands on the way, as they had to pass close to them anyway.

Life on board the ship was by all accounts very amicable. For the first few weeks the focus was on making as much progress as possible. In addition to sailing duties, the men caught a good supply of fish to supplement their diet. Anders painted and decorated his cabin, put linoleum on the floor, carved a bookshelf and arranged guns and weapons as a feature on the wall. In the daytime he sketched aspects of life on board the ship in his diary, and in the evening he played three-cornered Boston with Bull and Koren.* On Sundays Bull led a service, which Anders recorded as being remarkable for its poor hymn-singing, featuring uneven pitch and individuals singing the wrong words. Anders describes his own performance as being of unwavering seriousness and discordant shouting. Even so, he thought it was good to hear the lovely old melodies ringing out over sunny waters.

---

* Boston is a card game, usually played with four people.

Beef was troubled by the heat when they were in the tropics, and his master kept him on a strict diet of bread and milk in what proved to be a successful attempt to stave off illness. Interestingly, most ocean-going sailing ships had at least one pet on board, often more, to act as vermin hunters and/or companions, and it was not uncommon for captains to be accompanied by their own pets, with which they appeared to form particularly close bonds. One such relationship was that of Captain Sven Eriksson, on the ship *Herzogin Cecilie*, and his Alsatian dog Päik, as recorded by Eriksson's wife Pamela in a book she published about her travels with her husband.* Päik was an aggressive dog that provided security and companionship to his young, apparently insecure master. Another example is that of a different Captain Eriksson, sailing on *L'Avenir*, and his cat Frassie. This pet was so important to the captain that he commissioned a portrait of himself with her and, when she went missing during the voyage, he was so distressed that he lost his appetite for several weeks.†

It is likely that captains found particular solace in their pets. After all, they had sole responsibility for a ship and its crew and cargo for long stretches of time, and they could become very isolated in their roles. Their pets represented all the security and domesticity they went without in order to live the life of a sailor. Anders had just such a close relationship with Beef. In the *Cathrine* diary he makes repeated fond references to his dog. After two months at sea, he wrote: 'Never have I seen or heard about such a little creature as my pretty little dog. Now when I ask him if he is alright, the old dear doesn't hang back – he nods his head, barks and jumps all over me.'

On 11 June, their nineteenth day at sea, Anders was awoken by a terrible crashing sound. The mainsail fastening (halyard) had given way and the sail was lying half in the water. However, the crew managed to salvage the undamaged sail and raise it again. At this stage of the voyage *Cathrine* was carrying a great deal of sail and travelling rapidly south at 7–10 knots.

---

* Mäenpää, 2016.
† Ibid., p. 487.

Sailors are superstitious folk and like to relate stories of strange happenings at sea, and Anders recorded some of the yarns that were told on the voyage. With this incident involving *Cathrine's* mainsail he would have done well to pay heed to the story he recorded about nissens on board ships, and the help or hindrance they can be.[*]

One evening while they were on the Dogger Bank,[†] homeward-bound, the skipper was sitting in his cabin writing. He heard a strange voice calling 'I'm hanging on, captain.' 'Yes, hang on,' said the skipper. Shortly after there was another shout, 'I'm holding on, captain.' 'Yes, hold on, mate,' said the skipper. He thought it was one of the boys having some fun, but he was becoming a little annoyed. Then there was another shout, 'I'm holding on, captain.' 'Yes, you just hold on,' shouted the captain, now quite angry. 'If you get sick of it then let go, dammit.' No sooner had he said this than the whole topgallant rigging came crashing down through the roof of the cabin. Since that time the skipper would have known that he had a nissen on board, because that's who was holding the rigging.

Similarly, a story told by the steward about the perils of injuring birds that rest in the rigging may have resonated with the men on the day, their twenty- seventh at sea, Koren caught and stuffed his first bird, a tired, ordinary barn swallow that had sought to rest in *Cathrine's* rigging.

Aye, the birds have done a lot of good, said the steward, and, because of that, one should leave them in peace when they are tired and want to rest on board. It is a pity and shame to do them any harm, and there are those who have been punished for that, too. I was with a Sandefjord ship once.[‡] We were loaded with salt from Cadiz and were on our way home. In the French Bay,[§] three doves that had probably been blown offshore alighted on the ship. They stayed in the rigging all day. Really pretty birds they were. On board we had a

---

[*] Nissens are Norwegian goblins or leprechauns. In Norwegian singular is 'nissen' and plural is 'nisse'. I have Anglicised this to singular 'nissen' and plural 'nissens'.

[†] A large sandbank in the North Sea about 100 kilometres off the east coast of England.

[‡] Sandefjord is on the western side of the Oslofjord, 92 kilometres from Oslo.

[§] The Bay of Biscay.

deckhand who was from the north of Norway. He was a short-tempered bloke. He fought and drank on land and was nasty and unpleasant when in a foul mood at sea. So, he was not liked forward or aft. When he saw those birds, a real gleam came into his eye. He would get those in the evening, he said. I asked him what he wanted them for, but he just laughed at me.

Aye, just you look out, I warned him, because it has gone very badly before for those who have caught tired birds at sea. But the chap from the north of Norway only laughed and declared that he didn't believe in old wives' talk. He probably just had a lust to kill.

When the evening came the birds settled down to sleep in the rigging. One sat on the flying jib boom, one on the backstay on the mizzen mast and one right up on the cross tree. The northlander crept stealthily out along the jib boom like a cat and put his cap over the dove so that she fell into the sea and floated aft along the side. It was bad to see, and I begged him to leave the other two in peace. But no, he made his way up through the rigging and got hold of the one that sat on the backstay on the mizzen mast. He cracked her head on the boom and threw her to the deck.

'Look out now, Olaf,' I shouted up to him, but I saw that he was going up through the topgallant stays. I did not want to watch such awful things any longer, and so I went down into the galley. Immediately I heard a dreadful cry from up in the rigging, and when I looked up through the skylight in the galley roof, I saw Olaf come tumbling head over heels down through the rigging. I saw clearly that he hit his head hard against the backstay on the mizzen mast, just where he had killed the second dove. And then he came crashing headfirst into the deck just near the foremast. The whole of his head was smashed to pulp. 'What a terrible story,' said the cook. He thought about the little bird he had caught near the Cape Verde Islands. Good thing he had let it go.

These sailors' tales did not deter Koren, whose only purpose for being on the voyage was to procure specimens, albeit those more interesting than an ordinary barn swallow. Later in the voyage his attempts to capture albatrosses provided many hours of entertainment for the men.[*]

____

* It is likely that Anders would have seen several species of albatross on his

After a week in the doldrums the ship was visited by Neptune, whose task it was to ritually humiliate those sailors who had not previously crossed the equator and to give them permission to do so, as was the custom on all ships. Five of the men were subjected to Neptune's attentions, and Anders' diary was given over to pages and pages of a 'newspaper' created to mark the occasion, featuring drawings, paintings, poems and witticisms. Bull declared that 'this newspaper will, to a most important degree, veer from the usual papers with their straight, boring lines meant to assist a landlubber keep to a straight line. Our *Linepaper* … will be substituted here by many coloured curved lines to indicate the curvy forms of mermaids, mergods and mergoddesses.'* Readers were advised that copies of the paper could be obtained for a piratical price from the publisher.

It was at this stage of the voyage that Koren's efforts to capture birds started in earnest, as did the humour directed at his efforts. He fashioned a number of traps designed to ensnare birds, starting with the simplest approach of bait on a fishing line. He then progressed to a device that trailed behind the boat. His intention was to shoot birds, hoping they would fall into the water and be caught up in the trailing device. When this failed, he added sailcloth and wire, but the addition of these elements, together with the nails that were used to attach them, meant that the device simply sank when lowered into the water. It was some time before Koren began to have any success in catching birds. His first was a cape dove that had managed to ensnare itself in a line dangling from the ship, but the first albatross was caught by the carpenter, not by Koren. It had a 3.25-metre wingspan and weighed about 12 kilograms. Anders felt pity for the birds that were being so actively hunted, but he was a pragmatist and welcomed the addition to their diet. This was not the case with the crew, who expressed their dislike of albatross meat by heaving the carcasses overboard. Despite Anders' evident affection for Koren, he did tire of his

---

voyages south, however the most common, and the only one photographed and described in the accounts of these voyages, is the mighty wandering albatross, *Diomedea exulans*.

* The word 'line', in '*Linepaper*', is a play on crossing the line, or equator.

fellow traveller's obsession with birds, to the extent of wondering if his descendants would multiply by laying eggs. He was also prompted to write several poems mocking Koren, including this:

> *There flew a storm swallow under our stern,*
> *There flew one, there flew three, there flew twenty;*
> *When Koren saw them he was quite struck,*
> *And swore he would capture a'plenty.*
> *So off went he with industrious haste,*
> *His own patent he set to inventing;*
> *Alas, this was an illusion that burst,*
> *And now you'll hear of his experimenting.*

The crossing-the-line festivities and the beautiful tropical weather created a buoyant mood on board the ship. This buoyancy was checked slightly by the incapacity of the steward, but carried through to Bull's sixty-second birthday on 13 October. He was woken in his berth with a coffee tray and then presented with the many gifts that had been given to Anders to keep for the day. Among these was a mahogany framed portrait of King Haakon VII, who by that stage had been in the role for a little over a year following Norway's independence from Sweden. There was also a telegram from the King and the Prime Minister, which read 'Mr. H.J. Bull, leader of the expedition, our benign eyes are resting on you'. In honour of the birthday, they ate ptarmigan ragout, and the steward had baked a fruit cake and sponge for the occasion. The birthday toast was done with gooseberry wine, and the crew got a dram and a cigar each. The Norwegian flag flew from the mainmast, and Anders reflected on the remarkable age of the man who was actively leading a Southern Ocean expedition.

On 20 October Anders celebrated his twenty-fifth birthday, in similar vein to Bull's birthday a week earlier. He received a large parcel from his friends in Tønsberg, including a children's mug with 'GOOD BOY' inscribed on it, and a rattle and a doll in a tiny bathtub. On a more serious note, he received a telegram from Queen Maud saying, 'Follow our heed, be noble in deed'. These messages from the royal family indicated the ground-breaking nature of this expedition, coming as it did so soon after Norway had attained independence. But the best birthday present Anders received that day, he thought, was a good, driving breeze. He was keen to get to their destination as soon as possible and was pleased with the way *Cathrine* was performing. Bull was not so sure. He was concerned that Anders was sailing too recklessly. With the benefit of hindsight, we can see that this may well have been the case, while it may also have been an early intimation that Bull was a nervous passenger.

The bonhomie on the ship may give the impression that these were fourteen men off on a jolly jaunt but, as the days grew colder and the sea rougher, the serious task of preparing for the hunt began. The carpenter forged long-handled seal picks and others cleaned and prepared weapons and made stretchers of light coppiced pine and sailcloth to carry the skins and blubber. To prepare the men for the hunt Anders organised a shooting competition and was very pleased with the accuracy of some of the shooting. He led the prize-giving ceremony with a flippant speech thanking the men for travelling so far to participate in the competition, and he gave awards for the best and worst shooting. The winner, the bosun, received ten cigars. A medal inscribed 'Sic transit gloria mundi' went to the cook, who had managed to miss the target with all ten of his shots.

On their sixty-first day at sea, two of the men had a vigorous fight and Anders had to step in to separate them. He was a strong man and enjoyed this assertion of his authority. He was also not displeased to see the men's aggression, as he thought that it was an indication that they would apply themselves well when killing seals. However, as a counterpoint to this very masculine behaviour, on the evening of the fight Anders again recorded in his diary great affection for his 'pretty little dog', which he said needed little encouragement to return his affection.

Cathrine was performing beyond expectations in the windier conditions. They were recording 10 and 11 knots, although they had to cope with significant rolling of the ship. They tied down loose objects and struggled to eat with any finesse. Beef, too, found the conditions difficult and was off colour. Anders wrote a poem about the heaving, butting and rolling of the ship, the merry larks of the knives, plates and saucers, the mate falling from his stool and the skipper spilling food on his trousers. The poem ends by declaring that this was both satisfying and tiring. They did, after all, have a destination to reach, and for most of them, the sooner the better.

On the sixty-ninth day at sea they had their first real experience of the might of the Southern Ocean when *Cathrine* was chased down and passed by the biggest wave Anders had ever seen. He was at the helm when the second mate came running and shouted, 'Watch out, Captain!' Anders turned and saw the foaming crest of a tremendous wave rise up over the railing and high above him. As it came thundering down Anders took a firm grip of the wheel and waited for the deluge, expecting the wave to sweep the cabin overboard. Fortunately, at the last minute, *Cathrine* lifted her stern in the air, and the wave, mighty as it was, went underneath the ship. This wave reminded Anders of the first time he had seen New York skyscrapers, although those were man-made and stationary, and not at all threatening. He recalled reading a scholarly article that claimed, improbably, that waves cannot be higher than 10 metres, and that they are stationary. As the men on board watched the wave thunder past them to the east they were under no illusion whatsoever that it was stationary. As to the height, buoys in the Southern Ocean nowadays have monitored some waves almost 20 metres high, and waves commonly 10 metres and higher.

More worryingly, and the cause of some sleepless nights, Anders and the first mate were having difficulty with the compasses on board, with variations significant enough to require the factoring in of a four-degree declination error.* To check the compasses they altered their course towards

---

* 'Magnetic declination, sometimes called magnetic variation, is the angle between magnetic north and true north. Declination is positive east of true north and negative when west. Magnetic declination changes over time and with location. As the compass points with local magnetic fields, declination value is needed to obtain true north.' From https://www.ngdc.noaa.gov/ geomag/declination.shtml, accessed 18 October 2022.

the Cape of Good Hope until they could see land, and were pleased to find that their calculations were accurate and they could proceed with confidence. Anders and his officers were not the first northern hemisphere sailors to be thrown by the declinations in the southern hemisphere, which were different from those they were familiar with.

For two months they saw no other ships, so there was great excitement when a ship was finally spotted off the starboard bow. The members of the crew were given time off to write letters, and three hours later Anders rowed over to the barque *Dagmar of Lillesand*, together with a case of cigars in lieu of postage. The ship was en route to Port Adelaide from Cape Town, under the command of a Norwegian captain, Danielsen, who proved to be a man of few words and a poor host, offering Anders only bitter schnapps to drink. Danielsen was anxious about presenting the letters to the consul in Adelaide without money for postage, so Anders wrote out a bill to cover the costs, despite the gift of a case of cigars. Not surprisingly, Anders was unimpressed and he returned to his own ship as soon as he could.

The cruising part of *Cathrine*'s voyage was coming to an end, with the hunting fields they were seeking drawing ever nearer.

CHAPTER 2

THE NEW LAND LAY BEFORE THEM

Come, my friends,
'Tis not too late to seek a newer world.
Push off, and sitting well on order smite
The sounding furrows; for my purpose holds
To sail beyond the sunset …

Alfred, Lord Tennyson, *Ulysses*[*]

As they closed in on their first destination, the Crozet Islands, Bull and Anders both became anxious. They were now more than 44 degrees south and were having trouble interpreting their compass readings again, as the magnetic declination varied from what they were expecting. They also experienced their first Southern Ocean storm and were grateful for their warm bedding. Anders took delight in a fur rug that his mother had given him, which Beef was allowed to share once he had been washed in a solution of carbolic acid to kill his fleas.

The main destination for the expedition was the Kerguelen Islands group, which Bull had visited in his earlier voyage on *Antarctic*. Because they had to pass near to the Crozet Islands, which were reputed to carry large numbers of elephant seals, they decided to call there first. The Crozet Islands were discovered by Marc-Joseph Marion du Fresne aboard *Le Mascarin* in 1772, and were named after his second-in-command, Jules (Julien-Marie) Crozet. The islands are included in the group of subantarctic islands sprinkled around the Antarctic on or near the Antarctic Convergence. This

---

[*] Tennyson, *Poems*, 1842.

is where the cold water from the Antarctic meets the warmer waters from the north, creating vertical currents that bring nutrients to the surface of the ocean and provide a rich source of food for animals and birds, which in turn become a source of food for other species. Thus, these islands are home to immense colonies of birds and seals during the breeding and moulting seasons. The subantarctic islands offer the only land in the vast area of ocean between the Antarctic continent and Africa, Australia and South America.

The Crozet Islands are five small islands and a number of rocks and shoals sitting on top of a volcanic plateau, 45°57' to 46°29'S and 50°10' to 52°19'E. They are mere dots in the ocean, almost 3,000 kilometres from South Africa and 7,300 from Australia, buffeted by the persistent winds of the Roaring Forties that frequently develop into ferocious storms. These winds, working on the unfettered body of water that sweeps around the Antarctic continent, produce mighty waves that batter the islands, especially on their west. The average air temperature ranges from 7.9°C in summer to 2.9°C in winter, and it rains, sleets or snows on most days, with clear weather being a rare occurrence.

Like all of the subantarctic islands, the Crozet Islands are notorious for being fog-bound, the result of northerly air cooling near the Antarctic Convergence. As *Cathrine* approached the islands they were true to their reputation. To make matters worse, the bearings shown by the ship's compasses were wildly at variance with other indications as to their true bearings. Bull became concerned that Anders was a poor navigator, and Anders was not confident himself. On Friday 23 November, the navigation charts were suggesting that they should be near land, in around 180 metres of water. In thick fog, they took soundings but could not reach the bottom. Nonetheless, Anders was convinced that if the fog lifted they would be able to see land and so he posted crew members on lookout at several points on the ship and promised a dram for the first to sight land.

Suddenly the men shouted – land had been spotted right on their lee bow. All the men got a welcome dram, and Anders felt as happy as

Christopher Columbus must have been when he found the West Indies. The new land lay before them. They had arrived at Hog Island, a 67-square-kilometre island with mountains rising precipitously from the sea to 770 metres. They tacked during the night to avoid both Hog Island and the nearby jagged Apostle Islets, and Bull became increasingly nervous, thinking that any sudden movement might mean that the ship had hit a rock. In daylight they could see that any landings on the island would be impossible, so they decided to steer a course for Possession Island, another of the islands in the Crozet group, where they knew there were better harbours. While they were weighing anchor, they lost one of the best ones when the chain snapped, and they managed, by the skin of their teeth, to avoid hitting a nearby reef. They were learning quickly that the Crozet Islands were not welcoming to ships. Even so, Anders was tempted by the sight of beaches on Hog Island covered with elephant seals, but Bull was against any hunting there. In truth, the young skipper did not need much persuading to move on to Possession Island.

The largest of the Crozet group, Possession Island lies at 46°25'S and 51°00'E. Like most of the other subantarctic islands in the Southern Ocean, they are volcanic in origin and are bleak, wind-swept and mountainous. Possession Island itself is 150 square kilometres and has mountains rising majestically to 934 metres. Many ships have been shipwrecked on its shores, including seven sealers between 1804 and 1911 and several passenger ships.

In lovely clear weather, reminiscent of the conditions when she had motored out of the Oslofjord almost exactly three months earlier, *Cathrine* glided into American Bay and reconnaissance began at once. Thousands of animals lying on the beaches greeted *Cathrine*'s crew, enough to fill the ship with a full load of seal oil and seal pelts for fur. The new arrivals came across places where seal and whale hunters had lived decades earlier. A hut had blown down and its remains were strewn about. There were three iron boilers, which would have been used for boiling the blubber to produce oil. The men saw evidence of shipwrecks, including one wreck high off the beach and covered in sand, with chain sections, bolts, copper plates and other debris lying around. In case they needed further evidence of the dangers of these waters, they discovered a graveyard on a weather-beaten spot on a small rise. The graves were enclosed by a fence made from barrel staves. The memorial plaques on the wooden crosses marking two of the graves were still legible and identified the men as young whalers who had lost their lives there in the 1860s, one from Prussia and one from Iceland.* Another reminder of danger was a depot for shipwrecked sailors put on the island by the British government in the 1880s. The building had blown away and all the stores were strewn about, rusty and spoiled. There were rats in abundance. Nobody had visited the island in decades.

A flock of penguins had settled into the lee of the graves. When Anders sat down to photograph them one came over to him, quite unafraid, and stood for a while seemingly in deep reflection about what sort of creature it had before it. It quacked, turned round, went over to three of its companions, chatted for a while with them, then all four came back to inspect him. When Anders clicked the camera, it looked as though the penguins were laughing, but unfortunately the film had become moist and that and other photographs of this new land were unsuccessful. These would have been the first photographs ever from the Crozet Islands.

The beaches and hinterland were packed not only with seals, but also with birds, penguins of various sorts, and many other species. Koren was beside himself and over-zealously shot so many birds that he was asked to restrain himself. One day he disappeared on the island and came back so heavily laden with birds he could barely walk. He had no idea that the crew had returned to the ship and then had to come back for him. Inevitably, Beef the dog was also over-stimulated by this environment and chased penguins and barked like crazy at the seals, which paid him no attention until he bit the tail of a cub and was forced to make a rapid retreat when it turned on him and roared.

Anders was excited by the riches he saw before him and by the

---

* Prussia was a German state located on the southeast coast of the Baltic Sea.

imminent hunting. Although he recognised the brutality of sealing, and acknowledged that the seals, which had no fear of humans, were relatively easy pickings, he had developed a taste for hunting during his first whaling experiences north of Norway and was energised by his chosen profession. Above all, he was hoping to make his fortune.

On the first full day's hunting they killed sixty-nine seals, mostly small, and filled four whaleboats with skins and blubber to take back to the ship, which lay anchored in the bay.* The animals were killed on the beach. They were then skinned; the meat was cut off the skin and then the blubber was cut into pieces. On the ship the men slid the blubber straight into the burners in the hold, where the oil was rendered for transport, and the skins were salted down to preserve them.

This was hard work and the animals, although they did not attempt to escape or defend themselves, were still difficult to kill. One of the animals Anders shot on their first day on the island was a large bull elephant seal, probably a beach master attempting to protect its harem, that rose on its flippers with a dreadful bellow. Anders fired an explosive bullet between the animal's eyes and an ugly red fountain of blood spurted several metres into the air.† This did not kill the seal, which then came lumbering towards Anders, who retreated in fear and shot it in the throat. It fell and looked to be dead but, when he approached, it rose up again. Anders shot it twice more, and Bull also shot it several times, so that the animal had eight to ten spurts of blood pouring out of its head and flowing into the ocean. The seal made its way into the water and could be seen from time to time with thick blood still streaming out of it. After this experience, to optimise the chances of a successful kill, the men first shot the seals between the eyes and then several others would attack the injured beast with lances. Even so, if a supposedly dead animal was left overnight, it was likely to have

---

* Bull elephant seals can grow up to 4.9 metres, weigh up to 4 tons and yield up to 100 litres of oil.

† The explosive, or expanding, Remington bullets used were designed to expand rapidly on impact and inflict the maximum possible damage, thereby improving the chances of killing the animals quickly.

disappeared by the following day, which suggested that it was not actually dead when they left it. To avoid this wastage, from then on they only killed animals that could be skinned on the same day.

As they went about their slaughter, the beach was teeming with birds gorging on the carcasses of the dead seals. Many of the birds on the islands were predators or scavengers, so this bloodbath, which none of them would have witnessed before, was a great gift to them.

The hunting was not unaffected by the notoriously capricious weather. For several days they experienced a tremendous storm, with hurricane-like winds, the sea in a fury and *Cathrine* rolling in the heavy sea and straining at her anchor chains. Anders was anxious and feared that the chains would snap, and Bull was opposed to shore trips when the storm had settled but the wind was still blowing a gale and the sea was high. He was concerned that the normal slackening and stretching of the chains was an indication that the ship was adrift. By this stage of the expedition Anders had come to the conclusion that Bull was not suited to the ever-present dangers on a sealing or whaling vessel. Whatever their state of mind, the men all took comfort from their cosy quarters and the presence of the Norwegian flag flying on the Crozet Islands. This provided a touch of home and domesticity in dangerous waters far from their native land.

Anders, excited by the huge numbers of animals on the island, started making ambitious plans. He thought of hiring a 2,000-ton steamer, hiring thirty to forty men, and returning for a more secure hunt than was possible with their small ship, *Cathrine*, which was difficult to manoeuvre and was dependent for the most part on her sails. He had in mind including a winch to transfer the skins in nets and haul them on board, avoiding the difficult and dangerous process of manhandling the skins through the rough surf to the whaleboats, which was what they had had to do on this expedition. With a stronger ship they would be able to load in any weather, and bigger holds would allow them to bypass the need to cut the blubber and meat off the skin. Instead of sailing with the wind to offload in Melbourne or Buenos Aires, both weeks away from the islands, in ten days they would be able to steam to Cape Town, where their catch would be processed. Anders calculated the likely return on this more ambitious plan, concluding that, taking all costs into account, a single hunting expedition could see a one hundred per cent profit, or 180,000 kroner (about A$2,000,000). This would be at least four and a half times the profit likely to be made on this expedition – and with much less danger. This ambitious and energetic young man was frustrated by the slowdowns caused by the weather and had begun to lose faith in the whole venture.

Towards the end of November, Anders thought they would be fully loaded by Christmas, and his spirits had improved. By now their hunting had been honed. They had learned that the most effective way to kill seals was to shoot them in the eye, and their processes were more efficient, but they were bothered by the miserable, cold weather. The driving rain, sleet and snow resulted in everybody having sores on their hands, and Anders became a doctor every evening, trying different remedies to deal with them. He found that applying naphthalene helped. Despite the weather, they were trying to remain healthy, supplementing their diet with seal and penguin meat, but unfortunately found that the native cabbage plant, a valuable source of vitamin C, was too bitter to eat.[*]

On 1 December the ocean demonstrated its power again by overturning one of the whaleboats when it was hauled up onto the beach, threatening to drag it out to sea. In strong wind and rough waves, the men struggled to right the heavy and cumbersome boat. The bailer had disappeared when the boat was overturned, so they had to bail it out using their boots. With only two other whaleboats, they desperately needed to save this one, which they just managed to do.

This episode was, however, trivial in comparison with what followed.

---

[*] The Kerguelen cabbage, *Pringlea antiscorbutica*, belongs to the cabbage family and grows on several of the subantarctic islands, including the Crozet Islands.

CHAPTER 3

COOPED UP ON AN ISLAND

> *Here I am, cooped up on an island far too long.*
> *With no way out of it, none that I can find,*
> *While my spirit ebbs away. But you tell me –*
> *You immortals know it all – which one of you*
> *Blocks my way here, keeps me from my voyage?*
> *How can I cross the swarming seas and reach home at last?*
>
> Homer, *The Odyssey**

On Sunday 3 December, it being a day of rest, Anders and the crewman Thiis went for a long walk on the island and returned to the ship late in the day as a ferocious easterly wind was developing. American Bay is unprotected from the east, where it is totally exposed to the full ocean. The men knew that their ship was at risk from easterly winds at its anchoring site, but winds from this direction were rare and, for the sake of expedience, they had chosen to moor as close as possible to their hunting sites.

Despite being exhausted from his long trek, Anders turned his attention to the threat they now faced. Setting the sails in an attempt to sail out of danger would almost certainly have resulted in the ship running aground on the nearby reefs, and the motor was not powerful enough to make headway against winds of such force. Their only course of action was to let out more chain and put a drogue on the strongest chain, and they used the motor to try to lighten the knocks from the sea.[†]

---

* Homer, 1996, 4.524–29, p. 139.

† A drogue is a device used to slow a boat down in a storm or prevent the hull

25

By ten o'clock at night the wind had risen to a full storm and the sea had grown huge, hurling monstrous waves over the bow of the ship. Suddenly the port anchor chain snapped, leaving them with only their starboard anchor. Anders called together the ship's council – the most senior and experienced men on board – and suggested that one of the whaleboats should be used to take some of the crew to shore. The council decided, however, that all the crew should remain on board and they should closely monitor the weather.

The storm increased as night fell.[*] All hands had their lifebelts ready and were prepared to battle the elements. Anders noticed that Bull had put on his lifebelt and was checking the barometer and compass in the cabin whenever the wind gusted. He felt pity for the older man. The nervous tension was almost unbearable; more than one crew member said that it would be a relief if the anchor chains broke and the ship was thrown onto the reef. At least that would resolve their situation.[†]

It was hard to believe that the remaining chain held, despite the shuddering jolts it had to withstand, but it did. The ship, however, was drifting, and even in the dark they could see that they were a mere two ship's lengths from a reef. They held a second ship's council. The first mate and Bull wanted to release the anchor and try to get the hull beached and pour oil on the water to settle the waves. Anders respected the first mate's experience and views but he was against this action, believing that the likelihood of saving lives would be very small, given the undertow that raged close to shore.

The second mate came running to report that the hawsehole had gone.[‡] Anders rushed to check, but discovered that only part of it had been damaged, and so he had to hope that the remaining section would continue to function. Some thought the rigging should be cut, but Anders

<hr>

from being side-on to the waves.

[*] At this location, on this day, the sun would have risen at 4.10 am and set at 8.29 pm. See www.calculatorsoup.com/calculators/time/sunrise_sunset.php.

[†] Evjenth, 1938, p. 120.

[‡] The hawsehole is the hole in the ship through which the anchor chain runs.

was against that idea because he was afraid that the rope would become caught in the propellor and the propellor shaft would then break. He thought their only option was to try to wait out the storm. He also prayed, which was something he did not often do.

In the grey morning light a heavy shower of rain came and, with that, the wind leapt abruptly to the northwest and then gradually to the west. They felt a glimmer of hope, but the sea became terribly turbulent with the sudden change of wind. As rain began to fall, the waves subsided a little, but they were still in huge seas and were unable to move away from their perilous position. Anders reflected on this dreadful night, wondering whether or not he felt afraid for his life. He trusted his strength and thought he would probably have made it to shore somehow, but he shuddered at the thought of being a castaway on this desolate island, perhaps for years, because it was rarely visited by ships. During the night, standing in the dark and cold and thoroughly wet through, he found himself humming a comic negro song,[*] and wondered at the workings of the mind. He also thought about his family at home in Norway.

Anders attempted to reassure the crew. He spoke encouragingly to them and told them that, however bad it was then, it was still much better than if they were to be shipwrecked out at sea. They had the island nearby, and perhaps it would be possible to reach it when it became light.[†] Bull admired Anders' handling of the crisis, saying later that he was 'the very picture of ease and tranquillity, … [giving] orders in his usual quiet and easy way'.[‡]

In the middle of the following night Anders was woken by the man on watch and told that the wind had turned to the east again and was rising. They attempted to set sail, but it was impossible. They were drifting slowly towards the reef again, and the decision was made to put a boat ashore with half of the men. Anders resolved to stay on board as long as there was a splinter of the ship left. He recorded in his diary that

---

* Anders used the word 'negro'. This word is now unacceptable.
† Evjenth, 1938, p. 120.
‡ *New York Times*, 15 December 1907, p. 50.

should he not be able to save his own life, there were six siblings at the farm Store Ree who would be able keep up the family traditions, and he asked those at home to send greetings to a person he chose not to name, with the comment that they would know whom he meant. In what might have been his final message to his family, he said that, if he were to go under, he would be at his post to the last, and that he was quite calm and content – in a way.

Their chances of survival were miniscule. The sea was breaking dreadfully over the reefs astern and the storm was raging and growing in strength. Six of the fourteen men, including Bull, the second mate, the naturalist, Koren, the steward, an able seaman and a deckhand scrambled into one of the whaleboats, taking with them just the most essential clothes and food, and rowed off into the stormy sea. Those left on board saluted them by raising the flag (which, unfortunately, was hoisted upside down) and then kept an anxious watch on their six shipmates in the boat. In their small boat the men struggled against the wind and surf and at times disappeared completely from view in the troughs of the waves, but eventually they could be seen making land and dragging the heavy boat far enough on shore to secure it.

Anders asked the remaining men if they would like to go ashore in one of the boats, but they all chose to stay to try to help save the ship. Each was fortified with a dram and then they faced the storm again. With great difficulty they lowered one of the remaining whaleboats down into the water and manoeuvred it around to *Cathrine*'s lee side where it was raised again and put in the blocks, ready in case they needed to abandon ship. To achieve this seaman Hans Antonsen had jumped fearlessly into the boat, which many times stood vertically and pulled violently on the slender hunting line holding the boat to the ship. According to Anders, Antonsen stood at the rudder as calmly as if this was just an ordinary embarkation and steered while the other men hauled the boat into position. Close astern, the sea was breaking. If the rope had snapped, the boat would have disappeared, complete with its brave occupant.

They were taking frequent soundings and realised that they were drifting inexorably towards the reef. Anders gave the order to cut the rig and grabbed an axe. The bosun leapt up into the rigging to rig a hook onto a boom, and Anders stood ready by the harpoons. But then the ship shuddered violently and dipped in her stern, and Anders shouted to the men to get into the whaleboat. Seven men threw into the boat what they could readily find and were swiftly on board themselves. Anders stood by to lower the boat. The mate called on him to join them, but Anders said he would stay with the ship. The mate responded by saying that he would also stay, and then all the men said they would, too, so Anders then relented and joined them in the boat, and together they cast off into the furious sea. They were dragged into dense kelp near the reefs, could not get traction with their oars, and struggled to make headway, but by facing the boat's bow into the wind they were able to free themselves from the kelp, bit by bit, and slowly advanced towards the shore, rowing like men possessed. Without warning, a huge wave lifted the boat high and threw it well up onto the beach. The men leapt out and dragged the boat even higher to clear it from the waves.

And so they were all saved. They were, however, ashore on a barren, uninhabited island thousands of kilometres from civilisation, without a house, in the cold, rain and sleet. Anders walked over to a small cave where Bull was sheltering and was met by an excited Beef, who had gone ashore in the first boat. For Anders, this reunion was a little ray of sunshine in an otherwise catastrophic situation.

The fourteen men sat and watched *Cathrine* go under. They could see that she was low in the water. She floated for a while on the blubber in the boilers, but soon her stern dropped, and they saw steam and smoke issuing from the engine as the seawater engulfed it. For a while the rig swayed backwards and forwards, but then the ship snapped in two. Pieces of it could be seen flying in the air, the main mast with its flag broke off, the foremast came crashing down and the boilers tore loose and floated off. In less than ten minutes the ship – their home, their transport, their security and the means of achieving their dreams – was just a heap of wreckage.

They had been able to save very little. They had two of their boats, the ship's logbook, some woollen blankets, a small amount of clothing, a roll of canvas, a rifle with 200 cartridges, five tins of butter, some cookware and matches. The crew were sent off immediately to salvage as much of the wreckage as possible. Most of it had drifted past the bay where they had landed into a small bay to the east that they could only get to with great difficulty because of the loose scree on the steep approaches. On this first foray most of what they salvaged was of little value. Anders had sent some of his clothes, a blanket and some tobacco in a chest with the first boat, but most of his things were lost in the wreck.

When darkness descended that night some of the crew sheltered from the cold and rain under one of the boats, which they had upturned. Others sat in the open, exposed to the bitter weather. Bull lay in his bedding in the little cave, and Anders sat at its entrance, wet, cold, and shivering so much that his teeth chattered. Bull offered to share his blankets, but Anders declined, saying 'I am young, but you are old, and I can manage without'.[*] Every so often he got up and ran a little, trying to get a bit warmer. At daybreak they all shared some bread and tinned milk that the steward had packed onto the first boat, and then they were off again to salvage whatever wreckage they could find. This time they were luckier, as a lot more had come ashore during the night. They found good clothes and salvaged tins of butter, a tub of salted fish, three drums of oil and wood. They hauled everything up as high as possible to prevent it being carried out to sea again. They could see the cabin and scullery intact on the reef, but they could not get to it because the sea was still rising high from the east.

For dinner they had fried penguins on a spit, using one of the boilers left by earlier sealers as a fireplace. They also tried some corned beef and bread from the depot that had been left decades earlier for shipwrecked sailors. The penguin tasted good and the corned beef was passable. The bread, however, was spoilt and they ate it only out of necessity. They made

* Ibid.

sweetened tea from tea in boxes from the depot. Anders declared that he could not tell if it was tea or rat poison.

They hauled the two boats together, tilted them against the mountainside and covered them with wet peat and a strip of sailcloth. These boats were to be the castaways' accommodation for the next ten days, with the exception of Bull, who continued to sleep in the cave. The men spent the evening huddled together for warmth and were generally in good spirits. Despite the fact that his plans had come to naught, and they were stranded on the island, Bull managed to appear cheerful. Anders told sailors' yarns. He recorded in his diary that one of the crew – an able seaman – had behaved like an old woman during the shipwreck. This criticism of a crew member who, Anders felt, had not risen to the occasion during the crisis, was a small matter at the time, but it showed that Anders had little tolerance for those who, in his opinion, lacked courage. As we shall see, this was subsequently to prove a major issue for him.

The sea had settled somewhat overnight and they were able to row out to the reef to salvage what they could. Unfortunately, however, all the food that was not in sealed containers was ruined by exposure to the kerosene that covered the surface of the ocean all around the ship. For breakfast on their second day as castaways on Possession Island they had 'bread soaked in sea water, flavoured with kerosene and mixed with no small quantity of fine, flying sand from the beach, and the ashes from the open fireplace, mixed together with plenty of corned beef',* which tasted dreadful, but the men ate it anyway. Over the coming days they found a great deal of food and clothing that they were able to get ashore in good condition, all their ammunition, four more Remington rifles, two lamps (which they could use with seal fat) and a great deal of other useful material. Their main diet became penguin, morning, midday and evening. Anders declared that the soup made from these birds was delicious.

It took ten days for the carpenter, with help from others, to construct a hut out of salvaged material, mainly timber and sailcloth, and seal skins

____

* Ibid.

and peat. It was lined with moss and sailcloth and, although not completely watertight, felt like a palace to the men after their makeshift shelter in the upturned boats. They recovered a stove from the wreck and erected it in the middle of the hut. It smoked dreadfully and only managed to take the edge off the pervasive cold, so they all slept fully clothed. There was no fuel on the island, but they expected the salvaged timber to last a good while. To entertain themselves and to keep their spirits up, in the evenings they played 'My ship is laden with …' and other games,* performed match tricks and played ball on the sandy beach.

Cathrine was not the first ship to fall victim to the capricious weather and ferocious seas battering the rocky, inhospitable Crozet Islands. The evidence of this had been all around the men as they hunted the seals. History has not recorded many of these wrecks, but in June 1875, in the pitch black of night and in heavy fog, the Scottish clipper *Strathmore*, en route to New Zealand, struck a reef on the tip of Grand Island, the most northerly of the Crozet Islands, and was immediately wrecked. *Strathmore* had been built in response to the immigration demand and on this, her maiden voyage, she was carrying fifty passengers and cargo, including casks of cement, crates of earthenware, casks and cases of spirits, 623 tons of iron goods, 145 tons of railway iron, and kegs of gunpowder. In the chaos of the night half the passengers and crew were drowned, including the six second-class passengers who were unable to get out of their cabin and drowned in their bunks. The captain, Charles Macdonald, was amongst those who drowned that night. Forty-seven men, a two-year-old boy, named Walter Walker, and one female passenger and her son survived the wreck. One of the survivors appeared crazed and died just days later. Another died after two weeks from frostbite that had become gangrenous, and a third three months later after suffering dementia and protracted diarrhoea. In October the quartermaster, one of the oldest of the survivors, succumbed to the cold and dreadful conditions and, at noon on Christmas

* This is word game that has a number of variants. It can be objects starting with the same letter, or with consecutive words starting with the last letter of the previous word, for example.

Day, little Walter died, after having wasted away over the previous months. The castaways spent seven long months on the island, enduring constant damp and cold, subsisting mainly on penguins and albatross eggs and flesh, and using penguin skins for fuel. After several heart-breaking sightings of ships that they were unable to alert, the remaining survivors were spotted by a passing whaler and were released from their ordeal.[*]

This, then, was the sort of grim prospect facing *Cathrine*'s castaways and, even while their hut was being built, Anders started to plan a rescue mission. He realised it was possible, or even likely, that they might not be found on the island for some years, and so he decided that the only realistic option was to strengthen one of the whaleboats and attempt to sail it to Australia. Before making his plan known to all the men, he consulted the bosun Thorvald Johansen, and seaman Hans Antonsen, who both expressed their willingness to join him. Both were experienced sailors, and Antonsen had impressed Anders with his courage during the storm. Importantly, all three men were unmarried – Anders thought the mission was too risky to take along a married man who, if lost in the attempt, would leave behind a widow and family. When Bull heard of the plan he was adamantly opposed to it. His immediate response was 'Are you crazy?' He argued that the chances of the three surviving a 7,300-kilometre voyage in a small open boat in the wild and stormy Southern Ocean were, at best, slight. Anders, however, was a man of action, and to him the thought of living, or perhaps dying, on the island was a worse fate than the possibility of dying in a desperate rescue mission. Anders also pointed out the danger of the men losing either their patience or their sanity, or both, on the island and the difficulties that would create. This was not an unrealistic concern. Such issues had arisen with the *Strathmore* castaways, resulting in a great deal of conflict as well as the deaths of several of them. Bull then pleaded with Anders to consider his widowed mother. Anders acknowledged that his death would be a hard blow for her, but said that she had three other sons and that, perhaps in time, she would forget him.

---

[*] This information is drawn from Church, 1985.

It would take over a month to prepare the boat. In the meantime, the castaways did their best to improve life on their bleak island. The capricious sea decided to join them in their efforts, delivering from the depths a Christmas parcel that had been stored on the ship and then lost in the wreck. Although it had been on the seabed for twelve days and was, therefore, badly damaged, it was a remarkable, surprising, and very welcome delivery. Useful items in the parcel included knitted mittens for everyone. For Anders there was a fine new shirt and underpants from his mother and grandmother. These he planned to wear on the rescue voyage. Those who had packed the Christmas parcel would have been astounded to hear that it had come to the men from the bottom of the sea. The men had also found a copy of Asbjørnsen and Moe's fairy tales amongst the rocks on shore and dried it out.* This together with a copy of the Bible were at first the only books they had, and both gave them great comfort.

Anders was pleased that his family members were not aware of his plight, and he hoped that the first they would hear about it would be after he had successfully reached Melbourne. One night he dreamt that he was in the boat en route to Australia and was met by a big ocean steamer that picked him up. He woke to discover that he was still lying in their poor hut, but the dream gave him comfort. He was not starving or desperately cold, he was in good spirits and had courage, so he felt that the rescue mission would go well.

Not surprisingly, some of the men were beginning to feel downhearted, needing to be chivvied out of their bunks and encouraged to row out to the wreck. The younger ones seemed to be the most affected. They were all suffering with stomach complaints. To vary their diet the steward made a sort of black pudding from seal blood, and this was declared very tasty. Penguin cooked in various ways, however, continued to be their main diet, with the most popular form being soup. In lieu of salt for cooking the steward used salt water. They continued to salvage from the wreck whatever

* Peter Christen Asbjørnsen and Jørgen Engebretsen Moe were collectors of
  Norwegian folktales. The tales, which were published in numerous editions
  from the mid-nineteenth century on, quickly became beloved by Norwegians.

they could, whenever the sea was calm enough to allow it. One day they secured the smith's anvil, a frying-pan, two oil drums and a couple of knives, so their supply of useful items was slowly growing. Every evening after the men had gone to bed Anders read aloud from Asbjørnsen and Moe, and the men laughed at the stories about the trolls and nissens and the mischief they made.

One day they made a long rowing trip around the island to another bay called Ships Cove. It was a nice little harbour, but also open to the east and southeast. On the beaches there were countless numbers of penguins and seals and, in a colony of king penguins, they found eggs as big as a fist, or bigger, and collected some, although they were not quite fresh. They were fascinated by these strange birds that carried their eggs in a pouch under their bellies and waddled along with them. In Ships Cove there were also three giant boilers – the remains of sealing decades earlier – among which the seals were lolling about. They left a bottle in the cove with a message in it, just in case any ship called there, but they did not think there was much hope of that. There were a number of birds in the cove that Anders called ptarmigans that were almost embarrassingly tame.[*] Koren took his shoes off and they pecked him on the toes, pulled his socks off and kicked sand and dirt into his rifle.

Anders thought it would be possible to kill four or five thousand seals in a fortnight in this cove, if he could return with a steamer and enough men for the hunt. This ambition strengthened his determination to sail into the hazardous Southern Ocean in their little whaleboat, despite the storms and the mighty seas he would face. He had also realised that Bull's grand plan, which had resulted in an expedition with a small ship not suited to the dangerous conditions, was ill-conceived. It seemed odd to Anders that Bull, despite his advanced years and the experience of this expedition, was also keen to return with a bigger vessel and more hunters. The balance of power between the two men had, however, fundamentally

---

* There are no ptarmigans in the subantarctic – these were probably snowy
  sheathbills.

shifted. In the beginning Anders had been full of admiration for the older man, a person with great drive and an Antarctic explorer. As the *Cathrine's* expedition progressed, however, Anders' youthful confidence and willingness to take on the elements was at odds with Bull's more cautious nature. Anders was determined that if he was to continue in partnership with Bull he, Anders, should have unrestricted authority and work according to his own judgment. Nevertheless, the two men still had great affection for each other. Tension between expedition leaders and their captains was not unusual and was often the cause of conflict. Indeed, Bull had had a poor relationship with Leonard Kristensen, the captain of *Antarctic* on the 1894–95 voyage. Even though Bull had organised the expedition, he was on board in the loosely defined role of manager. Tellingly, in the accounts of this voyage written by both men, each barely acknowledges the other.[*]

The castaways on the Crozet Islands were lucky to have a good carpenter, both for his capacity to make use of what they had to hand in order to live comfortably, but also to work on the rescue boat. The carpenter, bosun and second mate forged metal and shaped and secured timber in order to strengthen the keel and lower it by 15 centimetres. They bolted the new keel in place, clad the underside with a big iron strap that was lying on the beach from an earlier shipwreck, and attached a rudder. The carpenter only had an axe to work with, so the preparations progressed very slowly. Desperate for materials to reinforce the boat, they salvaged whatever they could. One day, in a gale-force storm, Anders and the first mate walked to Hell Bay looking for nails in the timber tossed onto the beach from the wreck. The wind was so strong that Anders had to carry Beef to prevent him from being blown away. They found a thick iron bar that the carpenter was able to place along the length of the boat to secure a sailcloth that would provide some sort of shelter for the provisions and the men when they were not at the helm. Antonsen, who was one of the three embarking on the voyage, sewed the sails. Lifebuoys from *Cathrine* formed

------

* Kristensen, 1896, and Bull, 1896.

an inner buffer all around the boat, and this was reinforced with a belt of cork, salvaged from the wreck, for which Anders sewed a covering out of sailcloth. In this way they significantly improved the boat's buoyancy. The men spent as many daylight hours as they could preparing the boat for its difficult journey. In the end they felt that it was a strong, solid, and possibly unsinkable vessel. Anders named the boat *Hope* and carved this into her bow.[*] Rarely could so much hope have been placed in such a small vessel.

For provisions for forty to fifty days they planned to take most of the canned meat from the wreck, as well as preserved fruit, condensed milk and hard bread. Everything they had on board would have to be eaten cold.

The days leading up to Christmas were particularly dreary, with driving, drenching rain. Many of the men were dopey and slow or contrary, and not at all pleasant. Anders was aware that his authority as a captain was now only a formality, but he was pleased that the men still obeyed him. He turned his mind to the traditions that would be underway at Store Ree, with family members gathering from various places, and baking, frying and cooking for Christmas. He particularly imagined the cakes, which are a special feature of a Norwegian Christmas. The low spirits of the men were a further reminder that rescue must be sought. One positive note was the return of the dinghy, their most nimble boat, which had broken away from the ship weeks earlier. It must have been blown about in the open sea before an easterly wind brought it back to the reef, where it was spotted and retrieved when the sea conditions permitted.

Christmas Eve brought some welcome relief to their difficult life.[†] The weather was unexpectedly fine and they were able to sit inside their hut

---

[*] The Norwegian name was 'Haabet', which means 'hope' (literally, 'the hope'). No other ships' names have been translated in the text, but the name given to the rescue boat has an obvious, particular, significance, and so it is used in its translated form.

[†] Christmas in Norway is celebrated on Christmas Eve. Christmas Day is a day of rest.

without being dripped on, because even though they had done their best to waterproof it, it still leaked whenever it rained – which was most of the time. The men washed for the occasion, and Anders went so far as to shave, using a scrap of a shaving blade that the steward had brought with him from the ship. Koren found some heather and microscopic white star-like flowers that they used to decorate the hut.* For supper they had traditional butter porridge and all ate heartily.† They sang some Norwegian Christmas hymns and Bull read a lesson from the Bible and delivered a sermon he had written for the occasion. Koren read a comic piece he had written. Finally, they all got a dram from a bottle that had been saved.

At nine o'clock in the evening, after the others had gone to bed, Anders went outside into the darkening night. It was quiet and clear. The contours of the wild backs of the majestic mountains were silhouetted against a red sheen in the west and the Southern Cross was clear and shining in the sky to the south. Anders felt that God on high saw these fourteen men who were castaways on Possession Island. Then he went to bed to the sound of a snoring chorus coming from the bunks around him. The first mate was apparently a terrible snorer, so Anders kept a stick nearby to prod him. He thought he was being bitten by fleas, but Anders knew better!

After months of difficulty with the steward, another of the men, Hans Lysacker, took on his duties and proved to be an excellent cook. Their diet continued to be seal meat, penguin in many forms and blood pudding, but they discovered that albatross eggs were very tasty, quite like hen's eggs, although ten times larger, and so these were added to their pantry. They found that they could just walk up behind a nesting albatross, tip it forward and take the single egg from the nest. After this the bird would settle down again, not noticing that its egg had gone. They also took eggs from the pouches of the king penguins, and sometimes the penguins would replace their lost egg with a stone and proceed to incubate that.

----

* This could have been Antarctic pearl-wort (*Colobanthus kerguelen*) or subantarctic bedstraw (*Galium antarcticum*).
† 'Smørgrøt' (in Norwegian) is a porridge usually made by boiling down butter.

Worryingly, they observed that the seals had started to leave the island, as they do each year after the breeding season. This would have a serious impact on the availability of food. By the end of the year only a few big ancient males and an occasional skinny young seal remained on the beach. They observed a few females who had crawled high up into the island and surmised that this might have been to avoid the brutal amorous advances of the males. A seal 2–3 metres long would yield up to eight buckets of blood, in addition to the meat. They hung up as much meat as they could to dry and put up with its smell in order to ensure some supply after the seals had completely left the island, and they started fishing in the bay and collecting mussels from the rocks.

In the evenings they read from another salvaged book, Bernard Nordahl's account of the *Fram* expedition,* but, owing to the descriptions of the food, this was something of a mixed blessing – Nordahl described the cauliflower, pear puree, oxtail soup and chocolates that they had, which were in marked contrast to the limited diet on Possession Island.†

To add to their problems, they also had difficulty getting out to the wreck because of the high seas, and their supply of timber for the stove was running low.

On New Year's Day, 1907, Lysacker woke the men with pancakes and a drink they called coffee, which Bull later reported was brown, looked good and was hot, but was not actually coffee. It was another pleasant day, although an easterly wind was building again. Despite the fact that the *Admiralty Sailing Directions* said that easterly winds were rare in these islands,‡ they found this to be wrong, at least on this voyage, where they had already experienced four periods with easterly winds. Anders wondered if this would be his last year on earth. He expressed this tangentially by

---

* *Fram* was built by Colin Archer for the Norwegian Arctic explorer Fridtjof Nansen. This ship was also used by Amundsen for his first expedition to Antarctica, and was the most famous ship prior to *Titanic*.
† Nordahl was the first engineer on the 1893–96 voyage of *Fram* when she drifted in pack ice in the Arctic Ocean.
‡ Produced by the United Kingdom Hydrographic Office.

saying 'perhaps I won't get any older than the writer of this diary this year'. However, he was reconciled to the possibility that he might not survive the rescue mission and felt that he could not have done more to avoid their current situation.

They had a New Year's guest, a beautiful little black albatross chick that Koren had caught on one of his many excursions around the island. The chick's main talent was to shriek like a circular saw. There is no record of its fate. Koren had emerged as one of the most valuable men in the group, playing a major role in keeping up the men's spirits. He led by example, fascinated by his surroundings and constantly exploring, but he was also a cheerful and thoughtful person. Not only was he the main supplier of their important food, eggs, he and Thiis made and illustrated a pack of playing cards that was used nightly, and he produced a newspaper, *Crozeteer*, that featured droll accounts of life on the island.[*] *Crozeteer* was billed as a 'political, economic household magazine and maritime newspaper, the first and hopefully only volume.'[†] The cards were made by sticking thick white paper onto old newspaper with gum. Rounded corners were then cut onto each card and each mark and illustration was carefully drawn with ink – with not a feature missing.

By this stage Anders thought there were four or five men who were lazy and not contributing, and he hoped the group would manage without any serious incidents or problems until help arrived. The coal boiler, which contained a good supply of coal and had drifted to shore from the wreck, had been washed out to sea again. Anders had repeatedly asked the men to secure the coal, but this had not been done and now the coal was lost. This highlighted the problems the men would have if the rescue mission was not successful. Anders wondered if he should remain on the island, because he was the only one who still had some authority, but he was more worried about the possibility of living there for years, and so did not seriously consider abandoning his role in the rescue mission.

* Unfortunately, the whereabouts of the magazines are unknown, if indeed they still exist.
† Evjenth, 1938, p. 127.

By 10 January the boat *Hope* was ready. She was rigged and her sails in place, so now all that remained to be done when the weather was favourable for their departure was to get the boat into the water, position the ballast and store fresh water and provisions. Anders was full of praise for the skill and ingenuity of the carpenter and recognised that, should the mission be successful, Pedersen would be due the most honour. In fact, Pedersen was prepared to be in the party that went to sea, but he was a married man with dependants at home. Others had also expressed a willingness to be included, but the boat would not hold more than three men and the provisions they needed for the forty-five days Anders had calculated it would take them to reach Melbourne.

In readiness for his departure Anders gave his diary to Bull, with the hope that it would eventually reach his family in Norway. He also secured a promise from Bull that he would do everything in his power to get Beef back home. Anders recorded thanks to his mother, grandmother, brothers and sisters for always having been so good to him, 'who so little deserved their love'. He advised them that *Cathrine* was fully insured and so the money he had borrowed from them for his share in the expedition would be repaid, and he asked Bull, in the event of his death, to distribute his earnings to the crew, who would have the distinction of being his first and last crew. Bull dreamt that Anders' sisters were on board to say goodbye to him when he set off. Anders did not know if this should be interpreted hopefully or pessimistically, and suspected the latter, but thought it more likely that it was an indication of the pessimism Bull felt in his current demoralising circumstances. Anders' own dream some time earlier, that he was picked up at sea by a large ship, signalled a more optimistic state of mind.

In concluding his diary, Anders gave thanks to Bull for everything they had shared together, which he said was only good and enjoyable. While this may have been heartfelt, it was no doubt conciliatory, written in the knowledge that Bull would also read the less flattering comments Anders had made in the diary.

To his comrades who would remain on the island, Anders wrote this poem:[*]

> *When today we set sail*
> *On the stormy sea*
> *From Crozet's weather-beat isle,*
> *We will take with us our God*
> *Who rescue gave,*
> *Here from the raging sea.*
> *You who are left,*
> *Don't lose heart too fast –*
> *We'll be back, God willing.*
> *If the rescue is late*
> *And your feelings black,*
> *Maintain your happiest smile.*
> *You know that we do*
> *What we possibly can*
> *To bring you rescue one day.*
> *If we die on the sea*
> *Each man, all three,*
> *Has fought his mightiest deed.*
> *If we do not arrive,*
> *If our boat does us fail,*
> *Even so, you will get away!*
> *Then take greetings to home,*
> *Say our duty we did,*
> *And say, happily so.*

In response, Bull also wrote a poem about the perilous journey the three men were embarking on. Writing about how small the boat was and what a scrap of a sail it had with which to battle the stormy Southern Ocean, he focussed on the courage and skill of the three men, invoking

---

[*] This poem rhymes in the original Norwegian.

the image of Vikings. Of Anders he said that he was the sound offshoot of a hundred years' tree, and that only if forced by storm would he retreat to the lee of an island. Of Johansen and Antonsen he said they were not seeking personal glory, but were prepared to join their leader in order to secure the best possible chance of a good end to the predicament faced by *Cathrine*'s castaways. Of all three he said the blood that ran in their veins was that of true Norsemen, and the way their deeds would be spoken of would be that no warriors with sword by side had with greater courage given their all or expected so little in return. He said that the three men would be tried in a battle that would make their countrymen's breasts swell with pride and spark a desire in youngsters to emulate them. Of course, the men remaining on Possession Island knew this voyage might not end well, and in his poem Bull considered this possibility, pointing out how stormy the southern Indian Ocean is, but he promised that the remaining men would always remember their comrades and the battle they had fought on their behalf. And, if the voyage was successful, tears would flow, and a thousand hoorays would sound across the globe.

Bull was an excellent writer and an accomplished storyteller, which is evident in a tale he told on *Cathrine*'s voyage south, recorded by Anders, about the final, disastrous voyage of a Norwegian ship named *Valhalla*. Although written before they were stranded on the island, this story highlights the fact that Bull would have been mindful of the risks they were facing, and that he had good reason to be cautious about Anders' confidence that courage necessarily engenders luck. Anders introduced the story by saying: 'We sat together chatting companionably in the cabin on board *Cathrine* and the talk, as usual, got around to shipwrecks and the like. Bull said that one of the ugliest shipwrecks in living memory was that of *Valhalla* off the Newfoundland coast, and he told this story':

It was the spring of 1864 and trade activity from the cities of Norway to Canada was at a peak. Freight charges were high and so were the profits. Foreign ships were bought each year and wealth increased in many homes.

A healthy competition had gradually evolved between the captains who travelled the Canada route over who could be the first in Quebec on the spring voyage. Year after year Captain Blom from Tønsberg, commanding a vessel bought from Hamburg, had taken the prize, and it was generally accepted that nobody could get to Quebec before him. But he certainly had a vessel that could sail, and sail it he did! Indeed, there would be trouble for any officer who took the liberty of reducing the sails without informing the captain if he was in bed. That was not acceptable, and the unfortunate officer got a proper dressing-down from the captain.

Without doubt Captain Blom was a capable sailor and, as far as luck gives courage, he probably often let his ship run where an older and more careful man would perhaps have taken more heed of the weather. But when one is in the full strength of youth and has faith, hope and trust that the luck one has had for many years will continue, one can easily dismiss concerns and choose the much more appealing path, to place all one's faith in luck.

There was, though, a peculiar trust in Captain Blom's unfailing daring and splendid good humour that seemed to have its origin in his perpetually buoyant mood. I can recall that he could be heard long before he entered a room, because even in the hallway his merry laughter was in full swing. When he then appeared in the doorway with his fine, strong sailor's carriage and always cheerful face, his good humour spread to all of us in the room. He understood like few others how to enliven his surroundings, and I imagine it would have been the same on board his ship.

Then came the time that spring when one started to wait for news of the Canadian voyagers. The telegraph from America was, as far as I remember, hardly in use at that time, or at least it was not used by ships' captains to notify their arrival. The first information one got was through shipping gazettes, which possibly got their information by telegraph.

One day I saw in my club's newspapers that a couple of Norwegian ships had arrived in Canada, but, in contrast to the usual custom, not Valhalla. *I thought this was strange. Could she really have been left behind in the race to be first? Several more days passed until the next mail arrived from England, where there was news of a couple of ships that everybody knew were poorer sailers than* Valhalla. *The tension I had felt while reading this now changed to anxiety. Then in a tiny notice I found the remark, '*Valhalla *wrecked in the ice. Two men of the crew arrived this morning on a Glasgow ship'. Oh, what news! But what of the rest of the crew – the captain and the other twelve or thirteen men – surely they must have been saved by another vessel? And then there followed desperate times in many homes as people waited every day in fear and trembling for more information about the dreadful catastrophe.*

Who did not have deep sympathy for the captain's young wife and her many little ones, for the officer's old mother, and for all the others who were left, who had now probably lost their providers and their dearest on earth?

Yes, unfortunately, the worst fears came true. When the Consul's letter eventually arrived, it told how Valhalla *had struck an iceberg and only two of the crew had been saved. The others had all gone down with the ship. The son of the Consul, who was on board as a passenger, was amongst those who perished.*

Several years afterwards I met one of the sailors who had been rescued. He had been a junior deckhand, and he told me his tale.

> *We had a quick trip to the Newfoundland coast and, in his usual way, the captain gave the ship her head, so she went like lightning through the fog, despite the many icebergs we could glimpse now and then. One night the watch on the roof of the forecastle warned that there was an iceberg straight ahead, but at the speed we were travelling it was too late to manouevre to avoid an accident.* Valhalla*'s bow ploughed into the iceberg and the rig shuddered. The ship's carpenter discovered that one section of the hold in the bow had been rammed in and water was pouring into the ship. It was impossible to stop such a flood. The skipper gave orders to put the boats on the water, then saw to it himself that the steward got sacks of bread and barrels of water clear in order to be able to keep hunger and thirst away while we waited for rescuers from other vessels, if necessary. One of the boats*

shattered against the side of the ship in the high sea. Then we got out a dinghy and a man jumped into it to hold it clear of the ship. This was his salvation, because the line that held it broke and the dinghy drifted away from the doomed vessel. He was rescued by the same ship that picked me up later in the day. Before the other lifeboat could be launched the ship filled up with water and, as it sank, we were all pulled under with it by the whirlpool that develops when any large object sinks.

I think the rigging touched me, and I believe one of my comrades touched me, too, although it could have been part of the rig that brushed me as the ship slowly sank.

Somehow, I got to the surface again and crawled onto a small flake of drift ice that was nearby, where young F., son of the Consul in Quebec, managed to join me. The ice was just large enough to hold the two of us. However, F. must have been out of his senses, because not long after he jumped into the sea again and disappeared. Then I was alone on the scrap of ice! The chances of rescue were not great. Dawn approached, but it was half dark and the fog was thick. Even worse was the fact that the ice under me was melting and growing smaller with every hour that passed. Eventually it became so small that it could barely hold me. In the end I am sure that it was no bigger than our dining table at home, and I had to lie down flat so as not to lose my balance and fall into the sea again.

When it became light the seagulls started to become bothersome. They probably considered me sure prey. I had to hit out at them with my sou'wester to keep them away, but this movement doubly became my salvation. Suddenly I heard a shout in English, 'Hello there!' Turning around I saw the rig of a big barque that was streaming towards me. I am utterly unable to describe the feelings that passed through me at this sight.

Within minutes I was on board and rescued! My surprise and joy were even greater when there I was reunited with one of my comrades – the one who had drifted away from the ship in the dinghy, and whom we then presumed to have drowned. But as for all the others, where might they be? It only became clear to us when arrived at Quebec that they must have remained out there, all of them.

The English captain said he thought I was a seal when he saw me flap the sou'wester, which he took to be a flipper, because there were seals on the drift ice. The captain was aiming at me with his rifle when an officer realised that I was a man. I can therefore say that I was doubly saved from a certain death.

Here the young sailor finished his tale.

'But what about the first mate?' I asked. 'Did you not see anything of him?'

'No, at least I did not notice him specially. He was probably occupied with the boat and the crew.'

The first mate was, however, of special interest to me, so, many years later when I met the other man who happily had escaped from Valhalla, I put the same question to him. 'Yes,' he replied. 'Just as I got into the dinghy they started to lower the other lifeboat, and I clearly saw the first mate, who was standing by the boat hoist. One of his fingers was caught in the block and, despite his most strenuous efforts, he could not tear himself free. So I assume that he was pulled under in this desperate position, with his finger still fast in the block.'

Bull finished this story with the words: 'That dear, kind, young first mate. He was my brother.'

CHAPTER 4

INVESTING IN HOPE

Nine whole days
I was borne along by rough, deadly winds
On the fish-infested seas.

Homer, *The Odyssey**

At four in the morning of 11 January 1907 Anders woke to radiant sunshine, a thin covering of fog across the bay and a light breeze from the west. He rallied the men with the cry 'Turn out, all hands!', and the process of getting *Hope* underway commenced. The boat was pushed out into the bay on rollers and anchored while the ballast and provisions were stowed on board. By nine they were ready to sail, and Anders carried out some deviation tests with his compass. As they said farewell to their comrades, many were close to tears. Those who were to remain on the island wished the travellers good luck and 'God be with you'. Anders kept sentiment in check by speeding up the process as much as possible. The three who were leaving went on board *Hope*, hauled up the anchor, hoisted the sails and started to sail out from American Bay. They heard a ninefold hooray from the men on shore and replied with a rifle salute and hoisted the Norwegian flag. The men on shore responded with a rifle salute of their own, but this was heard by those at sea as an indistinct noise as the figures on the beach receded and the high, snow-covered ridges of the mountains loomed larger and wilder in their silent, majestic beauty.[†]

* Homer, 1996, 9.92–94.
† The description of *Hope*'s voyage is drawn primarily from Australian and Norwegian newspaper articles. A number of the Norwegian articles were

Soon the small craft's crew were aware that they were moving out of the protection of the bay, and *Hope* started to rise and fall noticeably in the ocean swell. When they were in the troughs of the waves they could no longer see the peaks of Possession Island. Almost immediately the wind rose to a gale. *Hope* responded by flying across the sea, and the three men were soon wet through. They put on their oilcloths and took care to remain seated whenever they were at the helm, or they risked being washed or bumped overboard. Anders became seasick for just the second time in his life. The boat was so small that men were either at the helm or under the tarpaulin that had been stretched across the bulk of the boat to provide some sort of shelter for their provisions and for them when they slept. By the end of the day they had settled into a roster of four-hour shifts. From the outset the air was foul under the tarpaulin, but the men realised they had little choice but to put up with it. Anders was too tall and broad to be able to sleep comfortably under the tarpaulin; he spent most of the time tossing about trying to position his body at different angles, failing to get much sleep.

At midnight on the first night Anders took the helm and found it so strange to be sitting there all alone in the black night trying to keep the boat clear of the mighty waves that were thundering down on them. The bioluminescence triggered by the passage of the boat trailed a long way behind them.[*] Anders was struck by how very small the boat was, and he strained every nerve and muscle to try to keep clear of the breaking waves.

Nonetheless, *Hope* was sailing well and they experienced three days of reasonable weather, making good distance north and east with just the occasional wave dumping enough water on board to require bailing. The men were in good spirits. But on the fourth night a storm sprang up from the northeast, the waves rose in height and became turbulent, and the boat repeatedly took on water. They decided to furl the sails, beat the sea with

---

written by Anders. See: *The Argus*, 15 February 1907, p. 5; *The Brisbane Courier*, 21 February 1907, p. 6; *Morgenbladet*, 31 March 1907, pp. 1–2; and others.

[*] Bioluminescence is caused by tiny marine creatures or algae.

an oilcloth in an attempt to dampen the waves,* and put out a canvas sea anchor to help the boat ride the rough seas.† However, they struggled to bring their craft's bow to the wind. *Hope* lay across the waves, which then broke over her time and time again, notwithstanding the fact that the men had put out the sea anchor. They took up the anchor again, hoisted a small sail and leaned away from the wind, while still beating the water with the oilcloth.

Everything in the boat, including the men and their clothes, was soaked through, and they were bitterly cold. The storm increased in strength and the men realised that they were battling for their lives. Two of them bailed while one steered. Anders described this as the worst night of his life, eclipsing those experienced when *Cathrine* was battered by the storms that ultimately destroyed her, but he was impressed by the attitude of the other two men who worked in silence for the most part, not complaining, just asking for help when it was needed or making an occasional understated comment such as, 'It's a bit rough tonight'. The exceptions to this stoicism occurred when waves washed Johansen's tobacco and one of Antonsen's clogs overboard. The men had little hope of surviving the storm but chose not to talk about it. They did pray, though, and felt that that probably helped.

At daybreak there was a heavy downpour that lasted for several hours. It did not make them any warmer but it subdued the sea and little by little they could feel the wind easing and then blowing from the west. They had had to steer south during the storm and had sped along, so were a good distance south of where they wanted to be, but that could not be helped. At the end of the day the sun broke through the clouds. The men hung their clothes on a line to dry them, then they ate preserved apricots and meat, which they thought made a fine meal.

---

* This would be intended to have the same effect as pouring oil on the sea to calm the waves.

† A sea anchor, which is a parachute or cone-shaped piece of fabric, is attached to the bow of a vessel and is used to keep a drifting boat's head to the wind and waves so that it can ride rough seas more comfortably.

Over the next few days, the weather alternated between rain and wind, and calm. They made good distance north again and their spirits rose, although much of their food had become mouldy and they had to resort to killing albatrosses and eating the meat raw, even though that did not sit well with their stomachs. The eighth day was calm, but the sun went down in dense, fiery red clouds in the west and a heavy sea began to roll up from that quarter. 'It's coming, Captain,' exclaimed Hans. They tore down the sails and prepared for another storm, but the night passed quietly and calmly, with only an occasional fierce gust of wind from the north. At four in the morning, Anders relieved the bosun who was at the helm and then waited for the storm to arrive. He thought they had little chance of surviving. He looked around the horizon in the hope that he might see the sails of a passing ship, but to no avail. He dozed a little, glanced from time to time at the ominous storm clouds in the north and thought sadly of the poor men they had left behind on the Crozet Islands. They had pinned their faith on the three men in a miniscule boat who were now about to face another, probably fatal, battle with a mighty storm on the wildest ocean on Earth. He thought it was good that they did not know what was happening.

The wind began to freshen and Anders readied himself for the storm. At the same moment he became aware of albatrosses circling the boat. He counted, three, then four, then seven and finally thirteen of the majestic birds flying around them. Aware that these birds often followed ships on their passage across the Southern Ocean, he turned around and was astonished to see the slender black hull of a large barque in full sail at some distance but sailing directly towards them, with foam streaming from her bow. He bellowed out to the two men under the tarpaulin, 'Hey, boys, a sailing ship! Bring our rifle and flag!' They came scrambling out and stared at the ship, then raised their flag and got out the oars and rowlocks in readiness to row to her. They watched as the ship's sails were lowered – first the mainsail, then the royal and topgallant sails, and finally the forecastle sail. The three men in *Hope* could hear the sailors on the barque singing as they lowered the sails. They rowed up under the lee side, where the davits and hoists had been made ready, and *Hope* with her three plucky sailors was hoisted aboard the impressive ship. They had been rescued by the Dutch barque *De Ruyter*,* which was en route from Philadelphia to Japan with a cargo of petroleum. Although there was some irony in the fact that these three shipwrecked sealers had been rescued by a ship carrying as its cargo a product that was to dramatically replace the need for sealing and whaling, nobody commented on it. The captain, Heinrich Fuitjer, had seen *Hope* as soon as he had come on deck at five-thirty that morning, his attention drawn to her by the circling albatrosses. At first he thought he was looking at a large fish or seal, but through his binoculars he could see the small boat with a man at the helm. He immediately began the rescue operation, which proceeded quickly and safely.

Anders' dream had come to pass.

Hans, Thorvald and Anders' sense of relief cannot be overestimated. Their transition from suffering to paradise was as sudden and dramatic as could possibly be imagined. They were treated with great hospitality by the crew. They were suffering from exposure, of course, and their first actions were to have a warm bath and then dress in dry clothes. Afterwards they were provided with hot chocolate – hot chocolate! – and a delicious lunch and were assigned comfortable quarters. In Anders' case this meant a large, private, elegant cabin – such are the privileges of rank.

No sooner had they been hoisted aboard *De Ruyter* than the storm broke in all its fury. In order to weather the storm even on this strong ship all of the sails had to be lowered. Anders thought again that this storm would probably have meant the end of their rescue bid, in the worst possible way. His view was underscored by Captain Fuitjer's declaration, 'That was a madman's undertaking of yours to try to sail from the Crozets to Australia, and you would never have reached land in that boat.'† When, over the coming months, Anders reflected on their chances of success he

---

* Anders and the press usually referred to this ship and its captain as German, however both were probably Dutch.
† *Morgenbladet*, 31 March 1907, p. 2.

swung between thinking they could have reached Australia and realising that it was, in all likelihood, impossible. *Hope*, with all of her strengthening, had stood up very well, withstanding one furious storm, and was probably capable of withstanding more, but the men were suffering from exposure and their provisions would have been insufficient. Nevertheless, one key part of the rescue plan had been to get *Hope* up into the trading route between South Africa and Australia to give themselves a chance of coming across a ship, which was exactly what happened. They had sailed no less than 1,150 kilometres in the eight days,[*] and had reached 42°S and 62°E, a sailing feat of which they were rightly proud. It was, however, only fifteen per cent of the distance they needed to travel to reach Australia.

In the years to come their achievement would be favourably compared to Ernest Shackleton's extraordinary small boat voyage following the loss of their ship *Endurance* in 1915, but the immediate comparison at the time was with a similar voyage in the northern hemisphere, probably in 1892, following the wreck of the sealing vessel *Arctic*.[†] Like *Cathrine*, *Arctic* was a small sailing ship with a supplementary engine. She struck ground and was wrecked on Jan Mayen, a Norwegian volcanic island in the Arctic Ocean. The men rushed out of their berths into their four fishing boats with just the clothes they were wearing and a few provisions: a little bread, pork, butter and pot beer, as well as some canned food. They sailed and rowed along the edge of the ice until they saw the mountains of Greenland far away, but the ice stretched out a great distance from land and was impossible to penetrate. They experienced alternating rain and snow, and the temperature was often as low as -13°C,[‡] so they suffered a great deal from cold and wet. Occasionally the men walked on the ice to stretch their legs and get fresh ice to make water, and at times they were stuck in the ice unable to move. After getting clear of the ice they set sail for Iceland in a stiff gale and arrived in Akureyri at the base of Eyjafjörður in the north

---

[*] Anders said they had sailed 720 miles (1,160 kilometres). The press reported this as 1,000 miles (1,600 kilometres).
[†] *Norges Sjøfartstidende*, 17 April 1907, p. 2.
[‡] Eight degrees Fahrenheit is the equivalent of -13 degrees Celsius.

of Iceland after having been in the boats for fifteen days and on the ice for several more. Of the twenty-four men, which was the entire crew, four were admitted to hospital for the treatment of ulcers on their legs, but otherwise they were all healthy. Their boats, which had travelled a similar distance to *Hope*, albeit in much calmer waters, had performed well.

Not quite so fortunate was the crew of *Carnarvon Castle*, which met with disaster in the same waters as those travelled by Anders in *Hope* and at the same time.[*] *Carnarvon Castle* was en route from Liverpool to Melbourne when, on 31 January 1907, at 42°S and 100°E,[†] a fire broke out on board. After five hours of a gruelling and ultimately futile battle the crew, several of whom had sustained burns, were forced to abandon the ship. They set course for Cape Leeuwin, Western Australia, 1,800 kilometres away, in two lifeboats that were each 6.7 metres long and 1.5 metres wide. The boats were well-equipped but open, and there was a serious shortage of fresh water. The captain's boat, which had sixteen men in it, had only 140 litres of water, and the first mate's boat, in which there were eleven men, had only 110. The boats attempted to stay together, but after seven days they lost sight of each other. After twenty-five days at sea the first mate's boat met a fishing vessel some distance off Fremantle. The men, who were so weak from the combination of dehydration and exposure they were unable to walk, were taken into care in Fremantle. One man required hospitalisation, but all recovered after several days. A day later the captain's boat landed at Cape Naturaliste, just north of Cape Leeuwin. Two of the men had succumbed to their injuries and exposure but the others, despite being in a very poor state, recovered after several days' treatment.

Meanwhile, on *De Ruyter*, Captain Fuitjer made a detour from his planned route to take the three men to Melbourne, where processes could be commenced to rescue the remaining eleven men on the Crozet Islands. Twenty-four days after their rescue Anders and his companions arrived in Melbourne; it was the evening of 13 February 1907.

---

* *Norges Sjøfartstidende*, 1 May 1907, p. 2.
† The Crozet Islands are 46°S and 52°E.

⚓ ⚓ ⚓

The eleven men on Possession Island had watched from the beach as *Hope* sailed out of the bay early on 11 January. Their hearts were heavy and they had little hope for the optimistically named boat. Bull preferred to think of the tiny boat as a bird gliding its way to safety, rather than as a vulnerable vessel with their three colleagues on board in the middle of a wild and inhospitable ocean. Two hours after she set sail, the men lost sight of *Hope* as she slipped over the horizon, at which point a small, rarely expressed, sliver of hope lodged in their hearts and minds.[*]

After Anders had given his private diary and notebooks to Bull for safekeeping and return to his mother if he perished in his attempt to rescue the crew, Bull wrote in his own diary that, should that fate await Anders, he, Bull, would rather remain on the island than have to fulfill his promise to deliver the book to Emma Ree. He put his trust in providence and prayed that Anders, Johansen and Antonsen would not die. He thought that such a fate would shatter his faith, which, despite many difficulties in his life, had not failed him to that point.

Several weeks after *Hope* had left, when Bull had had time to reflect on the miserable outcome of the *Cathrine* expedition and the perilous future facing him and the other men, he added an addendum to Anders' diary, a very moving and personal account of his own life; the life of a man who had been one of the first Antarctic explorers. Bull also addressed Anders' comments about his – Bull's – own anxiety and suitability for an undertaking such as this, which Bull was able to read once the diary was in his care.[†]

The entry took the form of a letter, addressed to *Dear Captain Anders Harboe-Ree, Dear young friend*. He said that he had been unable to read Anders' parting words to the men and had asked Rode, the first mate, to

---

[*] The primary sources of information about the men's lives after Anders and the other two men departed from the island are five articles by Bull in the newspaper *The Pall Mall Magazine* 1907 and in *Verdens Gang* in March, April and May 1907.

[†] The full entry was published in *RePublica*, 1995.

read them instead, and that it had taken some time – eighteen days – to summon the strength to write the letter. He wrote fondly of their time together on the voyage, saying that this time with Anders would always be amongst his dearest memories, the shipwreck not included. In addressing the comments about his nervousness, Bull said that this was the result of all the hope he had invested in the voyage, and his explanation was as follows. As a young man in Norway Bull had enjoyed great success personally and in business, but he had then squandered his, and the greater part of his wife's, wealth in the 1870s through a combination of high living and unsuccessful speculation. In order to try to rebuild his wealth, regain his reputation and overcome his compulsions, he made the decision to go to Australia, where he believed greater opportunity lay. For the first five years in Australia he suffered loneliness, poverty and deprivation, working as a timber-feller, farmhand and general labourer, all occupations for which he was ill-suited. Eventually he secured a position as a businessman in Melbourne, and from there he attempted to mount an expedition to the Antarctic, where he believed great wealth could be accumulated from whaling. These attempts culminated in the voyage of *Antarctic* to the Antarctic. However, this voyage was not successful commercially. Svend Foyn's death during that voyage precluded any further expeditions funded from that source, and it was eleven years before he met Anders and persuaded him to contribute to, and captain, an expedition to the south, where he continued to believe there were riches to be had. In that period, from 1895 to 1906, Bull had tried many times in vain to persuade people to back a similar voyage.

Anders and Bull's circumstances in 1906 were markedly different. Bull, although he was working in Norway, had not regained the fortune he had squandered, and was of an age when he could no longer expect to do so. Anders, on the other hand, was young, courageous and energetic, and came from a well-to-do family that was able to underwrite the risk he was taking. At any rate, he was young enough to begin again if the trip was not successful. For Bull this voyage was an all-or-nothing last deal of the cards. As they approached the Crozet Islands Bull's anxiety started to build and, as they started to hunt seals, he began to dream that this time he would gain the fortune he so desperately wanted, and thought about constantly. For him this was the chance to restore his reputation, redeem himself in his wife's eyes and finally free himself from his pecuniary worries and dependence on others.

Bull wrote that when the barometer fell and the weather hung threateningly over the mountains he became afraid that everything was slipping away: what they had begun to harvest from 'Canaan's Land of milk and honey',* and the great hope that had driven him on for so long, was in danger of slipping away. He wished that he had told Anders at the time that it was not so much that he feared for his life, although he would have dearly loved to die at home amongst his own instead of far away across the world, but rather feared that it would be unbearable to be so near his goal only to have it snatched away. Once *Cathrine* was lost and the men were stranded on Possession Island, Bull admitted that he was overcome with bitterness directed against God. He acknowledged that all the crew had been saved, but he could not understand why God would let him see that it was possible to regain his wealth in the way he had planned, and not let him finish the task. Despite his protestations of bitterness, Bull also started to imagine another expedition – one that he and Anders would undertake together, saying that it would be difficult for either to mount another on his own.

The letter to Anders, a letter that it seemed in all likelihood Anders was never to read, ended by urging Anders to live, and pleading with God to protect the boat. Bull was desperate for the rescue mission to be successful, in part to ensure that he would not have to live with the knowledge that the three men had died for his sake. He could not fathom how he would be able to face going back to Norway unless Anders reached safety.

It would not have been surprising if Bull had been unable to lift

---

* This is reference to Exodus 3.8, where God promises Abraham he will bring them to a land flowing with milk and honey.

himself out of his depression, but that was not the case. Writing about this critical period some time after they had been rescued, Bull spoke about visiting the graveyard near where they had built their cabin. He said that, 'Although no loving mother or sister will ever have the opportunity to place flowers on these remote graves, Mother Nature herself seems to keep a friendly eye on her sons. A thick green blanket covers the small burial mounds, and a beautiful little star-shaped white flower grows in great abundance on them. The first rays of the rising sun, showing its radiant face above the immense sea, shine and glitter on these graves and here, far from their relatives, the bodies of the young sailors will rest undisturbed by the noise and clamour of the civilised world.'

He could hardly have ignored the possibility that one or more of those remaining on the island would join those in the graveyard before rescue came, and he wondered if he might be the first, given his age. In spite of these morbid reflections, he rallied himself in the knowledge that he had a responsibility to do his best to keep his comrades in good spirits, and that is what he resolved to do.

Bull drew on his store of humorous tales to amuse the men. One that he told was of an ice merchant in Norway who wanted to give his beloved son a special birthday present, so he sent a telegram to his agent in London and asked him to send '1–2' monkeys. However, the message was converted in the telegram to '102' monkeys, and the arrival in the ice merchant's town of the first shipment of seventy-six caused a riot that would never be forgotten. The merchant, in nervous excitement and feverish haste, immediately sent another telegram to his agent, begging him, for God's sake, not to send the remaining twenty-six!

After the intensity of the period prior to *Hope*'s departure, with the focus on building the cabin, preparing the boat and securing a supply of food, life on the island was, relatively speaking, less active.* Obtaining

---

* *Verdens Gang*, 3 May 1907.

and preparing food were the main tasks, and they had to ensure that they managed their provisions as carefully as possible, at the same time trying to provide satisfying meals. While birds, seals and fish comprised their main diet, anything that could be considered a luxury, such as sugar or milk, was kept under lock and key.

With responsibility for the cooking, Lysacker took a great interest in his work. He fired up the stove at five or six in the morning, and breakfast was served at seven. This usually consisted of fried fish, some cakes made from flour and water and the drink they called coffee. Every man except the first mate and Bull took turns at being the cook's assistant. The first mate took on the role of manager of the Ministry of Fisheries, as they called it, responsible for supplying fresh fish when it was needed. He caught the fish and cleaned most of it himself. The lack of salt was a problem, but one of the men solved it by setting up a 'salt factory', boiling salt water until all the water had evaporated. Bull wryly noted that they would have been unable to support an export industry in this way, but they did produce sufficient for their needs.

During this period Koren was indefatigable, exploring as much of the island as possible. In good weather he climbed several peaks a day, but this was no leisurely stroll in the park. Possession Island has a rugged landscape of volcanic mountains rising to two high peaks, with Pic du Mascarin the higher, at an elevation of 934 metres. The mountains are cut by deeply glaciated valleys, and scree and treacherous bogs make walking very dangerous. Anders had suggested that the men should not walk about on the island on their own, but this did not stop the ever-adventurous Koren. For a naturalist, this was an unexplored island paradise. The coastal areas and valleys were covered with herbaceous subantarctic vegetation, and the bird life was extraordinary. At least twenty-six breeding species have been identified on the island, including king, northern rockhopper and macaroni penguins, wandering, sooty and light-mantled albatrosses, northern giant petrels, medium-billed prions, and Kerguelen, soft-plumed and South Georgia diving petrels. It must have been very frustrating for Koren to be surrounded by these novel birds, which museums and universities would have dearly loved to acquire, knowing that he was unable to transport any of them away from the island. Nevertheless, he developed an intimate knowledge of the birds and their breeding and nesting habits, and continued to be the chief supplier of eggs and birds for their larder.

Koren also continued to produce the island newspaper that he had initiated, the illustrated weekly, *Crozeteer*, which he read aloud in the evenings to a very receptive audience. Controversy over certain topics reached fever pitch, with some contributors resorting to pseudonyms to shield their identities. The hottest of these topics was a disagreement about whether fish or meat was the tastier food. Koren's good humour, and his modelling of very positive and constructive behaviour, contributed greatly to the castaways' amicable, healthy and overall successful imprisonment on the island.

Hope and her crew were never far from their minds. Predictions about the possible date of rescue were made daily and discussed at length. Bull had set 25 March as the last possible date for *Hope*'s crew to have reached safety, and they all agreed that they should not expect to hear anything before 1 April. After that date they felt that there was little chance that the rescue bid had been successful. In the meantime, they kept themselves as busy as possible. They set up gymnastic equipment on the beach, including a balance rope, with the challenge that, in order to leave the island, each man must walk the rope without losing his footing. It seems that none succeeded, but that was not really the point of the activity.

When Anders left the island, he found it very difficult to leave his dog, Beef. He extracted a solemn promise from Bull that he would look after Beef and make every effort to get him back to Norway. Beef was such an important part of the lives of the eleven men who remained on Possession Island that Bull featured him in the extended articles he later wrote about their time on the island for various newspapers and magazines. He described Beef as their faithful friend, on board as well as ashore; a merry, kind little dog and a good companion to everyone. Beef excelled as an entertainer. He was the self-appointed commander-in-chief of the beach, despite his diminutive size in comparison with the mighty elephant seals, and spent many hours frolicking about and herding penguins and young seals into the sea, at which point he looked very happy with himself, mission accomplished! He was called on to demonstrate the many tricks he had been taught by his master, especially sitting up on his haunches, which was such a characteristic pose that Anders sketched him like that and gave the drawing the title, 'The famous polar dog Beef'.

Beef was an integral player in a sport devised by the men for their amusement, involving the seals dozing on the beach. When elephant seals are lying down humans can get quite close to them without any risk of being harmed, but the seals are very sensitive to touch. The sport was to get a rope looped around the tail of one of them and then watch it try to free itself. This was dangerous sport (for the men, not the animal), because elephant seals can strike a damaging blow with their tails. When the men succeeded in roping an animal, it would spring up and jerk itself around, while the men tried to hold fast to the rope. Beef's contribution was to increase the overall excitement of the sport by running around and barking like mad, a role in which he excelled.

Throughout their time on the island objects of all kinds from the shipwreck were washed onto the shore, sometimes causing great merriment. Chief of these was the arrival of Bull's formal tails, soon to be followed by his top hat. Garments less suited to their circumstances could hardly be imagined. One morning the first mate discovered a photograph of Bull's oldest grandchild, a twelve-year-old girl. It seemed to Bull that she was saying to him, 'Grandfather, if you have forgotten me, I have not forgotten you, and so I have come to you.'

The castaways chafed at the physical restrictions of their situation and often talked about visiting one of the other islands in the Crozet group. They thought there was a depot on Hog Island, but that was about 100 kilometres away, and the idea of rowing there with the only boat that remained with them was too risky. East Island, however, was supposed to be just 16 or 20 kilometres away, or about two hours rowing, and the prospect of going there was very tempting. Thus, on a beautiful, clear and calm day, four of the men set off, making good speed. They had with them nothing but an empty butter tin filled with water, because this was intended to be only a day trip. They were expected back to Possession Island by nightfall, but failed to appear. By the second night they still had not returned and nor had they by the time the remaining seven men turned in to their bunks on the third night, so great anxiety was felt for their safety. Shortly afterwards they heard loud footsteps and voices, and were relieved to know that their comrades had finally returned. The four men were exhausted and hungry and wolfed down the meal provided for them, before telling their story.

On the first day they had rowed for six hours before they found a cove where they could get ashore. Immediately after their arrival the weather set in, and they had spent two days exposed to rain and cold with nothing to eat except some penguins they managed to fry. This in itself was a miracle, because they had not taken any cooking gear with them, and it was fortunate that one of the men discovered a match in his pocket. On the third day they made several attempts to leave the island in the heavy seas, with the boat at severe risk of overturning and the men in danger of drowning. They were not successful until their third attempt, by which time their hands were raw and bleeding.

Their experience put paid to any further discussion about excursions to neighbouring islands, although on East Island they had found rabbits and greater quantities of albatrosses than were on Possession Island. There is a curious reference to a shipwreck survivor living mainly off rabbits on Hog Island for five months in 1883.* It was reported that a woman named Alice Armitage was the sole survivor of a ship wrecked on the island. According to the article she was rescued by a New Zealand whaler, whose captain saw the smoke signals she had put up when she saw the ship. Remarkably, she was said to have appeared to be none the worse for her ordeal. Despite the

---

* 'Lady Robinson Crusoes', in *Pearson's Weekly*, 27 June 1907, p. 3.

fact that the article refers to this as a 'well authenticated' case, no other references to this shipwreck or survival tale have been found.

The week after their adventure, Koren produced an extra copy of *Crozeteer*, making fun of the intrepid sailors, which included himself, and evoking much laughter.

The men were obviously aware that the rescue attempt on *Hope* might be unsuccessful, and they speculated on other ways to draw attention to their plight. It occurred to them that they could use albatrosses – those mighty ocean wanderers – to take a message to the wider world and thus trigger a rescue mission. At first they could think of no way to achieve this, but then the inventive carpenter came up with a plan to put messages in the empty cartridges, of which there were hundreds on the island. They wrote messages on long strips of paper, rolled them up to insert into the cartridges, then made each unit watertight. Fifty cartridges were prepared in this way, and these were taken to a nearby bay where there were many albatrosses. The birds sat on their nests with great patience as the cartridges were fixed to their legs with wire, oblivious to the mission that was being entrusted to them. The hope was that one or two of the birds would end up on a ship and the cartridge would be noticed. The messages read: 'Most respectfully! Please inform the Norwegian consulate at your destination that the schooner, *Cathrine* of Tønsberg, was completely wrecked in American Bay on Possession Island Crozet Islands, December 4, 1906. January 11, 1907 Captain [Harboe-]Ree and two men left the island in one of our boats in the hope of reaching Africa, Australia or a ship at sea. The rest of the crew, 11 men, remained here waiting for help. In his gracious efforts to save us, the consul would do me a great service by sending a telegram to the address 'Stormbull, Kristiania' informing them of our present position and that all is well at present. Kindly give notice to the local press on your arrival and set the bird free as a thank you for the service it has done us.'

Although a great deal of effort went into this exercise, the men were not overly optimistic that it would result in their rescue. In any event, the services of these particular albatrosses were not required, although they presumably carried the messages that had been attached to their legs for the rest of their lives. As it was, another group of albatrosses helped deliver the castaways from Possession Island by circling *Hope*, thus alerting the captain of *De Ruyter* to the little vessel.

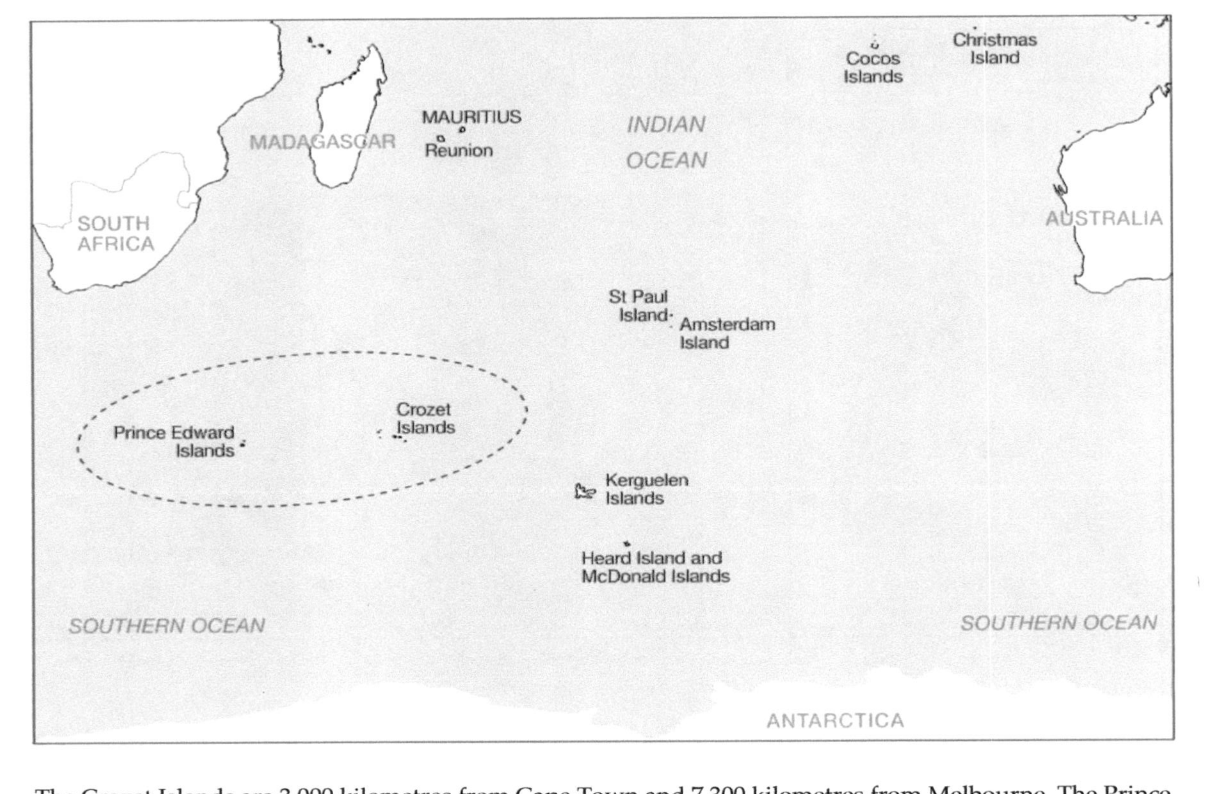

The Crozet Islands are 3,000 kilometres from Cape Town and 7,300 kilometres from Melbourne. The Prince Edward Islands are 2,150 kilometres from Cape Town and 8,140 kilometres from Melbourne.

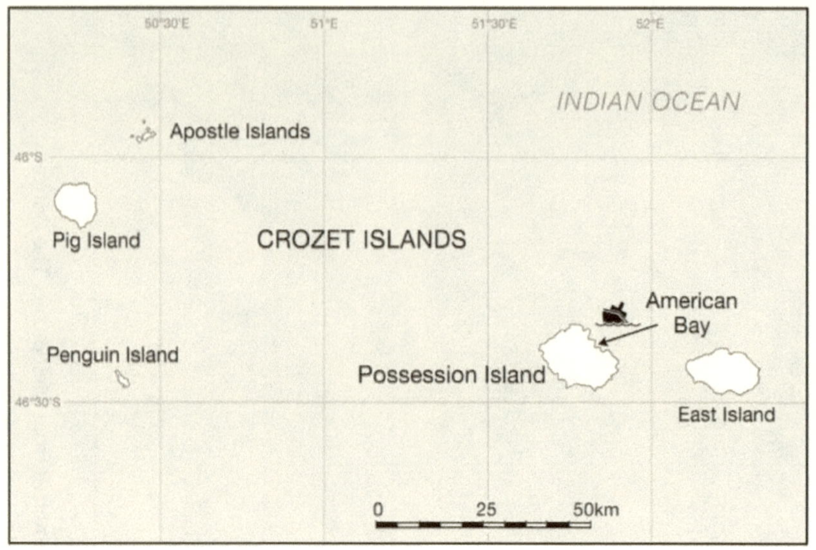

The Crozet Islands are a district within the French Southern and Antarctic Lands. The French name is Îles Crozet, or officially, Archipel Crozet. The islands' names are: Apostle Islets (Îlots des Apôtres); Hog, or Pig, Island (Île aux Cochons); Penguin Island (Île des Pingouins); Possession Island (Île de la Possession); and East Island (Île de l'Est). Prince Edward and Marion islands, which together comprise the Prince Edward Islands, are part of South Africa.

Anders Harboe-Ree as a young man prior to his voyages to the Southern Ocean. *Photographer and date unknown.*

Anders at 26 years of age, wearing his Order of St Olav medal and a cap made for the *Solglimt* crew, featuring the *Solglimt* logo, which was also on the ship's funnel. *The photograph was taken by Chr. Grundseth, Hamar, Norway.*

A photograph of *Cathrine* taken just prior to the ship's departure to the Southern Ocean in August 1906. *Cathrine* is anchored adjacent to Husøy in the Oslofjord, 100 kilometres southwest of Oslo. *Photograph by Joh. Henriksen of Tønsberg, 1906.*

Anders illustrated the diary he kept during the *Cathrine* voyage. This watercolour of the ship, from Wednesday 5–10–06, the forty-third day at sea, is titled 'After the squall'.

This photograph shows nine of the fourteen men who were on *Cathrine* for her voyage south. Henrik Johan (H.J.) Bull is second from the right. The man on the right, who appears in a number of photographs, is likely to be a senior officer, possibly the first mate, B.E. Rode. The man standing second from the left may be the naturalist, Johan Koren. Also in the photograph is Anders' dog, Beef. The photograph was probably taken by Anders. Handwritten on the back is 'M/S "Katherine" [sic] 1906'.

Drawings of the dog Beef and H.J. Bull in the *Cathrine* diary. The text relating to Beef is: 'The famous polar dog "Beef"'. The text referring to the sketch of Bull is: 'In unshaved slack-wind humour/A rare occurrence.' The page in the diary is from Sunday 2–09–06.

barometer. Vinden øger saa jeg fik gjort
fast til stormseil. Voldsom "norsejø".
Det er ingen lek akkurat at ligge her-
nede med slig en liten skonnert fille. —
Idag fiskede tømmerman-
den den 1ste Albatros

En svær fugl. Den maalte 3.25 meter
mellem vingespidserne og veiede c.a. 12 kg.
Ja der var sjau. Alle mand baade fri-
vagt og vagt hi'kei's stod agter paa halv-
dækket og fiskede eller saa paa fangsten og
tømmermand var selvfølgelig dagens løve. Det var
greit. Den blev fisket paa et triangel
af blik   der ser ud som paa teg-
                     ningen her. Der surres en
                     flaskebete i den spidse vinkel
                     og et triangelen fast spigret paa
                     et stykke træ for ikke at fyn-
                     ke. Naar saa fuglen hakker
                     efter flasket, blir den hæn-
gende fast i den kroken, den har yderst
paa nætbet og blir saa halt ombord.
Den skal spises. Jeg har aldrig smagt
sligt vildt før, men det skal kanske gaa
an. Vi har fanget flere andre fugle og saa

Pen and ink drawings of an albatross and bird-catching device, from the *Cathrine* diary, on Tuesday 30–10–1906. The drawings are part of a discussion about the naturalist Johan Koren's attempts to catch an albatross for his collection. Although this was primarily a sealing voyage, Koren was on board as a scientist to bring information and specimens back to Europe.

This untitled pen and ink drawing from the *Cathrine* diary shows storm petrels behind the ship. The drawing follows a poem mocking Johan Koren's attempts to catch a storm petrel. The image appears in a section of the diary dated Sunday 30–10–1906 to Saturday 6–10–1906.

On the long journey south the men on board were entertained by Koren's often unsuccessful hunting efforts. This pen and ink drawing titled 'Albatross hunt', dated Monday 19–11–1906, is another of the many references attesting to this in the *Cathrine* diary.

When *Cathrine* was journeying through warm parts of the globe the men rigged up an outdoor shower, as shown in this drawing from Anders' diary. It is dated Thursday 20–09–1906, and Anders records that they were at this time becalmed near the equator.

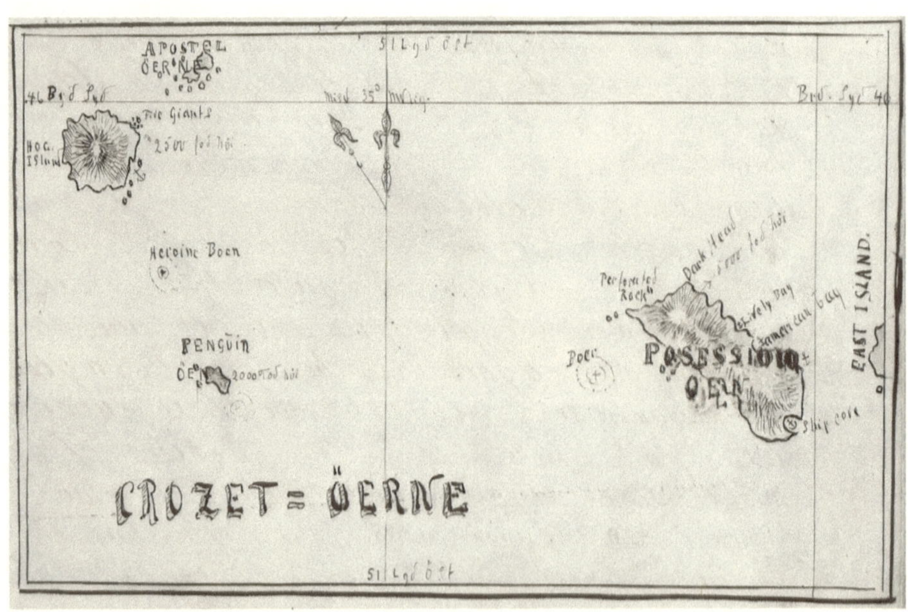

In a curious mix of French, Norwegian and English, this map of the Crozet Islands from the *Cathrine* diary shows Hog Island, Penguin Island and Possession Island. Features identified on Possession Island include: Perforated Rock, Lively Bay, American Bay and Ship Cove. The diary entry is from Wednesday 28–11–1906, so was done two days after their arrival at the Crozet Islands.

This page from the *Cathrine* diary marks the beginning of fourteen pages dedicated to the crossing the equator festivities, which are traditionally carried out for those doing this for the first time. The heading is 'Illustrated equato-realtime'. 'Realtime' translates as 'science', so is an ironic lead-in to the humorous entries in the following pages. This section of the diary is dated Sunday 30–9–1906 to Saturday 6–10–1906.

Another page from the *Cathrine* diary in the section relating to crossing the equator. The overall heading is 'Christmas Eve in the North Sea'. The caption under the top cartoon reads: 'Captain: If only those at home knew where we were. Cook: If only the Captain himself knew.' The caption under the second cartoon reads: 'Bosun (to one of the able seamen during a discussion about the ship's mate): And he talks about cleanliness, that pig. His hands are as dirty as my feet.'

A lengthy article by H.J. Bull about the *Cathrine* wreck and life on the Crozet Islands was published in *Pall Mall Magazine* in 1907. The illustrations in the article were done by Simon Harmon Vedder, 'from drawings supplied by the crew', most probably Anders and Johan Koren. The caption to this illustration on p. 692 says: 'Right astern of the vessel was a reef of small rocks, on which the waves were dashing with terrible fury and violence'.

The caption of this illustration from p. 694 of the *Pall Mall Magazine* article, referring to the second – and last – group of men who abandoned *Cathrine,* reads: 'We could now count the eight men on board, and saw that all would be saved as soon as they came successfully through the reef.'

The caption on p. 694 of the *Pall Mall Magazine* article, referring to *Cathrine*, reads: 'At the next bump the whole vessel suddenly split asunder … In less than fifteen minutes there was nothing left but a mass of wreckage upon the treacherous rocks.'

This photograph is of the remains of *Cathrine* lying on the reef in American Bay, Possession Island. It is not known whether this photograph was taken in the months following the wreck, in late 1906 or early 1907, or twelve months later when Anders returned to the Crozet Islands with *Solglimt*. The photographer is unknown. Any photograph that can definitively be linked to the *Cathrine* voyage was probably taken by Anders. Photographs that can be linked to the *Solglimt* voyage are likely to have been taken either by Anders or by the ship's secretary, Asbjørn Bjørnstad.

This illustration appears on p. 695 of the *Pall Mall Magazine* article. The caption, referring to *Cathrine*'s castaways on their first night on Possession Island, reads: 'Under the upturned boat a party of seven made their arrangements for the night as well as they could.'

The *Cathrine* castaways built this hut on Possession Island after they were wrecked. The sign on the hut, which says 'Cathrine', was presumably salvaged from the wreck. The castaways always referred to their hut as Christmas Cottage, to mark where they spent Christmas 1906. This hut was used again during *Solglimt*'s 1907–08 voyage, and it is not known which voyage the photograph is from.

The heading of this drawing in the *Cathrine* diary is 'Our Christmas table on Crozet, 1906'. Christmas was – and is – a very important occasion in Norway, and the castaways went to a great deal of effort to make their Crozet Islands Christmas as special as possible, under the circumstances. The table has a cloth on it, as well as jars with Norwegian flags, and flowers and twigs collected by the scientist, Johan Koren. For their meal, they somehow managed to produce a version of the traditional Christmas porridge that in Norway is made from butter.

The caption of this illustration from the *Pall Mall Magazine article*, p. 690, reads: 'Christmas Eve on the Crozets. We had two candles on our table, besides a couple of bouquets of native flowers planted in empty milk-tins, a small table-cloth, and two tiny Norwegian flags, so that the table, to us, looked almost dazzling with light and glitter.' To mark the occasion, the men sang some Christmas hymns, and H.J. Bull read from the Bible, as well as a sermon he had written. Then Johan Koren read a humorous story he had written for the magazine he produced while they were on the island, which they called *Crozeteer*. The table as illustrated by Anders in the preceding image does not look big enough to allow the fourteen men to sit around it, so the artist has used some creative licence for this illustration.

This photograph from the *Solglimt* voyage in 1908 shows a whaleboat being prepared for a rescue bid. The intent was the same as for the *Cathrine* rescue bid two years earlier when Anders, the bosun, Thorvald Johansen, and able seaman, Hans Christian Antonsen, set sail from the Crozet Islands for Australia. There are no photographs of the earlier boat, which was named *Hope*. It can be seen in this photograph that a mast has been added and the top is being readied for a canvas cover. The keel would have been strengthened and flotation devices would be fitted around the outside of the boat. The caption for this photograph in a privately owned album says: 'The rescue boat is almost ready. God willing, the nearest land is Durban.' This suggests that the target destination was to be South Africa, not Australia as it had been for *Hope*'s voyage.

This image from p. 699 of the *Pall Mall Magazine* article shows *Hope* on her journey across the Southern Ocean in early 1907. The caption reads: 'How infinitely small the boat looked on the vast ocean, even more so under canvas than without.'

CHAPTER 5

HONORED OF THEM ALL

... I am become a name;
For always roaming with a hungry heart
Much have I seen and known; cities of men
And manners, climates, councils, governments,
Myself not least, but honor'd of them all.

Alfred, Lord Tennyson, *Ulysses*[*]

De Ruyter arrived at Port Phillip Heads off Melbourne on the evening of 13 February 1907 and raised the three-flag signal KDA indicating the presence of shipwrecked sailors on board.[†] The tugboat *Alacrity* was dispatched from Queenscliff to meet her and take on board the three men, Anders, Johansen and Antonsen, who were then taken to Hobson's Bay where they disembarked and found accommodation at the Sailors' Home at the foot of Spencer Street.[‡] They were immediately welcomed in Melbourne as heroes. They had always intended to go to Melbourne, probably in April, but this was to have been with a full hold of oil and seal skins, not as shipwrecked sailors.

The Australian newspapers were, not surprisingly, very engaged with this sensational maritime adventure. A journalist from *The Argus* secured first access to the shipwrecked sailors by boarding *Alacrity* when she was off Queenscliff. Anders initially said that he would prefer to tell his story

---

[*] Tennyson, *Poems*, 1842.

[†] This does not appear to be a current signal.

[‡] In 1904 a sailors' home was established in Siddely St., where it operated until the 1960s.

once he was in Melbourne, but he relented and granted the journalist an interview. Over the following weeks newspapers across Australia featured stories about the three daring Norwegians and their life-threatening experiences. Headlines such as 'A Thrilling Story', 'Castaways in Polar Seas', 'Terrible Privations of the Crew', 'Crew on an Uninhabited Island', 'The Fate of a Sailing Expedition', 'On a Desert Island' and '1000 Miles in an Open Boat' provided leads into hundreds of articles about the misadventure and daring resolution.* Anders, as the captain and the one of the three with the best English, gave numerous interviews in the first few days after their arrival in Melbourne, and was overwhelmed to see his photograph repeatedly in newspapers and shop windows announcing his heroic deed.

In the interviews he gave, Anders explained the plight of the eleven men left behind on the island and the circumstances that led to the disaster, as well as his rationale for attempting a rescue mission in a whaleboat. He was unable to remember many of the crew members' names, even though there were only fourteen men on board the ship and they had spent an eventful four months together. This was probably a reflection of the social distancing on board, where some crew members were simply referred to as 'one of the boys forward'.

Anders said that his intention all along had been to track in a northeasterly direction to reach the regular shipping routes, in the hope of meeting a ship there. Failing that, they would try to make their way to Madagascar with the aid of the trade winds. He praised the captain and crew of *De Ruyter*, saying that they were rescued by them and brought back to life from a numbed and frozen state, the result of being in an open boat for nine days, hardly knowing if they were in the boat or submerged in the ocean. Anders reported that the remaining castaways were not in danger of lack of food or fresh water, at least until the breeding animals and birds left the island, but they were at risk of physical and mental illness.

---

* The first articles to appear in Australian newspapers were on 14 February in *The Argus*, p. 7 and *The Age*, p. 5, and others. There were also brief reports of the shipwreck in Norwegian newspapers on that day, including in *Kysten*, p. 2, *Norges Sjøfartstidende*, p. 2 and *Social-Demokraten*, p. 2.

One journalist described Anders as a sturdily built Norwegian with fair curly locks and full, pleasant features that immediately disclosed his nationality. Another claimed that Anders had gone to sea at the age of 10 or 12.[*] The newspapers were agog that that this young man was already a captain, and of a shipwrecked crew at that, and they were interested to learn, although he was every inch a sailor, that his capabilities had a wider scope. They reported that for six months he had abandoned the sea, earning his livelihood as a pictorial sketch artist on a Philadelphia newspaper.[†] Anders said he was keen to return to Kristiania as soon as possible in order to mount another sealing expedition to the Crozet Islands. Johansen and Antonsen were to make their own way back to Norway working on another ship, which was the standard practice of the time.

Anders visited the Norwegian Consul, Hans Gundersen, on their first day in Melbourne, but not before he had acquired clothes to replace the patched sailor's garb and clogs that he had been wearing when he arrived, in order that he could present himself with more dignity. In Gundersen's house he was greeted with a multitude of objects that were like a greeting from the Crozet Islands. Gundersen had been to the Kerguelen Islands in 1897 on his own ship, *Edward*,[‡] and had on display memorabilia from that trip, including photographs, shipping objects and natural history specimens, as well as, one newspaper claimed, a photograph of *Cathrine*, which he had bought in 1903 intending to mount a second sealing expedition to the subantarctic islands.[§] *Cathrine* did not change hands between 1899 and 1906, when Bull acquired her, so this cannot be right.

While the castaways were in Melbourne, Gundersen conducted an investigation into the circumstances surrounding the loss of *Cathrine*, and his report was forwarded to the Maritime Office in Norway. Anders presented Gundersen with excerpts from the ship's logbook, which had been copied to accompany the men on *Hope*. He explained that the actual

---

[*] *The Argus*, 14 February 1907, p. 7.
[†] Ibid.
[‡] McConville, 2022, p. 164.
[§] *Norges Sjøfartstidende*, 25 March 1907, p. 1.

logbook had remained on the island with Bull for safekeeping. The excerpts stated that there were 157 skins on board and 20 tons of oil, and that the estimated value of the load was 8,000 kroner (A$89,000). Anders, the first mate, Rode, the second mate, Hansen, the bosun, Johansen, the carpenter, Pedersen, and seaman, Antonsen, had all signed the excerpts, saying that they were a true and accurate record of the events.

At the Norwegian Consul's office there was mail waiting for the three men, including one for Johansen with a photograph of the young woman he was hoping to marry. Johansen was described by the press as a jolly-faced tar, of expansive build, who had sailed around the world on many occasions and had visited Australia three times previously. He was said to show no signs of the effects of exposure from his ordeal, and the news from home that reached him in the mail made him one of the happiest residents of the Sailors' Home.

The people of Melbourne were very hospitable to the three men. One day a delegation arrived at the Sailors' Home to invite them to be dinner guests at the Stock Exchange Club. Anders, the only one present at the time, went up to the Club expecting just an ordinary dinner, and was astonished to walk into a large room full of men. He was lifted up onto a table so everybody could see him, after which he received a volley of shouted hoorays, so loud that he thought the roof would crack open. He was very embarrassed and just wanted to get away, but he also admitted that it was a great deal of fun. He was treated to a splendid dinner with a number of speeches, to which he had to reply. The evening culminated with Anders being carried around the hall on a gold chair. When he arrived back in his room, he discovered that his dinner companions had put a considerable number of gold coins into his pockets, booty that he duly shared with Johansen and Antonsen.* Another highlight for Anders was a party given for him, on board a ship, by the Norwegian captains then in port. He was also a guest at the Melbourne Club (later reports in Norwegian newspapers said that he had been made a member of the

---

* *Morgenbladet*, 31 March 1907, pp. 1–2.

Melbourne Club, but that was probably a misunderstanding). He thought that Melburnians were great people.

There was a great deal of interest in the isolated nature of the island on which *Cathrine* had been wrecked, prompting a number of articles that debated which island was the loneliest, most desolate and most inaccessible in the world.* One article suggested that people would doubtless plump for one of the Crozet Islands because of all the news about the shipwreck there. The writer of the article, believing that *Cathrine*'s crew had spent their time on Hog Island, ruled it out as a candidate on the basis that it abounded with food supplies, including hares and rabbits, penguins, albatrosses and sea elephants.† Heard Island, in the same seas, was considered more isolated, as well as more barren, although it, like Hog Island, had a shelter hut built for castaways and was visited by whalers occasionally. The article was wrong on several counts, there being no remaining shelter on any of the islands in the Crozet group at that stage, and whaling and sealing had not been conducted on or around those islands for decades.

South Georgia made it to the list of possible candidates for remoteness because, although the writer claimed that it was visited by whalers, it had no shelter and was right out of the way of shipping routes, so anybody unlucky enough to be wrecked there would stand a very poor chance of getting off alive. Bouvet Island, a subantarctic island between South America and South Africa, was considered more isolated even than South Georgia because it was visited even more rarely, and the writer claimed that, on the last occasion a ship had visited there, five corpses had been discovered lying frozen on the beach, a grim memento of another unrecorded disaster at sea. Also considered as a candidate was Possession Island, not the one that is part of the Crozet Islands group on which Anders and *Cathrine*'s crew were shipwrecked, but the one that lies due south of New Zealand.‡ Ultimately, the writer gave the prize to Dougherty Island, on which no

---

* *Pearson's Weekly*, 28 March 1907, p. 6.

† They are more commonly called elephant seals.

‡ Correctly, this should be Possession Islands, which are a group of small islands and rocks in the western part of the Ross Sea.

landing had been made at that time, and which had only been sighted three times. Indeed, the writer stated that it had been named in the *Admiralty Sailing Directions* as 'the most remote and isolated spot on earth'. Since the time this article appeared in 1907, it has been determined that Dougherty Island does not actually exist, despite it having been reported in the South Pacific Ocean by ships in 1841, 1860 and 1886. Those ships must have sighted either fog banks or large icebergs, rather than land. Nevertheless, all of the subantarctic islands are very remote, with the Crozet Islands being no exception.

Anders left Melbourne on 1 March and arrived back in Norway on 25 April, travelling via Hoboken, New York, on the White Star Line steamship *Persic*. Anders' transport back to Norway included a curious connection with another shipwreck, that of *Suevic*, also a White Star Line ship. After arriving in England, Anders was to have travelled the home stretch on *Suevic*, but she was wrecked off the south coast of England on 17 March.[*] Due to human error, in heavy fog, *Suevic* ran full speed into the Maenheere Rocks, near Lizard Point off the Cornish coast. Remarkably, despite the difficult conditions, all 456 passengers and crew, including seventy babies, were rescued. The rescue was led by the Royal National Lifeboat Institution and involved just four open wooden lifeboats, each rowed by six oarsmen who were all volunteers. The whole operation took sixteen hours.[†]

Suevic went on to have an eventful life. Remarkably, her stern and bow were separated at the wreck site, using dynamite. The stern was taken under its own power to Southampton where, in due course, a bow that had been manufactured for her in Belfast was attached. There was a joke at the time that *Suevic* was the longest ship in the world, with her bow in Belfast and her stern in Southampton. *Suevic* returned to service, mainly carrying passengers between England and Australia, until she was requisitioned for

---

[*] https://www.whitestarhistory.com/suevic, accessed 31 October 2021.
[†] https://rnli.org/about-us/our-history/timeline/1907-the-suevic-rescue, accessed 31 October 2021.

duty in the First World War. In 1928 she was sold to a Norwegian company that converted her into a whaling ship and renamed her *Skytteren*.* In her final dramatic phase, during the Second World War *Skytteren* was stranded in Gothenburg, in Sweden, where she was wanted by both the Norwegians and Germans. While she was attempting to make a dash for England, *Skytteren* was spotted by the Germans, and her captain made the decision to scupper her, using pre-prepared explosives, rather than see her captured. The Germans took the crew as prisoners-of-war.

Anders had deliberately chosen a route that would take him via Cape Town so that, if necessary, he could organise a rescue expedition to free the castaways on the Crozet Islands. When the ship docked in Albany, Western Australia, he was delighted to learn that the rescue was already underway. On his arrival in Norway, it was reported that all signs of the hardships he had endured had disappeared, and he looked fit and well, with his seaman's courage and good humour intact, notwithstanding the financial loss incurred by the expedition. He expressed his appreciation of the kindness and hospitality he had received from everybody he had encountered. Bull, whose rescue is detailed in the next chapter, soon joined Anders in Kristiania, and together they threw themselves into a publicity drive to raise funds for their next expedition south. In this they were helped mightily by the Norwegian press, which was agog with the daring feat of its countrymen, who were hailed as true Vikings.

Two weeks after his arrival back in Norway, Anders' family, friends and the community of Stange held a big party in his honour. A reception venue was hired and it was reported that the whole evening was conducted in great style. The 120 guests entered the dining area to live music, and the room was beautifully decorated. In front of each guest's place there was a model of a whaling ship in full sail, with its crew on deck, all made from marzipan. Local dignitaries made speeches, ranging from humorous to serious, and Anders was said to have replied in his usual engaging manner. One of the speeches was given in honour of *Cathrine*'s crew, and a song

---

* 'Skytteren' translates into English as marksman, or shooter.

was composed for the occasion. The evening, which was characterised by good humour, ended with dancing.

The first lecture Anders gave in Norway was to the Kristiania Seamen's Association. The lecture, which was reproduced in full in the newspapers,[*] was presumably the same, or similar to, the many he gave over the coming months. He set the scene with vivid descriptions of the isolation of the rocky, mountainous islands and their exposure to the full force of the wind, rain, snow, sleet and relentless waves. He provided a history of sealing in the Southern Ocean, driven as it was in the nineteenth century by the high price of oil and abundance of seals, which resulted in seals being hunted almost to extinction. Drawing on the evidence of shipwrecks in every bay, the detritus of abandoned sealing equipment and the presence of a haunting graveyard, Anders spoke evocatively of the islands as being like a big, silent cemetery.

Anders said that, while the islands were at that stage treeless, there were fossils inland that provided a record of the presence of mighty trees in the distant past, apparently up to 200 years old, judging by his count of the tree rings. There are, however, no petrified tree trunks on the Crozet Islands. The petrified trunks that Anders thought he had seen are actually volcanic rocks. Of the other plant life on the islands, Anders spoke about the beautiful species of moss, the abundant grass that grows along the banks of the streams and a plant with a small white flower. Of the Kerguelen cabbage, he commented that even after twenty-four hours boiling it remained bitter and unpalatable, although it was nutritious.

He also recounted that the men were quick to discover the presence of mires, which were dangerous traps for the unwary. These mires, which form in peaty areas with a high moisture content, look like solid ground but give way immediately when walked upon. Anders himself fell into mires on more than one occasion, and several times had to come to the assistance of other men similarly caught out. As already mentioned, Anders had recommended that the men should not walk about on the

---

* *Norges Sjøfartstidende*, 2 May 1907, pp. 1–2.

island alone, a suggestion that Koren the naturalist had blithely ignored as he explored his fascinating, albeit temporary, home.

Anders reported in this lecture that rats were present in huge numbers on the island, and that they had ransacked the stores left in the depot. It is interesting to note that almost none of the other accounts of their life as castaways on the island made mention of the rats. Perhaps Beef kept them out of the cabin, where they would have been a terrible problem, and would therefore surely have been made much of. The rats no doubt had come to the islands on the ships wrecked there. Anders observed that they appeared to him to be living a comfortable life on bird eggs and dead animals. Anders had read references in the press to the presence of lemmings on the Crozet Islands, but he concluded that this was due to a misunderstanding caused by the fact that the rats on the Crozet Islands lived under tufts of grass, as did lemmings in their native environments.

Of 'lower' animals, Anders reported spiders, some small beetles and flies, as well as earthworms, but his audience would no doubt have been more interested in the larger animals, and Anders' descriptions concentrated on the extraordinary birdlife on the island and on the large mammals, the seals, that had enticed the crew of *Cathrine* to the south. Much of this would have been novel for the mariners in the room and even more so for the readers of the Norwegian newspapers that published the lecture.

Anders was enchanted by the penguins and included in his lecture a story about his first meeting with them on the island when several came to converse with him, only for this to be foiled by the lack of a common language. Anders said that he silently promised the penguins that he and his men had come in peace and would do them no harm, a resolve they had to break once they were wrecked and became reliant on the penguins in particular for a tasty meal. In describing the rockhopper penguins, Anders spoke about their feistiness and argumentativeness, telling how they stole eggs from each other and became hysterical when humans entered their colonies. He described the king penguins as being majestic and acting with great dignity, while the gentoos walked like arthritic old women. Most of the other birds he saw on the island were described only insofar as they were useful to the shipwrecked men. However, he singled out the southern giant petrels, which disgusted him with their scavenging behaviour and their habit of vomiting a putrid substance when they were defending themselves. The albatross eggs, of course, were a critical and appetising food source for the castaways, and so were highly valued. His descriptions of the elephant seals and the way the men learnt to kill them have been covered in an earlier chapter. Although these descriptions are confronting to a modern reader, perhaps this was less so for the audiences of the time.

The idea that Anders, Johansen and Antonsen were modern-day Vikings was stressed by the Norwegian journalists. It was, after all, merely a year and a half since Norway had gained independence, and the nationalistic foundation stories about valiant Vikings seeking wealth and new territories abroad were front and centre in people's minds. In fact, Anders absolutely fitted the bill. Like Anders, most Viking leaders were from old, affluent, land-holding families, were motivated by the pursuit of wealth and new territory and were involved in bloody battles to achieve their goals. In comparison, famous Norwegians such as Fridtjof Nansen and Roald Amundsen,[*] who were also often referred to as Vikings, were primarily motivated by an exploration impulse, rather than the pursuit of wealth. It is likely that they were also motivated by the pursuit of fame, which, in itself, was certainly a Viking impulse. Nansen himself thought that the country's sealers and whalers were its true Vikings. At any rate, the newspapers were very happy to make Norwegian chests swell with pride with tales of the deeds of the Vikings who had set sail on *Hope*, who had demonstrated the most valued attributes of courage, strength and the ability to survive.[†]

One journalist pointed out that, although Anders was born in the

----

[*] Brown, 2012.
[†] Drivenes and Jølle, 2006, pp. 115–116.

heart of Norway, rather than on the coast, it should not be surprising that he was drawn to the sea.* After all, several people from the same area Anders hailed from had been exceptional Vikings in the middle of the peak Viking era. In the year 999 or 1000, Ketil Kalv from Stange, Anders' home town, was a warlord Viking king who was among the chiefs at the side of Olav II (later Saint Olav) in the Battle of Svolder, the backdrop to which was the unification of Norway. Ketil Kalv married Olav II's half-sister, and their son, Guthormr, fought famous battles in the Irish Sea and emigrated as a Viking to Ireland where he established a settlement. Another rural countryman, the peasant king Sigurd Syr from the Ringerike district northwest of Oslo, and stepfather to Olav II, was also a sometime Viking seafarer, although he was primarily a farmer. These were not run-of-the-mill Vikings for Anders to be likened to.

In September, after innumerable public lectures and enthusiastic newspaper attention, the public acclamation of the extraordinary rescue mission culminated in Anders being made a Knight of the First Class of the Order of St Olav.† In August, Johansen and Antonsen had also received an award, of a lesser order. St Olav, who lived from 995AD to 1030AD, is the patron saint of Norway and is credited with establishing the unified nation, as well as converting it to Christianity. He is also said to have been the last great Viking chief, and so his choice as patron saint reinforced the importance of Vikings as part of Norway's foundations, which helps to explain the reception Anders received in his home country.

---

* *Dagbladet*, Friday 3 May 1907, p. 1.

† This was at the time the highest honour that could be bestowed in Norway. It was the equivalent of being knighted in Australia, although it carried no title, and it was awarded for exceptional contributions to the country or mankind. The 'knight' level has since been discontinued and the Order of St Olav is now almost only awarded to government officials or nobility, Norwegian or otherwise. For the remainder of the book this award is referred to as the Order of St Olav.

CHAPTER 6

SAVED FROM THAT FATAL SHORE

When you, by friendship's generous motives sway'd,
Flew to my help, and brought unhop'd-for aid;
Sav'd me just sinking on that fatal shore,
Where hope is lost and comfort is no more;

Elizabeth Scot, *The Friendly Rescue*[*]

News of the shipwreck reached Norway within hours of Anders raising the alert in Melbourne. The Norwegian Consul-General in Melbourne sent a telegram to the Norwegian Government advising that the eleven men on Possession Island were in need of rescue, and the Australian Prime Minister of the time, Alfred Deakin, cabled the Prime Minister of the Cape Colony,[†] Dr Leander Jameson, asking for his assistance. This is because the rescue attempt would logically depart from Cape Town, about seven days from the Crozet Islands by steamer.

These telegrams triggered the same fascinated response in Norway that Anders and his colleagues had elicited in Melbourne, with original and syndicated articles appearing in all corners of the country. Shipwrecks were not an unusual occurrence for this shipping nation, but the daring rescue bid was exceptional, and the press responded accordingly.

Just two days after Anders' arrival in Melbourne the Norwegian Government was able to advise that it intended to telegraph the Norwegian

---

[*] Scot, 1801, p. 121.

[†] In 1907 the Southern part of South Africa, including Cape Town and Durban, the two main shipping ports, was under British rule and was called Cape Colony.

Consul in Cape Town authorising the dispatch of a rescue vessel. As this was a matter of some urgency the approval to commit the government to the cost of the rescue mission was made without seeking Parliamentary approval, but Parliament was advised. The cost of the mission was expected to be around £550 (A$90,000). The Parliamentary President, Gunnar Knudsen, commended the Department involved, the Ministry of Trade, on its prompt response and said he was confident that everybody would agree with the actions that had been initiated. The Norwegian Consul in Cape Town, Charles Wilhelm Thesen, sent advice to Norway on the available options, and the use of a steamship was approved. The other possibilities were to deploy the British warship *Crescent*, which was at that time in Cape Town, or to hire a tugboat, which would be £100 (A$16,300) cheaper than a steamship.

In Norway it was thought that the steamship would be a more suitable vessel for those stormy waters. However, almost immediately – on Wednesday 20 February – it was announced that a modern, powerful tugboat would depart from Cape Town to rescue the castaway crew. In addition, a steamship that had left Cape Town the previous Saturday would divert to the Crozet Islands if the weather allowed, but would not expose itself to risk or delay. The steamship, *Turakina*, was a New Zealand vessel of about 8,000 tons that had departed from London on 21 January and was destined for New Zealand. The tugboat deployed for the rescue attempt, *Panther*, was reported to be a double-propellered, 400-horsepower vessel, 236 tons and 33.5 metres long, which had been built in Leith, Scotland.

No sooner had *Panther* reached the Southern Ocean than she had to turn back. She may well have been an exceptional tugboat, but she was not suited to the heavy seas of the Roaring Forties and had been swamped by the big waves to such an extent that the cabins had been inundated. The crew refused to make another attempt, and efforts to find a substitute crew in Durban proved fruitless.* The Norwegian press, perhaps with their

---

* Most of the references to Durban called it Port Natal. Possibly this remained common practice for mariners, however Port Natal was renamed Durban in 1835, and Durban is used throughout this book.

fellow countrymen's marine exploits in mind, thought the South Africans less than brave. Perhaps they would have been more sympathetic if they had fully considered the attributes of the tugboat that made it unsuited to the task. After this first rescue attempt had failed so signally, the Norwegian Ministry for Trade sent a telegram to Thesen giving him free rein to do what was necessary to retrieve the castaways.

By 23 February, nine days after Anders had arrived in Melbourne, the Ministry of Trade had received word that a steamship in South Africa was available to go to the Crozet Islands to rescue *Cathrine*'s crew. The offer, however, came with a price tag of 18,000 kroner (A$200,000) in compensation for the coal that would be needed for the voyage, based on travelling at maximum speed. This vessel, *Ingrid*, was owned by the Norwegian Consul Thesen's own shipping company.* It was an 85-horsepower steamship of 683 tons and was 58.2 metres long. *Ingrid* was normally deployed along the African coast carrying cargo. It was estimated that under good conditions she could make the return trip from Cape Town in fifteen to sixteen days.

As soon as news of *Cathrine*'s wreck and the subsequent rescue voyage started to filter through to the press in Norway, multiple arguments erupted about *Cathrine*'s suitability for undertaking the risky expedition to the dangerous waters of the Southern Ocean, the role of the Maritime Office in authorising the voyage and who should take the credit for *Hope*'s successful mission. These arguments began just days after news of the wreck and rescue voyage reached Norway – certainly before any of those involved were able to properly inform the discussion – and then continued once further information became available.

The left-wing press in Norway queried the suitability of 'fragile' *Cathrine*, which was by then thirty-six years old and had seen her best days, to undertake such a risky venture.† It was argued that, while shipowners

---

* *Kysten*, 26 February 1907, p. 2.
† *Social-Demokraten*, 9 March 1907, p. 2 and 13 March, p. 2.

were of course interested in speculating on old hulls, the Maritime Office should have taken action in the public interest and for the sake of the crew's lives and wellbeing. It was argued that had *Cathrine* been prevented from going on the expedition the Norwegian Government would also have avoided paying a considerable amount to rescue the crew and bring them home. The Director of the Maritime Office responded by saying that *Cathrine* had been assessed with an A2-star rating and should therefore be considered an absolutely fit vessel. Representatives from the Maritime Office had been on board prior to her departure from Norway and were satisfied that the ship was furnished with three good lifeboats (in fact she departed with four),[*] the required rescue equipment and appropriate instruments and tools. Furthermore, she had undergone major repairs in 1898.[†]

One correspondent, the Chairman of the Kristiania Seamen's Association, Commander Harold Lundh, challenged the Maritime Office in the press and privately, with the result that a copy of the inspection report was made available to the press.[‡] *Cathrine* was required to have three lifeboats with buoyancy aids, and one had to carry a light buoy. The safety equipment to be stashed in the boats was itemised. However, as active hunting vessels, two of *Cathrine*'s boats were exempt from some of these requirements, apart from the instruction that a supply of water and hard bread was to be in all the boats at all times. A further requirement was that the boats must be organised in such a way that they could be put on the water quickly, should be as free as possible from masts and rigs and must not be weighed down or obstructed by cargo or other goods. All ships were required to carry out practice launchings of their boats to check that everything was in order. Given *Cathrine*'s whaleboats had been launched almost daily when hunting was underway, and that two successful, if difficult, emergency launchings had taken place at the time of the wreck, it

---

* The boats on *Cathrine* were whaleboats that would double as lifeboats if necessary, as was the norm for whaling and sealing vessels at the time.
† *Social-Demokraten*, 13 March 1907, p. 2.
‡ *Norges Sjøfartstidende*, 10 April 1907, p. 1.

was clearly immaterial to the overall outcome whether practice launchings had been carried out previously in the interests of safety.

Some, including Lundh, thought that the Maritime Office should get the credit for regulating the type of whaleboat that sealing and whaling vessels were required to carry, thus ensuring that *Cathrine* had good enough lifeboats with her to make the hazardous voyage across the stormy sea. Others pointed out that this type of whaleboat had been in use in the northern hemisphere for many years, able to function successfully in all sorts of weather, long before the Office had control over shipping, and so the only people who should get the credit were those who carried out the daring voyage. Lundh argued that, because the Maritime Office had ordered three of *Cathrine*'s boats to be replaced with boats that incorporated the specified safety features such as buoyancy aids, it should get some of the credit for the successful outcome of the *Hope* voyage. Others disputed this point, saying that the boats were replaced, but not because they were condemned by the Maritime Office. It seems that there was great pride in the hardy little whaleboats that were such a feature of Norwegian whaling and sealing.

At that stage, of course, nobody in Norway was aware of the extraordinary effort that was put into strengthening *Hope* and making her seaworthy enough for the demands of her unexpected task. Anders, at any rate, was always at pains to give the greatest part of the credit to Pedersen, *Cathrine*'s resourceful carpenter, and the Norwegian press was soon lauding the efforts of its countrymen as enthusiastically as the Australian press. One newspaper said that, once again, a boat trip had been undertaken that Norwegians could be proud of, and another blasted those who would give the credit to the Maritime Office, saying that all the regulatory puffery imposed by it paled into insignificance when compared with the ingenuity demonstrated by the shipwrecked men and the fantastic sailing deed accomplished by Anders and his crew.

The newspapers, hungry for flesh to add to the early bare bones of the story, turned to a famous Norwegian-Australian Antarctic explorer,

Carsten Egeberg Borchgrevink, to ask for his views.[*] There was quite some irony in this choice of commentator, because Borchgrevink had been on Bull's earlier expedition in 1894–95 to the Antarctic and the two men had subsequently had a falling out. Borchgrevink was an ambitious fellow traveller on the vessel *Antarctic*. He became infamous for claiming that he was the first to set foot on the Antarctic continent. He said that he had leapt from the boat ferrying Bull, the captain and others to shore, in order to be the first to step on the continent, but also to investigate a jellyfish he had seen in the shallow water. The captain, Kristensen, also claimed this 'first', however it is now thought that a crew member, New Zealander Alexander von Tunzelmann, should be credited with having made the first substantiated landing on the Antarctic mainland because he got out of the boat to steady it before the others could disembark. It was believed at the time that this was actually the first footfall on the continent. However, as stated earlier, this 'first' almost certainly belonged to an American sealing expedition in 1821. Bull for his part simply said that the sensation of being the first men to land there was 'strange and pleasurable'.[†]

In 1898–1900 Borchgrevink led a scientific expedition to the Antarctic in the ship *Southern Cross*, and was the first to spend a winter on the Antarctic mainland. This expedition was financed by the wealthy British publisher Sir George Newnes, and was named the British Antarctic Expedition, even though its leader and most of the crew were Norwegian.

Borchgrevink painted a colourful picture of the situation facing Anders and the men on *Cathrine*. He advised Norwegian readers that the Crozet Islands were a constant terror for the seafarers who passed the Cape of Good Hope and continued further east towards Australia with the wind behind them. He said that these ships all set course far south of the barren and desolate archipelago that made up the Crozet group. However, because navigation in these waters was extremely difficult, it could almost be said that you had been unlucky if you found these storm-

----

[*] *Ringerikes Blad*, 19 February 1907, pp. 1–3.
[†] Martin, 1996, p. 106.

ravaged islands, where fjords cut a straight line into the islands, and a ship would be hopelessly lost if it were to be forced into one of them by a storm. Borchgrevink related the story of *Strathmore*, which was wrecked in 1875, as well as the sinking of *Prince of Wales* in 1821. *Prince of Wales* was a 75-ton cutter that was sealing around the islands in the Southern Ocean. As was the case when *Cathrine* went to the Crozet Islands, in 1821 there were abundant populations of several types of seals, as well as penguins. On the day *Prince of Wales* was wrecked, seven of the men were on land sealing, with eight remaining on the ship. When a storm arose the men on the ship tried to sail it closer to the land, but she ran aground and was destroyed in the storm, with all on board drowning. The men on shore were without provisions or shelter, but managed to survive on the island for two years, living on birds, eggs and seals, as well as the Kerguelen cabbage. The men were rescued in 1823, and one of the survivors, Charles Goodridge, published a Crusoe-style account of their experiences.[*] This is the first detailed account of the Crozet Islands.

In response to information in one of Anders' telegrams explaining that the shipwrecked crew had very little firewood, Borchgrevink suggested that, given the absence of any trees on the island, the men would have been able to burn albatross feathers as fuel, because the slow-moving albatrosses are easy to catch and their ribbed feathers burned well. In the event, there was sufficient timber from *Cathrine* to last the duration of their stay on the island, so the albatrosses' main contribution to the men's provisions was their eggs. Borchgrevink confirmed that there was a good supply of fresh water in the islands, noted the depots that had been established for shipwrecked crews and said the British, in consideration of the sailors who might be wrecked on these shores, had stocked the islands with goats, pigs and sheep and may also have thoughtfully left cookware and other useful items that could be of great use to the shipwrecked Norwegians. In fact, the only introduced species any of the castaways reported on Possession Island was rats, and these had made merry with the provisions left in

---

* Goodridge, 1938.

the depot. Borchgrevink said that he had himself visited several of these southern islands and found that, even on the best of them where vegetation was abundant, a number of graves could be found, bearing witness to the difficulties facing people trying to survive there, living solely on what the islands produced and the sea cast ashore. One could also say that they bore witness to the dangers of sealing on the islands.

When asked whether or not it would have been quicker for the three men in their makeshift sailing vessel to have gone north to try to reach Africa, Borchgrevink replied that it would have been almost impossible for such a small vessel to have made its way north against the constant westerly winds in the Roaring Forties. If the men were seeking Africa they would have had to sail north until they were out of the Southern Ocean and then set a northwesterly course. Borchgrevink was also asked to comment on the length of time it took *De Ruyter* to reach Australia after she had picked up *Hope* and her crew members, which was almost three weeks. Borchgrevink replied that sailing and navigation in these waters was extremely difficult, and the distances were huge. In 1889 Borchgrevink had sailed to Australia with the Norwegian barque *Valuta*, and he claimed they had made the fastest recorded voyage from the southern tip of Africa to Sydney, just twenty-two days. Anders had already told the Australian press that *De Ruyter* had to lower all of her sails when the storm hit just after *Hope* was taken on board, which showed just how fierce the storms could be, and how it was impossible even for a large sailing ship to make headway at those times.

The interview with Borchgrevink concluded with some rather self-serving and disparaging comments about Bull. Borchgrevink said that the shipwreck was of special interest to him because Bull, who was with *Cathrine* as a sort of manager, was also with him – Borchgrevink – on the *Antarctic* voyage in 1895. He said that Bull, now an old man, had gone through a lot, but his inexhaustible energy would probably ensure that he prevailed over the difficulties of this situation as well. In fact, Bull was not merely 'with' Borchgrevink on the expedition of 1895; rather, he was the driving force behind it. Similarly, Bull was not with *Cathrine* as a 'sort of manager'; again, he was the driving force behind it and was the expedition leader.

When he heard what had happened with the tugboat *Panther*, Borchgrevink wrote to the Norwegian press saying that this was entirely predictable because tugboats like this are low in the bow and not built for heavy waves and wind. Furthermore, he said that the need to carry coal on the deck to fuel the powerful engines would have further destabilised the tugboat. Borchgrevink had expressed the view in advance that a more seaworthy vessel should have been chosen, and one complete with good lifeboats. He noted with admiration how *Panther*'s experience had shown just how much Anders and the other two men had accomplished with their good whaleboat. He said that the rescue should be attempted by either a large steamship that would manage the stormy weather, or by a small sailing vessel like *Cathrine* herself that would be highly economical, light on the water and fly like an albatross, where a heavily loaded tugboat must wallow and work hard. A large steamship or a small sailing vessel could stand out from the island, wait for favourable weather and then send small boats in to ferry the men out, the whole exercise taking just a few hours once the boats could be launched.

On the morning of 21 February, the dog Beef behaved very strangely. It was his habit to share a bed with one or another of the men. He would lie there while Lysacker prepared breakfast and then rise when everybody else did. On this morning, contrary to his usual behaviour, he was so restless that at six o'clock Lysacker let him out of the hut, and some time later Bull heard him say, 'What the hell's the matter with the dog?' Apparently, Beef was running around on the beach, seemingly overcome with joy, behaving in a way the men had never seen before.

This was their seventy-eighth day of captivity on the island, a period during which their hope for rescue was tinged with scepticism and occasional despair. At noon, news spread like wildfire through the camp – a steamer was coming into the bay. They all rushed onto the beach, where they saw a magnificent steamship swinging around the headland and gliding into American Bay. The ship was flying the British flag and a rocket was fired to announce her arrival. The castaways speedily raised the Norwegian flag they had salvaged from the wreck, and six of the men, including Bull, immediately put a boat on the water and set out to direct the ship to a safe anchorage. Those remaining packed as many of their own and their colleagues' belongings as they could and brought them down to the beach, a task they completed before the rowboat returned, with the oarsmen pulling like men possessed. The ship was *Turakina*, which had left Cape Town on 16 February, taking just five days to reach the Crozet Islands. She was the most welcome of saviours. As the castaways were ferried to her, hundreds of passengers lined the rails and shouted hoorays while waving and swinging their hats in welcome.

The timing of *Turakina*'s arrival meant that *Ingrid* was actually commissioned to go to the Crozet Islands after the castaways had been rescued; she had left Cape Town on 1 March. After twenty-three days no word had been heard from her, and people were starting to worry. It was thought that she may have met bad weather at the Crozet Islands, making landing impossible, or that she had found no sign of the men on Possession Island and may have started to search neighbouring bays and islands. Despite the concern, *Ingrid* returned safely to Cape Town on 22 March.

In April it was reported that an English ship, *Mimiro*, had passed close by the Crozet Islands while the men were still there, but the ship's crew were unaware of this and the islands were only sighted briefly before fog hid them from view.[*]

Beef's odd behaviour had started at least seven hours before the rescue ship reached the island. Is it possible that a dog has such superior senses that it can hear, smell or feel a steamship's approach at such a distance? Or

---

[*] *Lloyd's List*, 15 April 1907, p. 3.

could it have been pure intuition that enabled Beef to know that help was coming? It does seem improbable that his strange behaviour was purely coincidental.

When talking later about their rescue, Bull declared that people who had not undergone the maddening, tedious and uncertain existence of a shipwrecked sailor could not begin to appreciate the feelings of the eleven men when they saw that fine steamship come round the corner of the bay. When he had gone on board *Turakina* and shaken the hand of its master, Captain Francis Forbes, three months of depression simply evaporated. The men were embarrassed by their rough and ragged clothing. There are no descriptions of what they did about this for the three weeks they were on the ship, but on their arrival in Hobart the Norwegian Consul in Hobart provided them with clothes and other necessities. Nevertheless, their reception and treatment on *Turakina* was full of kindness and compassion. One can only imagine their joy when they heard that the three men in *Hope* had been picked up at sea and were safe.

While on board *Turakina* Bull gave a lecture about the shipwreck and their life on the island, including the preparations for *Hope*'s voyage, as well as reciting long poems that he had written for his wife. Bull was an accomplished speaker and writer, and his lecture was enriched with drawings that Koren had made of various key episodes in the affair. The lecture was received with vivid interest and Bull was rewarded with enthusiastic applause. The audience was especially excited to hear about Anders' decision to seek rescue by sailing *Hope* to Australia, and they demonstrated this by way of a threefold hooray for Anders, Johansen and Antonsen.

Koren's reaction to their rescue was summarised thus: 'Talk about a dramatic transition! Eight days ago we walked about like miserable prisoners, dirty and horrible, living in a sooty hole of a hut lit only by a smoking stove and existing on a diet of penguin, seal meat and lard. Today we are passengers on a first-class English steamship, admittedly not elegantly dressed, but we are hailed as today's heroes (I do not understand why) and live like counts."* He went on to marvel at human nature, saying that while on the island they had salivated at the thought of a mere potato, or a piece of freshly cooked bread, but several days later they were already so blasé that they frowned at most of the English sauces and considered the coffee to be insufficiently strong.

The rescue by *Turakina* had almost not been accomplished. The captain had made it clear that he would not risk the safety or lives of his hundreds of passengers or crew by approaching the dangerous islands if the weather was unfavourable and, for three to four days on their approach to the Crozet Islands, the weather was exactly that. On the day they expected to reach Possession Island, a priest on board was asked to pray for the weather to clear, which it did almost immediately, with the sun shining in a blue sky just half an hour after the prayers were said. When they subsequently learned about this, the castaways gave praise for their good fortune. In a further indication that the gods were on their side, one of the engineers reported that the engine had been playing up all the way from Cape Town, but it had freed up just in time for the captain to risk approaching the island.

On 8 March *Turakina* arrived in Hobart, where the men rescued from Possession Island disembarked. Of the eleven, six, including Bull and Koren, went on to Melbourne, and the remaining five were able to secure working positions from Hobart to Europe on a Norwegian ship transporting lumber. Two of the crew members who travelled to Melbourne were taken on there by Norwegian ships, and three remained in Australia. Bull spent a little time in Melbourne, where he spoke at the Royal Geographical Society, amongst other activities, and then made his own way back to Norway. One report commented that Bull showed some signs of his ordeal, whereas the younger men appeared not to, being described as big, strong-limbed men, brown with exposure but well-padded, with no sign of privation.

The crew members – those whose English was good enough to be

---

* *Nedenæs Amtstidende*, 20 April 1907, p. 2.

interviewed – confirmed that their life on the island was more monotonous than difficult, and they certainly were not at risk of starvation.* However, the men spoke about almost losing their lives as they tried to make shore after abandoning the ship during the storm. The first mate, Rode, who was described as a powerful, broad-shouldered man, of middle age, with a reddish beard and light blue Norwegian eyes, said that he did not mind the stay on the island, but the worst thing was finding things to do. Pedersen, the carpenter, described as a tall, slow man who might have passed for Kipling's 'Hans, the blue-eyed Dane',† qualified those comments by saying that things were pretty lively in the beginning when they were busy making the cabin to live in, and then preparing the boat.

Pedersen spoke about the urgent need to build the cabin, saying he thought they would all freeze once they were stranded on the island – he used the word 'refrigerated', trying to find the correct English word to describe their predicament. He described the cabin they made as rough, since he did not have very many tools. In fact, he only had an axe, which Rode had seen lying on *Cathrine's* deck where it had been thrown just before she struck the reef. Pedersen confirmed the comments made by Anders about the wreckage from many ships that was lying on the beaches in all of the inlets. To make their own house they collected timber from their own and other wrecks, extracted all of the nails and bolts, then dug deep holes in the ground and stood uprights in them. These made the corner posts, and then Pedersen nailed the planks onto the four sides to make the walls. Everything was done with the axe, and all of the nails were those they had taken out of salvaged timber.

The roof was made from four thicknesses of sailcloth that had also been salvaged, and the house would have been comfortable enough if it

---

* The comments by crew members in this and the following paragraphs comes chiefly from *The Register* (Adelaide), 11 March 1907, p. 8.
† This is a reference to Rudyard Kipling's song 'The Ballad of Fisher's Boarding House', which features the sailor Hans: *And there was Hans the blue-eyed Dane, / Bull-throated, bare of arm, / Who carried on his hairy chest / The maid Ultruda's charm – / The little silver crucifix / That keeps a man from harm.* In the event, Ultruda's charm fails to keep Hans safe.

were not for the smoke generated by the stove that they had to keep alight in the middle of the cabin all the time. The smoke was so thick that it made the men's eyes water (the way they phrased this was that it almost melted their eyes). For a window, mercury was scraped off the back of a salvaged mirror. In readiness for a possible winter on the island they started to increase the insulation of the cabin with moss, but were interrupted in this task by the arrival of *Turakina*.

When asked if they had sufficient fresh water, the men laughed and said that that was certainly the case – because it rained every day there was far too much fresh water. They expressed concern that in March the seals and birds, which had been on the island for breeding and moulting, would go back to sea, thereby causing a serious shortage of food. The men agreed that, given the circumstances, they were not too concerned about the fact that most of their food tasted a little of kerosene and sea water, or that their tea and coffee were mixed with dirt, or that there was rust and mould in their food. They said that roast penguin and seal fat did not taste too bad, the depot food, despite its condition, was very welcome, and they supplemented their diet with edible greens they found on the island (the Kerguelen cabbage, despite its bitterness).

Rode and Pedersen spoke about the need to find things to occupy themselves or run the risk of falling ill, physically or mentally. Like Bull, they talked about the importance of the deck of cards Koren and Thiis had made, which was used every evening from dinner to midnight. They also described the sport that was had with the seals. Rode said, 'I'd like to know where we'd all have been if we hadn't done that sort of thing. When men are shut up on a little island they've got to have exercise and do work every day or they'd get all kinds of things wrong with them. All hands used to turn to and do something for about two hours every morning. It did not matter what it was – even dragging a seal around by its tail – if it kept the men active.' The two men declared that they had not worried about Anders, Johansen and Antonsen in *Hope*, saying there were some who did not think the men should attempt the voyage, but Rode and

Pedersen declared that anybody who knew the boat only laughed. They knew how staunch it was, and believed that it could be sailed all the way to London if there were sufficient provisions. At the time that they made these comments they were not aware of what the voyage had actually been like and that, after experiencing the full fury of a Southern Ocean storm, the three men were not at all confident they could survive another, even if the boat could.

The presence of the depot on Possession Island and the parlous state of the provisions found there by *Cathrine*'s crew were of great interest in both Australia and Norway. The British ship *Comus* had visited the Crozet Islands in 1880 for the purpose of establishing depots on the three main islands of the Crozet group. By this stage there had been many shipwrecks on the islands. Already mentioned are the first recorded, *Prince of Wales*, in 1820, and *Strathmore*, in 1875. In 1837 the French corvette *Héroïne* spent six days there rescuing the crews of two wrecked American sealing vessels and carrying out a survey. In April 1840 Sir James Ross in HMS *Erebus* also spent six days there but was unable to land due to rough weather, and in 1874 HMS *Challenger* had the same problem. In 1887 the French man-of-war *Meurthe* restocked the depots that had been largely exhausted by the crew of the French schooner *Tamaris*, which was wrecked on Hog Island in 1887. *Tamaris* was en route from Bordeaux to Noumea with a cargo of supplies for the penal colony there.*

In an interesting precursor to the efforts of *Cathrine*'s crew to enlist the aid of albatrosses to alert the world to their plight, the crew of *Tamaris* attached a message to the neck of an albatross. The message was punched into tin from a can. The albatross and its attached message were found on the beach at Fremantle by a young boy seven months later. Unfortunately, the method of attaching the message to the bird's neck meant that it was unable to eat, and when it was found it was dead. The message said

---

* *Bergens Aftenblad*, 5 March 1907, p. 1.

that thirteen shipwrecked sailors were in distress on the Crozet Islands. Australian authorities sent a search vessel to the Crozet Islands immediately but found no trace of the men.

In January 1888, *Meurthe* was dispatched from South Africa to look for the castaways. She went first to Hog Island, where *Tamaris* had been stranded. There the crew found a message saying that the men had exhausted the supplies from the depot and had decided to row to Possession Island, which was a larger island, and where they knew there was another depot. When *Meurthe* arrived at Possession Island there was no sign of the crew and the supplies in the depot had not been touched. Because shipwrecks around the islands were so common, for some time the Royal Navy had sent a ship there every few years to look for stranded survivors. *Meurthe* replenished the depot on Hog Island with a ton of preserved supplies, including cartons of biscuits, tins of sardines, twenty blankets, fifteen pairs of shoes and fifteen pairs of trousers, all carefully packed in boxes. The depot on Possession Island was not replenished because it had not been touched.

An amusing example of how the press can provide misleading information when in possession of some, but not all, of the facts, appeared in a report in an English newspaper describing how castaways from the Norwegian Antarctic Expedition – by which they meant the *Cathrine* expedition – had communicated their plight to the wider world by means of catching sixty albatrosses and fastening to their legs sealed cartridges containing messages asking for help.[*] According to the report, one of the messages came safely into the hands of the Australian Premier [sic] who duly communicated with the Cape Government, as a result of which a steamer was sent to rescue the men and they were safely brought to Hobart. The newspaper thought that this would remind readers of an episode in the novel *Foul Play* by Charles Reade,[†] where the characters Robert Penfold

---

[*] *Hartlepool Northern Daily Mail*, 12 March 1907, p. 1.

[†] *Foul Play* is an 1869 novel by the British novelist and dramatist Charles Reade (1814–1884). It tells the story of a clergyman, Penfold, who is wrongly convicted of a crime and transported to Australia. En route the ship he is

and Miss Rolleston are stranded alone on an uninhabited island in the South Pacific. Penfold catches wild ducks and attaches messages to their legs, giving the approximate position of the island, and sets them loose. One of the ducks is caught, and this leads to their rescue.

In due course the two captains primarily responsible for the rescue of *Cathrine*'s shipwrecked crew, Captain Fuitjer of *De Ruyter* and Captain Forbes of *Turakina*, were awarded the Order of St Olav in appreciation of their service to Norwegian citizens.

It has been possible to trace the movements of some of the men on board *Cathrine* after they were rescued, but not of all. In a number of cases the men parted company with Anders once they had been rescued and brought to Australia, but some went on to accompany him on later voyages. Bull and Anders were to continue their partnership, as we will see later. The two men who had made the hazardous rescue voyage with Anders, Johansen and Antonsen, would return to the Southern Ocean with him in 1908, as would Hans Lysacker, who had eventually taken on the roles of *Cathrine*'s steward and cook.

One of *Cathrine*'s crew members was living in Australia in 1958 when Anders visited his family there as an old man. At the end of his visit Anders was to leave Australia from Adelaide, and this information was reported by ABC Adelaide on the day before his departure.[*] To his great surprise, a sailor who had been with him on the *Cathrine* voyage came to the wharf to see him, and the two old comrades had a warm reunion.[†] This was Emanuel Thiis,[‡] the crew member who had been exploring Possession Island with Anders on the fateful day fifty years earlier when the storm that wrecked *Cathrine* sprang up. He was one of the three who elected

---

travelling in is shipwrecked on an uncharted island called Godsend Island in the South Pacific. Eventually he is rescued and vindicated of his crime.

[*] ABC News Service, Adelaide, 31 March 1958.

[†] The account comes from Rodney Clarke, the son of the ABC presenter Rhys Clarke, who recalls his father talking about the incident.

[‡] His full name, as it appears in Australian records, was Charles Emanuel Thiis.

to stay in Australia rather than go back to Norway immediately after the rescue. Thiis was born in Kristiania in 1881, the same year as Anders. He married in Australia in 1911 and, when he died in 1964, his occupation was listed as engineer.

Of the crew who chose to remain in Australia, most is known about Koren,* who had become one of the most important members of the group, deserving much of the credit for the mostly positive morale that was maintained throughout their stay on the island. In Melbourne Koren assisted Bull with his presentation to the Royal Geographic Society, providing the illustrations of the animals and birds they had found. Koren wanted to work in Australia to raise money to mount his own expedition to Siberia and, in this, he was helped by a young zoologist who had been at the Royal Geographical Society presentation, who arranged positions extracting eucalyptus oil on a property near Euston in New South Wales for all three of the Norwegians. They lived on site and earned 6 shillings (A$50) a day for work that Koren described as not very strenuous. Koren was soon promoted to the position of foreman, thus raising his pay to 7 shillings (A$60) a day. He spent his spare time studying the local fauna and soon had good knowledge of the local species, with an emphasis, not surprisingly, on birds. Attracted by a reported salary of 10 shillings (A$85) a day, in July the three men walked for fourteen days to reach Broken Hill, where they were all engaged doing mechanical work, which suited them, despite the contrast in climate from their time on the Crozet Islands. In Broken Hill, as summer approached, the temperatures were rising to 50°C.

One of the three, Hjalmar Jensen, who was little more than a boy, and who was close to Koren, asked to accompany him to Siberia, and together they took a working passage from Sydney to Japan. Four months after leaving Broken Hill, travelling on a series of ships, they arrived in east Siberia, very late in the season and with all their savings gone. They continued to travel westward along the coast of Siberia, collecting

---

* Information about Koren is drawn from a number of newspaper articles and Evjenth, 1938, chapters 6 and 7.

wildlife and bird specimens, as well as ethnographic information, for the University of Norway and European museums. While in a small boat on one of the great rivers in eastern Siberia they were overwhelmed by a violent storm and their boat capsized. Koren managed to cling to the upturned boat until he was rescued by Indigenous people who heard his calls for help, but Jensen did not. In this disaster Koren also lost all his equipment, a rich haul of specimens and his dogs. For the next ten years Koren continued to hunt and collect specimens in Siberia and Alaska, funded through a variety of means. He earned a reputation as an intrepid and pioneering Arctic explorer, and there are specimens collected by him now held in museums across the globe. In 1917 he was working for a Russian trading company, trekking through eastern Siberia conducting trade and supplying humanitarian aid parcels to communities affected by the Spanish flu. He contracted the flu himself and died in the Red Cross Hospital in Vladivostok at the age of 39.

There is no further information on the public record about the other six crew members.

On a happier note, Bull was able to keep his promise to Anders to get Beef back to Norway. Beef joined the eleven shipwrecked crew members on *Turakina* and, in due course, was brought to Hobart, where Australian quarantine laws almost scuppered the plans to shepherd him home. Australia's strict laws were well known to all sailors. Captain Eriksson's dog Päik,* for example, had been trained to stay on board in Australian ports because the captain would have been fined every time the dog stepped on land. Not surprisingly, then, Beef was at first refused entry to Australia, where Bull intended to find passage for him on a homeward-bound Norwegian ship. Bull's powers of persuasion were put to the test. He met with the Premier's secretary and twice with the Minister for Agriculture, and pleaded at least half a dozen times with people at Customs House. In the end he was successful, and a place was secured for Beef on a Norwegian ship. Given all the other pressing matters Bull must have had to deal with

---

* Mäenpää, 2016, pp. 488–89.

on his arrival in Hobart, this effort on his part speaks to his affection for, and loyalty to, both Anders and Beef. Two of the tricks Anders had taught Beef were to put out a lighted match with his paw and to knock the ash off the end of a cigar. Bull was pleased that he had done his part to ensure that the master would have his servant present in due course to fulfill his duties in the smoking parlour!

The strength of the bond between the man and his dog was dramatically demonstrated when they were eventually reunited. Anders came into the garden of Bull's summer house in Tønsberg, where Beef had been taken on his return to Norway. When Beef saw Anders he ran towards him, sat down in front of him then fell flat on his face in a fit, foaming at the mouth. Two buckets of water were thrown over him before he revived, after which he became quite mad with joy, tearing one of his master's trouser legs to shreds in his excitement. Many Norwegian newspapers ran with this heart-warming story, usually under the heading 'The soul of a dog'.*

---

* *Asker og Bærums Budstikke*, 2 October 1907, p. 1, and other newspapers.

CHAPTER 7

THE BELLY'S HUNGER

But there's no way to hide the belly's hungers —
what a curse, what mischief it brews in all our lives!

Homer, *The Odyssey*[*]

Up to this point in his life Anders had appeared in a rather heroic light, a man at ease with his responsibilities and interactions with the world. An episode following the action-packed voyage with *Cathrine* and preceding his second expedition south would provide a different perspective on his character.

Generally speaking, the relationships between Anders and the other thirteen men on board *Cathrine* appear to have been very amiable. The one exception to this was Anders' experience with the cooks and stewards, and even that seems to have been more a case of frustration on his part and managing with the limited number of personnel choices available to him, rather than any outright conflict. Nonetheless, his grievances about these roles on the voyage, perhaps heightened by the quality of the experiences he had on the ships that took him to Melbourne and then home to Norway, bubbled to the surface in a letter from him that was published in a Norwegian newspaper, bemoaning the poor state of preparation provided to Norwegian men who signed up on ships as either stewards or cooks.[†]

This was not the first time Anders had expressed his disapproval of other people's behaviour in letters to the press, and nor would it be his last.

---

[*] Homer, 1996, 17.313–314, p. 363.
[†] *Norges Sjøfartstidende*, 30 July 1907, p. 1.

In the winter of 1904, when he was 22, he had written to the press about the theft of skis from people participating in a skiing competition near Asker in Norway.* As he described it, many skis were stolen – including his own, presumably – while the competitors were attending the prize-giving ceremony. Anders asked if nothing could have been done to prevent the thefts, and he cited the example of the arrangements in place at another competition, at Frognersetter on the outskirts of Kristiania, where competitors delivered their skis to staff members who, for a small fee, took them into safe storage. Anders said that the situation at Asker was scandalous, both on the part of both the thieves and the competition organisers, especially given the fact that skis had been stolen at that same competition the year before as well. He went on to say that appealing to the thieves' honour would be useless, since those involved obviously lacked any honourable feelings. He concluded by urging nearby residents to report anything they might know to the police, if that would lead to the arrest of the thieves. He signed off giving as his address the name of the ship he was based on at that time, *Start*.

In 1906 Anders was prompted to write to the press again when he read an article in a Norwegian journal about the sorry behaviour of Norwegian sailors in foreign ports.† A young sailor in Hamburg had got drunk and had subsequently been robbed and beaten. As a result, there had been a call for the Norwegian Government to contribute financially to the Seamen's Missions, which to that point had operated only with donations. This was a small cameo of the darkest and worst aspects of a sailor's life, and could have been seen as an aberration, rather than the norm, but Anders acknowledged that such experiences were far too common occurrences. He argued, however, that similar episodes also occurred amongst people on land, and it was unreasonable to paint sailors in a more negative light than landlubbers. The author of the original article, Mr Dahle, claimed that Norwegian sailors had low morale and were a 'ravaged young forest'.

---

* *Asker og Bærums Budstikke*, 23 January 1904, p. 2.

† *Norges Sjøfartstidende*, 12 January 1906, p. 1.

Anders countered with the argument that his many comrades, all young Norwegian sailors, were fine, upstanding fellows who made their country proud, and there were thousands upon thousands of such people from Norwegian homes across the country. According to Anders, these men were the pride of their fathers, helped their mothers, provided younger siblings with friendship and love and were a positive example of how to behave. Anders did admit that there were some sailors, unfortunate fellows, who had lost their moral compass and who were a problem for landlords and acquaintances, but again he asked if there were more of these types among sailors than people living on the land.

Mr Dahle suggested that sailors should only be paid a portion of their wages, with the balance being sent to their families for safe-keeping. Anders was appalled at this suggestion. He devoted the remainder of his letter to urging family and friends to write letters to the young sailors on board ships, pointing out that loving letters from home would assuage homesickness and discourage consolatory drinking in foreign ports. Anders praised the many Norwegians who supported the Seamen's Missions with clothes that they themselves had sewn or knitted, then donated, but he urged them also to write letters, especially at Christmas time.

Revealing a fundamental shift in his views about Norwegian sailors, Anders did not pull his punches, when, in 1907, he took pen to paper to complain in a 2,400-word letter to the press about the poor quality of stewards and cooks on board Norwegian ships. Given how preoccupied he must have been in dealing with legal and administrative matters associated with the loss of *Cathrine*, as well as raising funds and preparing for his next expedition, his level of frustration with stewards must have been very high to cause him to write the letter.

Stewards were appointed to supervise supplies and inventories and to look after the needs of senior officers by cooking for them and cleaning their quarters. Cooks were responsible for catering for all other crew members. In his letter Anders is speaking about both stewards and cooks, although the letter is headlined 'Our Stewards and the Provision of Food on

Board'. In a comment that revealed both his expectations and his position in the social hierarchy, he began his letter with: 'One thing has always annoyed me on board Norwegian vessels. It's the cooking, and in general the conduct of stewards on board. It is just as important to have a good steward on board as it is for a housewife to have a good maid, but there is many a time, sadly far too often, that good food is spoiled and wasted on board.' He pointed out the importance of good stewards and cooks on morale, and the rapidity with which everybody becomes disgruntled if bad food is constantly served, as well as the risk that diseases such as beriberi and scurvy might develop if the men's diet was not satisfactory.[*]

Having maligned all Norwegian cooks and stewards in his letter, Anders then admitted that being a steward was not an easy job. He believed that the work was most suited to older, more experienced men, but the problem was that those in this group commanded big salaries and were hard to secure. He also acknowledged that some shipping companies provisioned their vessels with second-rate food, but suggested that this problem was declining, with most companies complying with the Norwegian Maritime Act guidelines. In his opinion, if followed, these guidelines were such that good stewards and cooks had the means to provide tasty, nutritious food, and so the blame for poor food lay with them. He particularly mentioned canned meat, which he complained was often just opened, cut into portions and then served fore and aft (that is, to both officers and crew). Anders commented that with a little effort more could be made of this meat, however it was neither his place nor within his ability to provide recipes.

The main purpose of his letter was to urge those charged with training stewards to deal with the skills and approach to work needed by those who applied for these positions on ships. He said that on his last three ships the cooking had been done by youths – high school students – and they just spoiled the food and lacked the experience to do better. He compared that

* Beriberi is caused by vitamin B1 deficiency, and scurvy by vitamin C deficiency.

with his own training. Although he had completed his training to become an officer on a ship, this did not mean that he was able to immediately take on the full responsibility of a ship's master, but that he needed to gain experience. Nor was there any reason why a crew member who was tired of deck duties should be transferred to the role of steward or cook without some experience in such a role, especially given the high salaries that stewards could earn, which were comparable to those of a first mate.

And, he asked, how was a captain who must hastily hire a crew going to be able to separate the sheep from the goats, when one said he was a good steward and another said the same, one produced an elegant certificate from a stewards' school, while the other had nothing to prove his qualifications in the culinary arts, one produced examination results that showed consistently good marks while the other claimed that he could cook good food and bread? The one with the certificate got the job, settled on terms and salary, and the captain was relieved to have made the appointment, but there often began the months of disappointment and frustration on board that only a poor steward could cause. Perhaps the one with no certificate would have been a better appointment?

Anders wrote of an appointment he had made of a steward with excellent grades on his certificate, who on his first day on board said that he wanted nothing to do with the provisions. Anders could only have been speaking about the steward on board *Cathrine*, as he probably would not have been responsible for recruiting for this position when he was a senior officer on his previous ships. Anders said that some of the other recruits on that first day on board were a little drunk, and he thought that could have been the case with the appointed steward as well. When the steward was asked who he thought should be responsible for the provisions, the answer was that it should be one of the officers. Anders put off further discussion with the steward at that point, and wondered if the behaviour he was seeing was something learnt in the training course.

The next problem was that, while he was accompanying the steward to the providore to get what was needed for the voyage, Anders was called away to deal with something else and he sent the steward to get the provisions on his own, with the instruction to get 'a little of everything'. The steward returned with only blood pudding and cans of stew. When challenged on his choice, and on why he hadn't thought to include some variety, such as lobster or grouse, the reply was that the blood pudding and stew should be good enough, and that the cans of stew were larger than anything else, so he was being economical. But this wasn't the end of the difficulties. The galley was apparently completely unsatisfactory, and certainly nothing compared with the galley on the steward's previous ship. Perhaps, thought Anders, there would be some benefit from this earlier experience, but the days went by and became weeks and then months, and all they got was the same ill-prepared food. The worst of it was that the steward thought he was serving excellent and delicious food, and said it was a bloody injustice if others couldn't see that. When Anders complained to the steward, he replied that Anders should have stocked the ship with better food. Then the steward became incapacitated with a sore back and could not work, but Anders claimed that not a man on board believed that. As a result, another crew member had to cook, but the meals did not improve.

Before they left Norway Anders had asked the steward how much of a supply of hops was required to make bread on a six-month voyage, to which the steward had replied 'a kilo'. When it was suggested that this might be insufficient, the amount was increased to three kilograms, however, after two months at sea the steward advised that there were almost no hops remaining, and so they all had to eat hard bread, which caused dissatisfaction fore and aft. And, despite the fact that the proud steward had received top marks for bread-baking in his course, he had consistently failed to produce any good bread, even when hops were available.

At the outset, Anders had agreed that the steward would be helped with some tasks, such as cleaning and water retrieval. The consequence of this was that he demanded help with everything possible, while he strutted around with his hands in his pockets and with a gilded brass chain hanging beautifully on his greasy vest, playing at being an officer. After his purported back injury, he was allocated full-time help, with the expectation that the food would improve, but in this everyone was to be disappointed. Unhappily, the saying 'too many cooks spoil the broth' came true. In addition to cooking, the steward was supposed to clean the cabins and keep the saloon clean and tidy, but it barely occurred to him that he had those responsibilities, probably thinking that they were beneath an important fellow like him. And if he did send his assistant to do the cleaning, he didn't even bother to check if it had been done. In reporting this, Anders remarked that there were even times when he had to sweep out his own cabin. The rest of the crew were patient people who did not complain in the beginning, but after a while everybody was complaining.

Anders asked what could be done with such people? For practical and regulatory reasons, in most cases they had to be kept on for the duration of the period for which they had been employed, but it would have made more sense for all stewards to have to serve an apprenticeship as cooks for a number of years, just as those who had their officer's certificate had to serve on board for three years before they were considered qualified. Anders wrote that, when he was a young man on board a barque from Fredriksstad the steward then also needed help, and the younger members of the crew were invited to take on this role. The steward took Anders aside and told him that he could teach him enough in three months to be able to get a position as a steward on a handsome salary. In fact, the young crew member who took on the role of steward's assistant for seven months then undertook the stewards' examination and received his certificate, presumably, Anders thought, with an A for bread-baking.

Anders concluded his letter by saying that the matter of stewards' training and capability was a rich field for the Maritime Office to explore, rather than some of the unhelpful things it was preoccupied with. He does not elaborate on the nature of those supposedly unhelpful things. However, as his frustration with the Maritime Office turned to fury over the next two years, he may well have had cause to wish that the Office had heeded his advice and focussed its attention on the training of stewards, rather than on what he saw as the persecution of captains.

As mentioned earlier, it was really quite odd that Anders took the time to write this letter, when he could be assumed to have had much more pressing things on his mind. Perhaps, by focussing on this relatively minor topic, he was attempting to deal with the greater anxieties associated with embarking on another expedition to the dangerous waters of the subantarctic, having just survived the trauma of a shipwreck in that part of the world. He was certainly prone to use the press to express hostility to people he thought had behaved badly, or let him down, as has already been seen and we will see more of subsequently. It must also be acknowledged that this criticism was usually aimed at people in subordinate positions to himself, which raises questions about the more negative aspects of his character.

Two and a half months after Anders' letter about the parlous state of stewards on Norwegian ships, a reply from a steward was published.* The correspondent, 'J.E.', who has not been further identified, admitted that in a number of ways Anders may well have been right, that there was a lot that could be corrected, that there were probably bad elements amongst Norwegian stewards and cooks, and that it was unfortunate that Anders had had such a bad run on board his ships. He pointed out, however, that talking disparagingly about stewards was something of a maritime pastime, to the extent that, if a steward was not pleasant or good enough, it was said that he should be hung, and he argued that some of these problems could be found on the ships of any nation, with Norwegian stewards no better or worse than most, and perhaps even a little better.

He pointed out that stewards actually have very difficult jobs. For example, on a sailing ship with fifteen or sixteen men, the steward must rise between four and four-thirty in the morning then stand in a hot galley all day, even in the tropics, and cook. Then bread must be baked and the provisions inspected. After that the steward must clean the cabins

---

* *Kysten*, 8 October 1907, p. 1.

and saloon before returning to the galley to provide another meal. J.E. argued that even the most capable of stewards would need help with that workload, and on those ships where some assistance was provided it was little enough. J.E. said that they often took the brunt of dissatisfaction on board, even if the root cause was something else, and he wondered if all of that was just too complex for the Maritime Office to attempt to resolve.

J.E. concluded by saying that there were two kinds of stewards, as there are of all people: one being better, and one being worse. No doubt Anders could agree with that sentiment.

CHAPTER 8

THE ENERGETIC YOUNG CAPTAIN ON THE MOVE

As you set out for Ithaka
hope your road is a long one,
full of adventure, full of discovery.
Laistrygonoans, Cyclops,
angry Poseidon – don't be afraid of them:
you'll never find things like that on your way
as long as you keep your thoughts raised high,
as long as a rare excitement
stirs your spirit and your body.

C.P. Cavafy, *Ithaka**

As soon as Bull arrived back in Kristiania in early May 1907, he and Anders launched themselves into an effort to mount another expedition to the Southern Ocean. If there were any misgivings on the part of either of them about going into partnership again, these seemed to have been resolved or brushed aside. Perhaps Bull was right when he said that neither of them would have been able to mount an expedition on their own. Both men were determined to exploit the vast riches they had seen but had not been able to capitalise on with their first expedition, and they wasted no time in preparing for a second, significantly more ambitious attempt. Just days after Anders' arrival back in Norway, but before Bull had returned, one journalist captured the zeal with which Anders threw himself into the

---

* Cavafy, 1975.

task by saying, 'We catch the energetic young captain on the move'.* He was asked whether or not they were thinking of a second expedition, and Anders confirmed that they were, and hoped to be leaving in the autumn, which was just three months away. He said that firm plans would have to wait for Bull's return, so they had obviously communicated with each other while they were in transit and committed to another partnership. Anders stated that a new expedition would be much larger, and there were sufficient numbers of seals to warrant it.

When asked about the financial implications of the loss of *Cathrine*, Anders replied that the whole expedition had cost 40 to 50,000 kroner (A$452,000 to A$560,000), but that everything was insured. His personal loss he thought to be about 1,000 kroner (A$11,200). The costs relating to the shipwreck did not include what the Norwegian Government had spent on the rescue attempts and repatriation, although the latter would have been quite small given the fact that all the crew except Anders and Bull had either got work on other ships or elected to stay in Australia. At that time it was standard practice for the government to meet the rescue and repatriation costs associated with shipwrecked or disabled Norwegian ships, although this policy was soon to become a hot topic, triggered by Anders' own disasters.

Anders was asked what had attracted him to a seafarer's life, and he replied that he had always been adventurous, had had trouble settling at school and had gone to sea early, spending three years on ships before undertaking his officer's certificate. He said that he had been on a voyage to the Arctic Ocean as an officer on a Tønsberg ship and then had met Bull, who was looking for a young captain who was prepared to take a ship to the subantarctic islands for sealing, and who had the capacity to invest money in the expedition. Anders said that he had not hesitated, and that he had no regrets, despite the outcome of the expedition. He said that Bull was a kind-hearted, sincere, gracious and distinguished person, and the fact that he was prepared to go on such a risky expedition at his age

---

* *Norges Sjøfartstidende*, 6 May 1907, p. 2.

indicated that he had old Norwegian Viking blood in him.

By early June, Bull and Anders had formed a whaling and sealing company in association with Storm, Bull and Co. The new company had share capital of 250,000 kroner (A$2,733,000), most of which, the public was informed, was already subscribed.* Two weeks later, and after a fruitless search in Europe for a suitable vessel, Bull and Anders visited England. There they inspected a steamship that they hoped to acquire and fit out as a well-equipped factory ship,† and the purchase was announced in mid-July. The ship, *Macfarlane*, was built in England in 1881 by the Sunderland Ship Building Company and first named *Harbinger*. She was 2,700 tons and had a two-cylinder compound steam engine of 170 horsepower. In 1906 *Harbinger* had been sold to a Norwegian company, Chr. Hannevig of Horten, and renamed *Macfarlane*. In the following year she was sold to Storm, Bull and Co and renamed *Solglimt*.

The ship's original name, *Harbinger*, means the forerunner of things to come. This could be something good or something bad, and the original name was to prove apt in both these senses. *Harbinger* had her first taste of damage in 1892, while ferrying coal in the North Sea and the Baltic, scraping her underside on the Hallgrund shoal in Finland. This in itself was an omen of the more catastrophic event that occurred in 1908.

Interestingly, Bull and Anders named the company formed for their venture Fangstelskabet Haabet, or Whaling Company Hope, and their new ship was originally referred to as *Haabet* (*Hope*) in honour of their little rescue boat, but they did not stick with this name, ultimately naming their ship *Solglimt*.‡ The word 'solglimt' can be translated into English as 'glimpse of the sun', or 'ray of sunshine' or 'sunbeam'. Even though they retained the company name, it made sense that they should choose another name for the ship, because the word 'hope' carried with it an implied possibility of failure, while 'a ray of sunshine' had no such connotations.

---

* *Morgenbladet*, 9 June 1907, p. 1.

† Factory ships, or floating factories, were designed to allow processing of blubber in onboard boilers, as opposed to on land. Basberg, 1988, p. 21.

‡ *Norges Sjøfartstidende*, 24 July 1907, p. 2.

Once acquired, *Macfarlane* was taken to a shipyard in Tønsberg, and then on to another in Moss,* where she was equipped with the means to render blubber on deck and with tanks for storing the oil that was extracted on board. The original intention was to fit the ship out with sufficient tanks to store 1,100 tons of oil. However, it seems that the capacity achieved in the fit out was closer to 800 tons. In addition, accommodation for seventy crew members was installed. By August the company had share capital of 300,000 kroner (A\$3,300,000), *Macfarlane* had been renamed *Solglimt*, work to equip and fit out the ship was well underway, and Anders had hired forty of the anticipated seventy plus men required for the expedition. At this stage all the men were Norwegian and came from Tønsberg or nearby districts. Most were experienced whalers or sealers in the Arctic. Three who had been taken on as crew managers were described as being 50 years of age, so Anders was clearly looking for mature leaders to manage this large crew.† This hiring process was conducted before Anders could have the benefit of the advice provided by the steward J.E., who urged captains to only employ stewards with experience. There is no record of the quality of the stewards and cooks on board for this voyage, good or bad.

The expedition was expected to leave Norway in mid-September and return by mid-April 1908, a round trip of seven months. The ship would return with all of its catch, to be sold from Norway. Bull and Anders were reported to be co-leaders of the expedition, with Bull described again, as he was on the *Cathrine* expedition, as the manager, and Anders as the captain. Included in the complement of crew members were Bull's son, Gustav, who was engaged as an officer, H. Svindal,‡ who was a medical student, and Captain Theodor Ring, who was on board as a scientist. Svindal would obviously relieve Anders from the responsibility of dealing with injuries sustained by the crew, and Ring would take up where Koren left off, collecting zoological and botanical specimens. Ring was a career

---

* Moss is on the eastern side of the Oslofjord, 53 kilometres from Oslo.
† *Norges Sjøfartstidende*, 12 August 1907, p. 2.
‡ Anders sometimes referred to Svindal as Svinland.

mariner who had served in the Siamese Naval Service for a number of years. He was a significant shareholder in the company formed for this expedition and had with him a student, Raknæs, who was a special envoy from the University of Norway.[*]

On 23 September 1907 all preparations were complete and the large, powerful and impressively well-equipped ship was taken on a test cruise.[†] On the morning of 24 September the crew signed on and *Solglimt* departed, carrying with it the hopes of Bull, Anders and their many friends, family and shareholders. They planned to stop in Newcastle to take on 1,500 tons of coal, enough for the entire voyage, and then in Cape Town for additional supplies. As well as the provisions required for their own expedition, *Solglimt* had on board a supply of goods funded by the Norwegian Government to replenish the depot on Possession Island that the *Cathrine*'s crew had used a year earlier, notwithstanding the fact that most of it had been spoiled by exposure. They would restock the depot with preserved food, blankets, clothing, matches and ammunition.[‡] Bull and Anders and their comrades had been grateful for what they could obtain from the old depot, and they had been at pains to publicly thank the British Government for establishing it in 1880, but they would have been amused if they had read a report of their adventure in a Scottish newspaper, which asserted that they 'did not suffer from lack of food, as a government depot well stocked with eatables was discovered'.[§] This article also said that the men 'spent most of their time in wandering about their island home on the lookout for passing vessels', which was perhaps not the most accurate description of the way they had spent their time while shipwrecked on the Crozet Islands.

Bull and Anders had chosen to return to the dangerous waters of the Southern Ocean and its tiny islands with a stronger and bigger ship, seeking to take a vastly bigger catch in safer conditions, but this new expedition

---

* *Moss Tilskuer*, 24 September 1907, p. 2.
† *Moss Tilskuer*, 23 September 1907, p. 2
‡ *Fredriksstad Tilskuer*, 27 September 1907, p. 1.
§ *Dundee Evening Telegraph*, 2 October 1907, p. 4.

was certainly not without its dangers. As if to illustrate these, just weeks before *Solglimt* was due to arrive at the Crozet Islands, the steamer *Star of New Zealand* experienced exceptionally fierce gales and dangerous seas just south of the Crozet Islands, while en route from New York to Melbourne. In addition to the immense seas that towered over the ship, threatening to engulf her, while driving squalls of hail and snow enveloped the vessel, the temperature hovered around freezing point and a large iceberg was seen nearby.* *Star of New Zealand* hove to and rode out the storm, but it was a dangerous situation, and that was without the added risk of being driven onto one of the islands or hitting a submerged reef. The Norwegian press reported that there were two large Norwegian hunting vessels in the south that season, *Solglimt* and *Fridtjof Nansen*, making the point that both were pursuing their trade in dangerous waters.†

Nevertheless, *Solglimt* arrived safely at the Crozet Islands on 26 November after a good trip from Cape Town. They anchored at the westernmost island, Hog Island, in beautiful clear weather and attempted a landing, but a high sea prevented this. They had a bad experience with one of the boats almost being wrecked, and hastily retreated to the ship. The next day the sea was even higher, so they hauled in the anchor and proceeded to Possession Island, about six hours to the east, where Anders and Bull had been with *Cathrine* the year before. They anchored in American Bay, and Anders found it very strange to be back exactly where he had been wrecked, and where he had lost so much. They could see the remains of *Cathrine* on the reef, and their 'villa' was standing intact where they had left it. They went ashore and up to the hut, but the door was blocked by a large elephant seal that was lying right across the doorway, showing no inclination to make way for such insignificant creatures as those who stood before it. They fired a rifle to scare the seal and it moved away, revealing an interior that was unchanged except for the ample evidence that immeasurable numbers of rats had taken advantage of the

---

* *The Daily Telegraph* (Sydney), 8 November 1907, p. 11.
† *Arbeidet*, 15 February 1908, p. 2.

hospitality afforded by the hut in the harsh winter months. The turf walls had collapsed a little, but this was soon fixed, and the following day a party of twenty-four men moved into the hut to use it as a base.

The catch then began in earnest and, in Anders' own words, 'a terrible massacre ensued'. The elephant seals were shot in their thousands, and for days the river that flows through the middle of the valley onto the beach and into the sea ran thick with the dull red blood of the seals. Anders was appalled by the carnage and repeatedly asked himself what right they had to slaughter the poor animals, but then he pushed those thoughts aside, as a seal hunter had to, and soon got used to it. They had perfected the art of killing the seals instantly with one well-aimed bullet, and so he thought that what they were doing should not be considered cruelty to animals. To a modern reader this is less than convincing, but it was good that the animals did not suffer the prolonged agony of a combination of bullets and lances, which had been their lot in the past. The hunt went quickly. The animals were shot and skinned, the skins and blubber were brought to the river on stretchers and these were floated down the river to be loaded onto the waiting whaleboats. Boatload after boatload was rowed out to the ship, where there was activity aplenty, with the rendering of blubber and the salting of skins.

In a week's time they had cleared American Bay of all its seals, and the whole valley, as far as they could see, was full of seal carcasses. They then made their way to another bay on Possession Island, Ships Cove, where there were even more seals. Ships Cove is a small bay well protected from strong winds. Between this bay and American Bay there are three small bays, which they charted and named Rings Bay, Bulls Bay and Svindals Bay, after three of the most senior men on board. It seems odd that they did not name a bay after Anders. In any event, the names they gave to the bays on this voyage have not carried through to the present day.

For the first fourteen days they had remarkably good weather, quite different from the Crozet Islands experience of the year before, but the weather soon reverted to type, the gale-force storms came, and they were compelled to go out to sea or, when possible, lay to in the shelter of the islands.* The storms brought howling, furious winds that swept down through the valleys, wrenched at the ship and whipped the sea up into mighty peaks that were higher than the ship's masts. Anders quipped that there was no more fun to be had than laying to in a stormy ocean and being tossed around on a dark night. And this was in a ship of 2,700 tons with a significant load on board. They found that after each of these storms abated the sea remained high in the bays, meaning that for several days they could not land and hunt on shore.

On the morning of 21 December, a fresh easterly gale blew up, so they had to head out to sea again and thought that their Christmas would be spoiled by a storm. In the evening the wind swung around to the southwest, so they were able to anchor in the lee of the land. The storm rose to what Anders described as a hurricane and they laid to with both anchors out. Many times during the night they felt as though both chains were going to snap, but they held. The storm continued through to Christmas Eve but then died down at noon, and by five o'clock all was quiet and the sun was shining. Nonetheless, the sea was still high and they had to have swing-boards on the Christmas table.†

In honour of Christmas they rang the ship's bells and the sound echoed against the steep mountain walls and rolled far up into the valley. The crew dined on pork and penguin roast and had punch afterwards. In addition, each man was given a pound of tobacco and a book from a parcel that had been brought from Norway for this purpose. They also had a small tree in a pot with them for the Christmas celebration, but it had not survived its voyage through the tropics. In the saloon the officers and senior crew members had a quiet and pleasant evening, ate well and went to bed early.

---

* In nautical terms, 'lay to' means to remain stationary and face the ship's bow into the wind.

† These were boards that could be fixed to the table to prevent whatever was on the table from being thrown onto the floor. The modern form of these are called fiddle rails.

Did Beef, Anders' dog, accompany them on this expedition as well and participate in the Christmas celebrations? There are no written references to him, but there is one photograph of Beef with Anders and four other men that is most likely to have been taken on Possession Island in late 1907 when *Solglimt* arrived there. Anders went to Possession Island twice, once with *Cathrine* and again with *Solglimt*. There are no confirmed photographs from the *Cathrine* visit because the cameras and film were lost in the wreck, which means that the photograph is most likely to be from the *Solglimt* voyage. If that is the case, then Beef must have been on *Solglimt* with Anders on the voyage. A famous polar dog, indeed. The photographs of the Crozet Islands from this voyage are the first ever taken there.

On Christmas Day they rested, both because it was the custom, but also from necessity, because the seas in the bay were too high to allow landings. On Boxing Day they had an excellent day's hunting, but they could see that the seal colony had started to go out to sea and the remaining seals were now quite lean, so it was no longer profitable to continue hunting on Possession Island. This led them to move to East Island, which is several hours from Possession Island, and is, as its name implies, the most easterly island in the Crozet group. East Island is wilder than Possession Island, but it, too, has several wide bays where it is possible to land in good weather. In every bay they found the remains of past sealing, especially huts and boilers, as well the wreckage of lost ships. Anders wrote that there were rabbits on East Island, and these provided a welcome variation in their diet. This was in addition to the other good food they could get from the islands, including penguins, ducks and several other edible bird species. Of fish, there were large quantities, but, oddly, they caught only one variety and this, while apparently ugly, was very tasty.[*]

They named three previously unnamed bays on East Island after their

---

[*] 'Ugly' is an insufficient description to allow identification of the fish they caught, but it could have been the South Georgian Spiny Plunderfish that lives near the coast of subantarctic islands, and is certainly not pretty. The scientific name for this fish is *Harpagifer georgianus*.

major shareholders, Sundt, Wedel Jarlsberg and Amundsen.* In Sundts Bay, which is open to the northeast, they had three good hunting days. They tried a number of times to land in Wedel Jarlsbergs Bay, which opens to the south and where they saw great numbers of seals, but the sea was always too high. They made a landing in Amundsens Bay, on the east, but were hit by such a violent storm that they were only just able to get the sealers back on board the ship. After this they returned to Possession Island, where, to their astonishment, they discovered that many seals had come back on shore. These were mostly females, pregnant and fat, and they provided a rich haul. In his various lectures and articles Anders spoke critically of the indiscriminate slaughter of seals, including breeding females, that had been carried out in the past, leading to the near extinction of the colonies,† but there is nothing in his reports of this expedition that hints at any awareness of the concept of sustainable hunting.

On 26 January 1908 a large steamship was seen approaching American Bay, where *Solglimt* lay at anchor. This was the first ship they had seen since leaving Cape Town in mid-November, and they were eager for news from the outside world. They signalled the ship and within ten minutes were moving towards it, but almost immediately a flag was raised on the other ship, it changed course and steamed away at full speed, to the great disappointment of all on board *Solglimt*. At any rate, their time at the Crozet Islands was coming to an end. The further the summer progressed, the more frequently the winds came from the north, causing heavy fog that hindered hunting. By this stage their provisions had diminished considerably and they decided to face *Solglimt's* bow homewards again. They set off on 1 February with a fresh breeze from the north. There was a party on board to celebrate their successful catch, and everybody was happy. Anders said, 'It's fun to come home with what is probably the biggest load of seal oil to have floated on a keel.'

---

* Amundsen is not an uncommon Norwegian surname. There is no evidence to suggest that this was the famous Norwegian Roald Amundsen. Indeed, it is highly unlikely that it was.

† *Lillehammer Tilsuker*, 10 February 1909, p. 1, 2, and other newspapers.

In mid-February 1908 *Solglimt* arrived back in Cape Town, where she stayed for a week and Anders, Bull and others visited the Prime Minister of the Cape Colony, Dr Leander Jameson.

While in Cape Town Anders wrote to the press in Norway reporting that they were on their way home with a good load after a successful trip.[*] In his letter he reprised some of the atmospheric descriptions that he had undoubtedly used in the many talks he gave in 1907 while drumming up support for this expedition. He said that with storm and rain, snow and sleet and wet clothes, hunting on the Crozet Islands was not a lot of fun. He reflected on the newspaper articles that had considered whether or not the Crozet Islands were the most desolate place on Earth, and thought that was a fitting description, saying that somewhere more barren, sad and inaccessible would be hard to imagine if you had not seen it for yourself. He described the wild mountains that rose up out of the sea, constantly whipped by fierce winds that, through erosion, had created marvellous shapes, and the slender towers, jagged peaks and mountain ridges with precipitous drops that made Beseggen look like child's play.[†] This dramatic landscape was punctuated with valleys where fresh green grass grew and where small rivers flowed. It was at the mouths of these rivers that the seals gathered in the summertime, and where the sealers went to hunt them.

They arrived back in Tønsberg on 28 March 1908, six months and four days after leaving Norway. Everyone was in a good mood and satisfied with the voyage. As if to underscore the successful nature of the expedition, they had enjoyed excellent weather all the way home from Cape Town. There had also been no serious illness or injury, just one report of a fractured arm. However, Anders praised the contribution made by Svindal, who was a medical student, and whose ability to deal with the arm injury was notably better than Anders' would have been, and he recommended that all such expeditions in the future should carry a doctor.[‡]

---

[*] *Morgenbladet*, 17 March 1908, p. 1.

[†] Beseggen is a spectacular mountain ridge in Norway, a popular trekking area, which rises to 1,743 metres at its highest point.

[‡] *Morgenbladet*, 3 April 1908, p. 3.

Four thousand barrels of blubber and oil, or 700 tons,[*] were to be unloaded and refined at Tenvik Tryworks.[†] In addition, *Solglimt* had delivered to Norway 1,800 seal skins that would be tanned and sold. Anders reported that they had returned with a full load, but could have brought more back if they had fitted extra tanks. Ring and Raknæs had brought back a valuable collection of plant and animal specimens for the University of Norway,[‡] and Svindal collected invertebrates.[§] In August Bull's son, Gustav, presented a large preserved male elephant seal to the Bergen Museum for its collection.[¶]

In response to a journalist's question, Anders said that they were constantly busy while actively hunting, basically working and sleeping, but the voyage there and back was a relatively leisurely time.

By May Anders had advised that he was planning a second expedition to the subantarctic islands with *Solglimt*, with an anticipated departure in July. In June it was announced that the company Storm, Bull and Co, which owned *Solglimt*, was offering her for sale. The ship was advertised as having an A1 rating from Lloyds, was 2,700 tons, was fitted out with new oil tanks with approximately 800-ton capacity, six new pressure boilers with pipelines, four whaling boats and a motor boat, and in all other aspects was completely ready for an expedition. By July a share offer for a new whaling company, Solglimt, was advertised under Anders' leadership. S. Theodore Sverre, who had experience with Arctic Ocean hunting, was

---

[*] Reports of the *Solglimt*'s fit out state that she had capacity of 800 tons, however all of the reports about her catch after this voyage refer to full tanks of 700 tons. It was also reported that she could have brought home more oil if she had had more capacity.

[†] The company name in Norwegian was Tenvik Transkogeri. Tenvik is a town on the Oslofjord, south of Tønsberg.

[‡] The samples gave rise to two articles by Baard Kaalaas in the German journal *Nyt Magazin for Naturvidenskaberne* [*New Magazine for Nature Scientists*], 1911a and 1911b. The articles note Bull's generosity in including scientists on the expedition, and that this was the first significant collection of plant matter from the Crozet Islands.

[§] Headland, 1989, p. 240.

[¶] *Bergens Tidende*, 8 August 1908, p. 2.

appointed as the manager, and the company was expecting to be very profitable, with a net profit of fifty-five per cent being estimated. Each share was 1,000 kroner (A$11,000) and the share capital was 200,000 kroner (A$2,200,000). It was advised that the ship was undergoing repairs and refurbishment at a shipyard in Tønsberg and would be ready for departure in mid-August. Once again the crew would be seventy-five men, including a doctor.

All of this suggests that Anders was parting ways with Bull commercially, however Storm, Bull and Co retained ownership of *Solglimt*, so it is likely that the Solglimt company was created under its auspices to mitigate against risks.

In the middle of all of these legal and commercial activities, 'this energetic young captain', at 27 years of age, had become betrothed to Marie Skar, who was from Lillehammer.* When he was writing his final words in his diary from the *Cathrine*'s voyage, he had hinted at the existence of a sweetheart, but had not named her. This must have been Marie. Marie was born in 1876 in her parent's house that was perched beside the Mesna River, which flows rapidly down through Lillehammer to the northern tip of Lake Mjøse, on which the town is situated. Marie's father, who was a master dyer, died at a young age, leaving his widow, Karoline, with three small children to raise, so Anders and Marie were both fatherless by the time they began courting, Anders' father having died when Anders was 17. Anders and Marie came from a similar class. Anders' was the older family, mainly of farmers, whereas Marie came from a family of distinguished intellectuals. By all accounts, both of the betrothed were very strong-willed people and a good match.

In May Anders had had an audience with the King,† who presumably was keen to meet this audacious young man who was the toast of the town. Although he could not know it at the time, Anders' life pivoted at this point. Notwithstanding the heavy responsibilities he had already

---

* Lillehammer is 150 kilometres north of Oslo.
† *Kysten*, 6 May 1908, p. 2.

carried on his young shoulders, gone would be the carefree, almost boy's own adventure, phase of his life, the high spirits and the derring-do that attracted public acclaim and honours. Indeed, it could be said that this audience with the King marked the end of his youth.

CHAPTER 9

THE WINE-DARK SEA

And if a god will wreck me yet again in the wine-dark sea,
Much have I suffered, labored long and hard by now
In the waves and wars. Add this to the total —
Bring the trial on!

Homer, *The Odyssey**

By 11 August 1908 the repairs and refurbishment undertaken on *Solglimt* had been completed and she was in dry dock to be scraped and cleaned in readiness for her new voyage to the Southern Ocean. She departed from Tønsberg on 15 August, en route to the Crozet Islands, as before, with plans to stop in Newcastle to take on coal, and then again in Durban to replenish coal and stores. Anders was planning to be away for seven or eight months, with the intention of returning to Norway with a full load for processing and sale, as had occurred on the previous expedition.

This time Anders had sole responsibility for the expedition, wearing both master's and expedition leader's hats. The first, second and third mates, Henry Fævang (aged 36), Henrik Hansen (aged 40) and Johan L. Henriksen (also aged 40) were significantly more experienced sailors and sealers than Anders. There were no scientists on board, but there was a doctor, Evald Hagbart Martinsen (aged 28), and a secretary, Asbjørn Peder Bjørnstad (aged just 19). It is not known how many of the men had been on *Solglimt*'s first voyage, but there were three men who had been on *Cathrine*'s voyage with Anders to the Crozet Islands in 1906, including

---

* Homer, 5.244–48.

the two who had accompanied him in *Hope* for the rescue attempt – the bosun, Thorvald Johansen, and able seaman Hans Christian Antonsen. Johansen was engaged as one of two bosuns for this *Solglimt* expedition, and Antonsen as an able seaman and the man in charge of one of the whaling boats. The third crew member from *Cathrine* was Hans Lysacker, who on that voyage had been taken on as an able seaman but eventually took over as steward and cook. He was engaged on *Solglimt* as a baker.[*]

Most of the crew were Norwegians, however there were seven Swedes, a Dane, a Finn, an Icelander and a German. There were reports that some of the crew hailed from Anders' own district in Norway, Hedmark, but it is not possible to tell from the crew list how many of these there were. Presumably none of the men from Hedmark had previously been to sea, but they were probably attracted to join the expedition by the publicity surrounding Anders' exploits. Almost all of the men, sixty-one of the seventy-five, were under 30, and more than half, thirty-seven in total, were aged 20 or under. Just five of the men were over 40, and two of those were over 62. The oldest, at 65, was an able seaman, Ole Christian Olsen, and the youngest were three 15-year-olds, two of whom were deckhands and one of whom was a mess boy. It was usual for the captain to hire the crew, and this was presumably the case for this voyage. Unless Anders knew the candidates, which would rarely have been the case, it is interesting to muse over how he decided whether or not to sign a man, or boy, on to his crew. The challenges of engaging a competent steward, for example, were highlighted in Chapter 7, while some of the difficulties of creating a functioning, peaceable community are discussed in the next chapter.

There is no evidence that Anders' dog Beef was on this second *Solglimt* voyage.

And what of Bull? As Anders was establishing the Solglimt company, Bull was involved in the establishment of another company, Kerguelen, again under the auspices of Storm Bull and Co, primarily for the purposes of whaling and sealing in the Southern Ocean. In 1908, aged 64, this

---

[*] *Solglimt* Crew List.

irrepressible man led an expedition to the Kerguelen Islands with Captain Ring, who had been on *Solglimt*'s first expedition, as master of the company's transport ship. Bull established a whaling station and guano factory on the Kerguelen Islands. The company operated with two whale catchers and a transport ship, and was a pioneer in Southern Ocean whaling. Poor catches put an end to whaling operations after just three years, but seal hunting continued.[*] In 1924, on his eightieth birthday, Bull received the King's Order of Merit, a gold medal, for services to exploration and whaling. He died in Norway in 1930, aged 86.[†]

On Friday 2 October 1908 Anders reported back to Norway that they had arrived in Durban, where they expected to complete loading coal and provisions in three days, departing the following Monday. The telegram advising this included the statement 'all well on board'. This must have been a relief to Anders. Although he was fully recovered by the time they arrived in Durban, he had been sufficiently unwell during the seven-week trip from Newcastle to Durban that the doctor had had to operate.[‡]

Early in the morning of 15 October *Solglimt* reached Marion Island, which is one of a pair of islands of volcanic origin, lying just 22 kilometres apart, that together comprise the Prince Edward Islands. At 46°36' to 46°58'S and 37°35' to 38°01'E, these islands are 1,000 kilometres west of the Crozet Islands and share many characteristics with them. Although each of them is only a tiny speck in a huge ocean, they lie on the Antarctic Convergence where the cold, northward-flowing Antarctic waters meet the relatively warmer waters of the subantarctic, which provides much krill and other food and, therefore, breeding grounds for sea mammals and birds. They are also bleak, poorly charted, wind-swept and rarely visited. Marion Island is just under 300 square kilometres and rises to a height of

---

[*] Tønnessen and Johnsen, 1982, p. 201.

[†] The medical problem is not identified in the article. *Morgenbladet*, 3 June 1930, p. 4.

[‡] *Oplandenes Avis*, 3 December 1908, p. 2.

1,230 metres. It is possible that the two islands were discovered in 1663, but formal discovery is attributed to the Frenchman Marc-Joseph Marion du Fresne, who visited them in 1772, on the same voyage that led to the discovery of the Crozet Islands. Cook sailed between the two islands in 1776 and named them the Prince Edward Islands. The first landing was probably by the sealing vessel *Sally*, between 1799 and 1802, with the American sealer *Catherine* making a landing in 1803. Bull had visited Marion Island in 1894–95, but had not landed. At least seven shipwrecks are known to have occurred on Marion Island, and others are suspected. The numerous reefs that surround the islands are a major hazard.[*]

As soon as they arrived at Marion Island, immediate steps were taken to assess seal populations and conditions along the coast. Very few sealing vessels had been to the island for fifty to sixty years prior to *Solglimt*'s arrival, so there would have been huge numbers of seals in the few small bays where it was possible to make a landing. Marion Island had not been identified as a possible destination for *Solglimt*, but, as it lay on the route to the Crozet Islands, it was not surprising that she called there on the way.

Soundings taken at a distance of 1.5 kilometres from land revealed consistent depths of 55–75 metres. Anders brought the ship to anchor in a bay, and hunting began. The men were all equipped with Krag-Jørgensen rifles with lead-pointed bullets,[†] and by evening they had winched six deeply laden boats back on board. On the next day, 16 October, it was not possible to land in that first bay due to high seas, so they went to another small bay and put hunting crews ashore for the day's work. Because this bay, which they named Solglimt Bay, was not a suitable site to anchor, they decided to take the ship back to the place where they had anchored the previous day. As the ship was swinging slowly around to head back in the direction they had come, all on board felt a hard bump, closely followed by a lighter bump. The ship immediately began to heel over, and the engineer came bounding up to the bridge, where Anders and the doctor were, to

[*] Cooper, 2010, and other sources.
[†] The Krag-Jørgensen is a repeating bolt-action rifle designed by the Norwegians Ole Herman Johannes Krag and Erk Jørgensen in the late nineteenth century.

report that water was cascading into the engine room. The carpenter, who had been sent to investigate the source of the knocks, then returned to the bridge with the grim news that the water level was rising fast.[*]

Anders and the first mate conferred and made the decision to try to beach *Solglimt*, rather than risk her sinking 2 kilometres from shore. Anders signalled the boats on shore to come to their aid, instructed the engineer to bring the ship to full speed and maintain that, and he ordered all the twenty or so men who were on board at the time to go to the midship deck and put on their lifebelts. In a state of panic, a group of crew members leapt into a motorboat that was in the davits, hanging off the side of the ship, ready to be lowered, with the result that the boat landed badly on the water and several of the men fell into the ocean. Although they were soon rescued, this could have had a more disastrous outcome.

In the sprint to beach *Solglimt*, Anders took the helm himself. He found the ship difficult to steer due to the listing, as he recounted later, perhaps also due to his nervousness. The strategy was successful and their luck held, insofar as they encountered no further obstacles. Ten to fifteen minutes after the grounding *Solglimt* rammed bow first into the black sandy beach of the cove that they had, perhaps presciently, named Solglimt Bay, but which was later named Ship's Cove. The ship rocked violently back and forth, then settled into the sand. The efforts of the engineer and a machinist to keep the engine operating at maximum capacity, with water rising around them and the ship listing heavily, were both remarkable and heroic. Once they had beached, the two men in the engine room stopped the engine and blew the steam off. By this stage there were just under 2 metres of water in the engine room.

At the hearing that would take place to investigate exactly what happened, there would be a great deal of discussion about whether or not soundings had been taken, or if there was a lookout. On the previous day soundings had been taken regularly but on the morning of the accident

---

[*] There are extensive official reports and newspaper articles about the loss of *Solglimt*. The information in this section draws on many of them, including the Shipping Inspector's report on the grounding.

no soundings were taken because *Solglimt* was only going to retrace her route, and near the spot where the accident took place 82 metres had been measured. For the same reason there was no specific lookout. However, the first mate was asked to keep an eye out while he was on the forecastle deck raising the anchors, and Anders had an unimpeded view from the bridge. In addition, one of the motorboats was on the water circling the ship, testing the engine, which had been troublesome. Another boat had earlier passed directly over the place where the grounding occurred. Nobody saw any sign of a reef, and there was no reef marked at this point in the *Admiralty Charts*,* although it was known that the charts were incomplete. Afterwards, when the shipwrecked men were looking for signs of the reef from land, they could only see it in bad weather. On the day of the grounding, however, the weather had been fine. Several crew members claimed to have seen some sign of breakers, but they said they thought what they had seen might have been a whale spouting. One crew member claimed to have told the second mate about the sighting, but the mate said in the inquiry that he had heard no such talk. As would later be established, the reef *Solglimt* struck was actually the sharp point of an underwater peak, with the sides dropping away steeply, and so sounding, even very close to it, would not have helped. Although the bay where *Solglimt* ended her working life in is no longer called Solglimt Bay, the reef, which is now marked in the *Admiralty Charts*, bears the name Solglimt Blinders.

As soon as *Solglimt* was beached the men set about salvaging everything they could from her. There were seventy-five men who needed to be sheltered and fed for an indefinite period of time on this bleak and inhospitable island, and so it was imperative that *Solglimt* be stripped of anything and everything that would improve their chances of survival and make their lives more comfortable. In this regard, the *Solglimt* survivors were in a better position than those from *Cathrine*, who at first had had to abandon everything on the ship. To get materials from *Solglimt* onto the

---

* *Admiralty Charts* are produced by the United Kingdom Hydrographic Office and are used in conjunction with *Admiralty Sailing Directions*.

island, mooring cables were secured between the ship and large boulders on shore, and lighter provisions and materials were transferred ashore in baskets. At the same time, all the boats were deployed to ferry heavier materials to shore. It took several days to salvage everything they could from *Solglimt*. The vessel had been rammed deep into the sand on the beach, and some of the cabins and storage areas were full of water. This had damaged or destroyed many of the provisions and made salvage work more dangerous.

Solglimt had a good deal of timber in her lower storage areas. This may have been to build huts for the hunters so that they would be able to work from shore, just as those on *Solglimt*'s voyage the year before had used the hut that was built for the crew of the shipwrecked *Cathrine* on the Crozet Islands as a base. It was absolutely imperative that this timber be salvaged to build huts on Marion Island, but there was a great deal of water in the area where the timber had been stored. The timber was being thrown back and forth between the bulkheads by the motion of the waves, and the access door had been jammed shut by the loose timber. In another instance of heroism, Anders and the first mate, Henry Fævang, stripped off so that they could squeeze through the hatch into the hold, where they proceeded to lift the timber piece by piece up through the hatch so others could in turn pull them onto the deck. Anders and his first mate were at constant risk of death or injury from the moving timber and also because they were standing in icy water for a prolonged period of time. The water in the bay would have been between 4 and 10°C.* Exhaustion and lack of consciousness would be expected between thirty to sixty minutes at such temperatures, and death within one to three hours. The fact of their deed is recorded, but not the length of time they were in the hold.

When Anders was lauded and awarded the King's highest honour because of the dangerous voyage that he undertook in *Hope*, there were several journalists and commentators who argued that he should not be

---

* This estimate was provided by South African researchers familiar with the conditions of the bay.

put on a pedestal for his actions. Their reasoning was that, as the captain, he had a responsibility to try to rescue the men who had been castaway by his failure to keep the ship safe. Perhaps those same journalists and commentators would argue that Anders also had a responsibility to risk his life in icy water with loose timber threatening to crush him at any moment, but the fact is that he did put himself at significant risk, and undeniably had done whatever he humanly could to ensure the preservation of the men on his two shipwrecked vessels. Anders may have been an unlucky, or worse, captain to sail with, but it appears that he was a capable and courageous man in a crisis.

The performance of expedition leaders and ship's captains varies significantly according to personal qualities and circumstances. As expedition leader, Ernest Shackleton, for example, led what was probably the riskiest rescue mission ever after the loss of a ship. His story is well known. After his ship *Endurance* was trapped and ultimately crushed in pack ice in the Weddell Sea in January 1915, he and the crew camped and trekked on the ice, and sailed across stretches of open water in their three lifeboats before successfully reaching terra firma on Elephant Island in April 1916. He then sailed a small lifeboat 1,160 kilometres through the stormy Southern Ocean to South Georgia, a journey of fifteen days, and trekked across that mountainous, glacier-ridden island to reach the whaling station Stromness, and thus was able to organise the rescue of the men who were on Elephant Island and at the landing point on South Georgia.* As was also the case with Anders, Shackleton was accompanied in this entire epic feat of endurance by other men, but the leadership credit goes to him.

By contrast, in 1906 when *Cathrine* was shipwrecked, Bull, despite being the expedition leader, became incapacitated by anxiety and played no part in the efforts to save the ship. Of course, he was not a sailor, but nonetheless he seemed resigned to whatever fate would deliver and was opposed to Anders' plan to attempt to get help by sailing a boat away from

---

* Lansing, 1959.

the island. An even more extreme example of a failure of leadership in a time of crisis was that of the captain of *Strathmore,* which was wrecked on the Crozet Islands in 1875. When the ship hit the rocks in the middle of the night Captain Macdonald was completely unable to act. He was overheard saying repeatedly to the first mate, 'I told you it would be so. I told you it would be so', and he was last seen being washed overboard by one of the waves that was battering the wreck.*

Solglimt's doctor, Evald Hagbart Martinsen, said of their first experiences of being castaways: 'I will never forget the first night ashore on Marion Island. It was pitch-dark all around us, it was difficult to start and maintain a fire out of the saturated materials, and it was bitterly cold. Outside, the sea moved in huge swells, and around us we heard the eerie roar of the sea elephants. It was not a good night for sleeping!'†

The following day they organised and stored the provisions and work started immediately on building the huts. Within ten days they had built eleven huts, one of which, the first to be built, was the kitchen and storeroom. With great difficulty they had been able to get a large stove ashore, which allowed them to cook bread daily. The other ten houses were for the men. They arranged themselves in friendship groups and built their own huts using timber, sailcloth, rocks and peat.

Anders shared his hut with the first mate, the senior engineer, the doctor and the secretary, a total of five men. Anders' team found a spacious cave that formed the basis of their hut. They erected a sloping roof and external wall of timber and canvas and later put down a plank floor. They salvaged a stove from the cabin on board, and with coal from the ship were able to keep their hut warm. A photograph of Anders in one of the huts shows that they also salvaged tables, chairs, a lamp and other useful objects from the ship, even including a tablecloth!

The men all gave their huts a name.‡ Anders' hut was called

---

* Church, 1985, pp. 32–33.

† The article quoting the *Solglimt's* doctor, *Aftenposten*, 13 January 1909, p. 1, refers to him as Marcussen. However, the Crew List has him as Martinsen.

‡ Most of the information in this section about the wreck and life on the

'Solbakken', which translates as sunny slope. It is possible that this means that the hut received good sunlight, but it seems more likely that it was an ironic name; Anders commented that it was named as it was because the mountain shone on it, that is, it was completely in the mountain's shadow. It is impossible to know why particular names were chosen. One hut was called 'Olafstua',[*] which refers to a cabin somehow relating to Olaf, so it was probably either named for one of the men who lived in the hut (one sailor was named Olaf, another Olav), or for Norway's patron saint, Olav. Another was named 'Kampen', which can refer to a battle, a round hill or a sporting event. More amusingly, perhaps it was a play on the English word 'camping'?

Yet another of the huts was named 'Grunerløkka', which is a suburb in Oslo. Perhaps this cabin had a central location, or it housed men from that area. Another, 'Blaasenberg', could relate to smoking or windiness and either is plausible – all of the shipwrecked men were likely to be smokers and if they had a stove in the hut it would most likely have been very smoky. However, the hut might have been more than usually exposed to the wind. Another, 'Bjönnehytter', or Bjönne's hut, was probably named after a person, and the hut used for cooking was just referred to as 'byssa', which means galley. The name of the 'Smedstua' hut suggests a blacksmith's hut, so either it was a workshop, which seems unlikely, or perhaps it was where the ship's carpenter was living, or there was another reason altogether why it was so named.

But whatever the reasons for the particular names, it is interesting to know that the huts were given names. This had also been the case with the hut built after the *Cathrine* shipwreck, which was named 'Julestua', or 'Christmas cabin'. It presumably gave the men comfort to bestow a name on the building that was to be their home for an indeterminate period of time. It was also a practical way of referring to a specific building,

island comes from an article by Anders published over two days in Norway: *Morgenbladet*, 29 December 1908 and 2 January 1909, p. 2.

* This hut was also referred to as Ola's hut, which, if correct, means it was probably named after one of the men from the hut.

particularly when there were eleven of them and, in some cases at least, it provided an opportunity to express a sense of humour about their situation.

In addition to the huts, the men formed paths by levelling the ground to link the huts that made up the small village they had created and by building steps to connect sections of the path on different levels. In an echo of the newspaper *Crozeteer*, which was created after *Cathrine* was wrecked, a newspaper was also started on Marion Island. Only one copy of this newspaper, which was called *Skravla*, was produced. Its main topic was in-depth criticism of the village's road system. The issue of *Skravla* can be seen in the photograph of Anders in the hut. 'Skravla' translates as something like a 'bit of nonsense', or 'idle chatter'.

The night after all the huts had been completed, the night of 27 October, a furious storm battered the island. Anders said that he had never seen a wilder sea than he witnessed that night. On one side of the bay where *Solglimt* was beached there is a small rocky island that rises in a sheer cliff for over 50 metres. During the storm the men saw colossal waves that rose on the seaward side of this island and, like raging waterfalls, hurled themselves over it and down into the bay. That night they lost both of their motorboats, despite them having been hauled so high up off the beach that it was thought the sea would never be able to reach them. The ocean was mighty enough to snap *Solglimt* – a 2,700-ton steel ship – in two in the middle. When this happened all of the empty barrels, which were still stored on the ship, came loose and were thrown up onto the beach, along with several of the big steel tanks that had been intended to store the oil processed on the ship. In the morning the men were faced with the desolate sight of storm debris, barrels, iron tanks and boats strewn all along the beach, with seals and penguins trying to make their way among the tangled chaos. They were unable to find the two motorboats but, with a great deal of effort, they managed to haul the whaleboats back onto shore and secure them.

One day news leapt through the colony like lightning: some of the crew who had been for a mountain hike across the island had found diamonds! They had brought back with them some shiny, glass-like slivers, which turned out to be capable of cutting glass, as can diamonds. The Finnish crew member, August Sjöblom, who had spent some time in the diamond mines of the Transvaal, said it was just a matter of finding the diamonds that were in good condition, and they would all be millionaires. Many believed this and spent countless hours combing the island for diamonds. What they had found, in fact, were just crystals. There is no record of when this disappointing fact became known, but the possibility of wealth to be gained had at least given some of the men something to do.

Anders spent one Sunday in the search, but did not record what he found, if anything. He did, however, record his impressions of the island, saying that the island seemed to grow in size and become wilder and stranger the further one explored inland. The island consists mostly of lava and annealed rocks that form the most extraordinary shapes. There are many craters from extinct volcanoes, and Anders said that in places the land resembled petrified rivers that had suddenly been stopped in their tracks. Anders likened the landscape to the surface of the moon, but noted that, while the moon had only one man, Marion Island had seventy-five.

As soon as Anders and his team had built their hut, they turned their attention to how to effect a rescue. Their prospects of being found on Marion Island were no better than had been those of *Cathrine*'s crew on Possession Island two years earlier. These were islands that had probably not been visited for decades, and there was no reason to believe that they would be visited any time soon. Marion Island was as bleak and inhospitable as Possession Island, with rain, sleet or snow falling, on average, 300 days a year, summer temperatures ranging from 5–13°C, and strong winds blowing almost constantly. They had ample fresh water, had salvaged provisions sufficient to feed all the men for about three months, and could supplement those with eggs, penguin-meat and fish, but the prospect of living on the island with such a large group of men who had nothing meaningful to occupy their days was daunting. In addition, they had said that their destination was to be the Crozet Islands, so even if a search was initiated in Norway after many months with no word from *Solglimt*, it was unlikely that this would include the Prince Edward Islands. The castaways very quickly made the decision to attempt to replicate *Hope's* successful rescue voyage after *Cathrine* was shipwrecked, and the first mate volunteered to skipper a boat. This time they were much better equipped to reinforce a whaling boat for such an arduous journey, but otherwise the methodology was the same: they strengthened the keel under the boat, attached a tarpaulin onto heavy iron hoops that had been fixed to it, placed flotation devices all around it so that it would be unsinkable and added a mast and sail.

A lookout for passing ships was kept every day, and on Saturday 14 November, almost exactly a month after they had been stranded on Marion Island, and when the rescue boat preparations were all but complete, two of the men on lookout duty came rushing to the huts yelling that they had seen a sailing ship. There was an instant flurry of activity throughout the colony. Anders and others flew up the hill near their hut and confirmed that there was indeed a small sailing ship within sight. Even though it was far out to sea, it appeared to be tacking towards them. They immediately put one of their boats on the water with the first mate and eight men to row, to try to reach the ship. At this point they must have been aware of what a great loss they had endured when the two motorboats had been lost in the storm.

High on a rise, those left on the island lit a huge bonfire made up of barrel staves, kerosene and petrol, after which some hours passed in great excitement. Anders followed the passage of the rowboat through his binoculars. At times it was lost in the valleys of the waves, and then he lost sight of it altogether. They could see that the ship was drawing closer to them, and eventually they were able to identify her as a little 'fore and aft' schooner of the very fine American type.* It did not appear that the ship had seen them, however, and she turned about, so they poured barrels of petrol onto the fire, causing the flames to leap sky high, and fired

---

* This refers to a two-masted, fore-and-aft rigged sailing ship.

rifles shots. This had the desired effect, and they saw the ship turn back towards them again. A short while later they could see that their rowboat had reached her. Those on shore had to wait for several more hours before their rowboat returned to the island, which it did, as fast as the rowers could manage.

The ship was indeed an American vessel. She was *Beatrice L. Corkum*, a sealer from Halifax, Nova Scotia, under the command of Captain Frederick Gilbert. She was hunting for fur seals, was just 81 tons and had come to Marion Island directly from Halifax. She was travelling with a second ship, *Agnes G. Donahoe*, but the two ships had been separated during a storm the previous night. Captain Gilbert reported that he was looking for his companion ship and would continue to do that before either coming back to rescue *Solglimt's* men, or, failing that, reporting their situation to whalers based on the Kerguelen Islands, which is where they were heading. How odd it would have been if it were Bull, then at Kerguelen setting up a whaling, sealing and guano factory, who was the first to hear that his comrade had been shipwrecked again.

Although *Solglimt's* men were disappointed by the news that *Beatrice L. Corkum* was to leave them, there was nothing they could do about it, and at least they knew that their plight was known, and help would come in due course. They could only hope that the two ships in the vicinity would soon return.

To the castaways' great relief, *Beatrice L. Corkum* located her sister ship, and both were seen the next day. However, the two ships were at first becalmed in the lee of Prince Edward Island and could not make progress towards Marion Island until the following day. When they were closer to the cove Anders rowed out to meet them to discuss rescue possibilities.

The second vessel, *Agnes G. Donahoe*, at 100 tons, was somewhat larger than *Beatrice L. Corkum* and was commanded by Captain Reuben Balcom. Both of the captains were experienced sealers in the Arctic and Southern Oceans, and the Balcom family were no strangers to the perils of their occupation. In 1892, Reuben Balcom's brother, George Washington

Sprott Balcom, was arrested for illegally sealing in Russian waters (it is said that a fictionalised version of his crew's escape from Petropavlovsk was the basis for Rudyard Kipling's short story: *The Devil and the Deep Sea*) and in 1904 their ship, *Agnes G. Donahoe*, was the centre of a diplomatic dispute between Uruguay and Great Britain after she was seized for illegally sealing in the River Plate. *Agnes G. Donahoe* would herself be wrecked at Point Prim, Nova Scotia, in 1913.[*] Anders was immediately impressed by Captain Balcom, whom he described as a characteristic old Nova Scotia sailor, bold and unpretentious, who had sent many a valuable load of fur to the London markets.

The two ships had sixteen and twenty men on them, respectively, so were not ideally placed to rescue seventy-five men. Nevertheless, Captain Balcom said that, room or no room, they had to take the shipwrecked men off the island, and the two captains agreed to take half the men each. Anders rowed back to shore and instructed the men to gather their belongings and prepare for the trip out to the ships. When half the men with their meagre belongings were on board the ships, a storm blew up and the high seas on the beach made it impossible to continue. With the storm rapidly increasing in severity the ships struggled to hoist sails and move away from the dangers of the island. The severe storm lasted for three days, during which time Anders, on board *Agnes G. Donahoe*, could see what excellent ships these American schooners were, riding the fury of the waves with relative ease.

Those remaining on the island, who were waiting for the weather to settle, were given a fright when an assistant cook came running and shouted that one of the ships had capsized and the sails and engine were underwater. On further investigation this turned out to be a huge iceberg drifting southwards. The rescue ship lay safely at anchor.[†]

On Friday 20 November, the ships were able to approach the island again and take on board the remaining men. Six men from each of the two

---

* Mitchener, 2015, pp. 112–115.
† Bjørnstad, 1908, *Diary Excerpts*, 27 November.

ships were left behind on Marion Island to make room for *Solglimt*'s men. Those left on the island were able to make use of the *Solglimt* village and could hunt for fur seals while they were there. Anders reported that the fur seals were just starting to arrive at the island. In fact, the ship's secretary, Bjørnstad, having no weapon to hand, had killed a beautiful specimen with his bare hands on their last day on the island.

On 30 November, ten days after leaving Marion Island, *Agnes G. Donahoe* arrived in Durban, and on 1 December news arrived in Norway via a telegram to Lloyd's in London that *Solglimt* had struck a reef near Marion Island on 12 October and was completely lost, but that all of the crew had made it safely to land.* *Beatrice L. Corkum* arrived in Durban five days after *Agnes G. Donahoe*, having encountered a terrifying storm on the way from Marion Island, with waves so huge they were breaking over the ship and flooding the cabin. *Solglimt*'s doctor was apparently so frightened that he had said his prayers, not something he was accustomed to do.†

Anders was impressed with how well the schooner sailed on this voyage, just as he been impressed with its ability to ride out the storm. The crews on both ships had had an uncomfortable voyage, packed as they were like herrings in a barrel, and the food had been less than ideal, but they all appreciated the fact that they were being brought back to civilisation and accepted their conditions without complaint. They had all lost most of their possessions, either at the time the ship was beached or because they were unable to take much off the island, but no lives had been lost, and neither had there been any injury or serious illness.

The rescued men were met in Durban by the Norwegian Consul, Jacob Egeland, who, Anders reported, received them with great kindness and did everything he could to help them to adjust. The crew were to be sent home to Norway on the first available ship, because working their own passage home (the usual practice in such circumstances) would not be

----

* *Norges Sjøfartstidende*, 1 December 1908, p. 1.
† Bjørnstad, 1908, *Diary Excerpts*, 4 December.

practicable when so many men were involved, and when so many of them were not working sailors.

As had been the case when Anders was in Melbourne after the loss of *Cathrine*, a marine inquiry was conducted by the Consul on the ground, in this instance by Egeland. Anders drew on excerpts from the *Solglimt* logbook and made a declaration about the circumstances leading to her loss.

CHAPTER 10

CAPTAIN HARBOE-REE AND HIS MEN*

But the crews began to mutter among themselves, …
Look at our captain's luck – so loved by the world,
So prized at every landfall, every port of call.

Homer, The Odyssey†

Although *Solglimt's* destruction had not resulted in any loss of life, or even injury, and the time spent on the island was blessedly short, the relationships between the crew and officers on this voyage had little of the camaraderie that had been a feature of the *Cathrine* expedition.

Trouble with the crew had begun in Durban when *Solglimt* stopped there on her way south to replenish her coal supplies and take on provisions. The crew had all signed on with a contract that forbade them to go ashore when in port unless they were instructed to do so, but many of the men ignored this agreement and went into the township anyway. The result was drunkenness, fights and arrests at all times of the day and night, until a police force of sixty men with bayonetted rifles was instructed to keep them on board. Anders' description of this was that 'when Norwegian hunting crews come to foreign ports they create a scandal, and our people did their best to keep this tradition alive.' He expressed the view that the greater shame lay with the older men, whose behaviour was the worst, and who influenced the younger men, and he reflected that the contract was of

---

* This chapter heading refers to the ubiquitous Norwegian tableware that features the text 'St Olav and his men' ('Heilag Olav og hans menn').
† Homer, 1996, 10.39, 43–44, p. 231.

136

little use, because, if the men were punished for breaches of it in the way they deserved, there would be mutiny on board.

Extraordinarily, and almost certainly injudiciously, these comments about the men were made in an article Anders wrote in Durban after his rescue and sent to a Norwegian newspaper.* The article was published before any of the men, Anders included, had returned to Norway. Referring to the panic on board immediately following the moment *Solglimt* struck the reef and the crew realised the ship was doomed, Anders stated that it was typical that men who were tough and big-mouthed when all was well were the worst cowards in the moment.

Not satisfied with those criticisms, Anders went on to say that, once *Solglimt* had been beached and the salvaging begun, the crew, with few exceptions, behaved badly. To begin with, he claimed, the worst were utterly terrified, but when it began to dawn on them that the immediate danger was over, they danced to another tune. Little by little they had sneaked away from the work and begun to roam the island to gather eggs and kill birds for fun. A lot of provisions were stolen, boxes were broken open, kegs were smashed to pieces and the contents of these were strewn all over the ground. Cans were half-eaten and then thrown away. The result of this terrible behaviour, asserted Anders, was that quite a few men got upset stomachs and obviously could not work. He qualified his criticism by saying that there were many who understood that it was not possible to proceed in this way, and thanks to those men, they were able to get things in order and salvage a great deal from the ship. After the supply hut had been built there were also thefts from it, and so steps were taken to secure all the provisions.

By contrast, Anders said that all of the ship's officers had behaved extremely well at all times and provided a good example to the other men, with the first mate, Henry Fævang, being singled out for high praise. Anders commended him as a skilled and unassuming man and noted that he was also the one who was prepared to risk his life by sailing away from

---

* *Morgenbladet*, 29 December 1908, pp. 1–2.

the island in a small boat to try to bring relief to the shipwrecked men. There is no mention anywhere of why it might have been that Fævang, and not Anders, was prepared to undertake this mission. Interestingly, the ship's secretary, Bjørnstad, was not in complete agreement with Anders about the quality of the officers. On the contrary, he said in his diary: 'Our second mate is, as usual, constantly whining and complaining and is unhappy with everything. He is a big pessimist and makes the worst out of every detail.'*

In a separate (unpublished) letter from Durban Anders provided more explicit details of the behaviour of some of the crew. Regarding the decision of the Consul, Egeland, to repatriate the men on an Aberdeen-South African Line ship named *Inyati*, Anders said that while the ship did not have accommodation for that number of people, the accommodation in the mid-deck was sufficient and everybody was provided with a sleeping bag and pillow. Long tables were set up and ventilation was provided through air valves in the hatch. Anders said that the man who behaved the worst during this time in Durban was the baker, Hans Lysacker, who had performed his job badly while on board *Solglimt*. Anders accused Lysacker of behaving pitiably during the grounding and refusing to participate in the salvage work afterwards. One of Lysacker's objections about boarding *Inyati* was that, as a baker, he should have his own room, even though Anders pointed out that he had shared a room with the stokers on board *Solglimt*. When he did not get his way he tried to get his comrades to help him attack Anders. According to Anders' account, three or four men came up behind him and he could hear Lysacker egging them on to commit a 'proud and glorious deed', but none of them had the courage or will to start the fight. Anders invited Lysacker to take him on, but he wisely walked away.

When the ship was about to leave, some of the crew, many of whom were drunk, refused to board the vessel, saying they would not be sent home like pigs. The men abused Anders and the Consul, hurling foul language and threats at them, saying they would punch their heads in

---

* Bjørnstad, 1908 *Diary Excerpts*, 18 November.

and give them a thrashing. With support from the police, all but two of the crew boarded the ship. As *Inyati* pulled away from the pier, Lysacker stood at the railing yelling threats to Anders, who was standing on the dock. Amongst other things, he said in English, so that everyone would understand: 'You, Captain Ree, sailed the ship onto the shore on purpose in order to claim the insurance. I know it because I saw it all and I will prosecute you when I get home and you will go to prison for many years.' Anders' response was to say that such a serious accusation should result in Lysacker's arrest in order that he could be questioned and punished.

The two men who had refused to board ship, arguing that the accommodation provided on *Inyati* was not good enough, and trying to incite the other men to also refuse the emigration officer's order that they embark, fled the dock when the police were called. According to Anders, after *Inyati* left they appeared at the Norwegian Consul's office and demanded to be accommodated in a hotel, where they said they would stay until further notice. Anders said that they were accommodated, but in a police cell rather than a hotel. In Anders' view the men had behaved despicably. He, representatives of the emigration office, his officers and the Consul had inspected the ship and the preparations being made for the repatriation of the men and all had agreed that shipwrecked sailors could not expect better amenities.

One of the most intriguing aspects of this incident is that Lysacker had been on *Cathrine* with Anders and had taken over the job of cook and steward when the original crew member could not perform those tasks. He appears to have done a good job on *Cathrine*, however there is not enough information on the public record to understand why his experience on *Solglimt* had turned out badly. As we will see in the next chapter, both of the two men who had been on *Cathrine* with Anders previously turned on him at some stage during the *Solglimt* voyage and its aftermath. It is worth considering that they may have thought they should get special treatment because they had been on the earlier voyage and, when this failed to eventuate, they became embittered.

What a contrast this public attack on his crew by Anders was from his defence in 1906 of the behaviour of Norwegian crews in port, when he thought that the main problem sailors suffered away from home was a lack of letters from loved ones.

Anders and Bjørnstad arrived in Southampton on 2 January 1909 and subsequently in Norway on 11 January, having left Africa on 10 December. They had travelled from Cape Town to England on a Union-Castle Line ship. The rest of the men arrived in England five days after Anders and Bjørnstad on *Inyati*. They disembarked in London and were sent by rail to Newcastle, from where they were repatriated to Norway on several ships.*

On his arrival in Norway Anders was described by a journalist as looking a little strained after the hardships he had endured. When he was asked how the crew had fared since their arrival in Durban, Anders replied that there had been a few ups and downs. Two of his men, he said, had been left in the hustle and bustle down there. He presumed that the men now faced a few months hard labour for having defied the emigration officer's orders.†

Not surprisingly, there was an immediate reaction to Anders' harsh comments in the press. Some of this was initiated by the newspapers, and some by crew members. The first article to appear made its sympathies clear by starting with: 'Last night in the Kristiania International Seamen's Home I met some well-dressed, quite good-looking sailors, who on closer inspection turned out to be part of *Solglimt*'s reportedly infamous crew.'‡ This was followed by a statement that the Home had vouched for the men's excellent behaviour while they were there. The journalist interviewed Øivind Hoem, a sailor and whaler, whom he described as a pleasant man. Hoem said that there was not much of a mutiny on board. He said that some of the men had got hold of brandy in Durban and then in their drunken state had had an argument with the captain when they were at sea. Hoem said that the men had complained to the captain about the

* *Aftenposten*, 7 January 1909 p. 7.
† *Morgenbladet*, 11 January 1909, p. 2.
‡ *Kysten*, 12 January 1909, pp. 1–2.

bread on board, which had been bad throughout the voyage, not properly cooked as a result of problems with the oven. Later he spoke to two men who had a bottle of brandy, and when he asked them where they had got it, they said from the captain. Hoem did not know if that was true. With regard to *Solglimt*'s grounding, Hoem claimed that there was nobody at the helm when it occurred. The journalist was shocked by this statement and had to gather his thoughts before he could continue. When asked about Anders, Hoem said that the crew saw little of him.

Hoem was also asked about the episode when they were homeward-bound in Durban, to which Hoem replied that the men were not satisfied with the quarters they had been allocated. The journalist asked if anything was wrong with them, and Hoem said, 'Yes, almost everything'. He claimed that they had been provided with nothing to sit or lie on, although there were three long tables with benches, and the Consul promised them good food and mattresses, after which most of the men went on board. They did get mattresses, but no blankets until they got to Cape Town. The diet was consistently poor throughout the journey.

Finally, Hoem was asked about the two men who had been arrested in Durban. Hoem agreed that they had refused to board the ship because of the poor conditions and had argued with the Consul before leaving the port. Regarding Anders' comments about the hard labour they might face, Hoem just looked at the journalist and smiled, as did a number of people within earshot. The article concluded with an editorial comment that the newspaper had thought that, given the strong statements Anders had made about the crew, it was only fair that the crew be given an opportunity to respond. The newspaper said it could not guarantee that everything stated was correct, and it had a particular concern about what had been said about there being no helmsman at the time of the grounding. The editor thought that this might have been a misconception, despite the statement being made quite firmly.

Two officers who were interviewed by another newspaper upheld Anders' comments about the crew, saying that some of them were not 'mother's best children', especially when they had some alcohol in them.[*] They said that the relationship between the men and officers was good once things settled down, and were full of praise for Anders who, they said, applied himself with vigour as a captain and worked like a horse throughout the salvage operation. In another interview the first mate confirmed that there had been a mutiny on board as they departed from Durban, when some of the crew obtained brandy and became argumentative.[†] When asked how serious the incident was he replied that it was not, that it was mainly the result of drunkenness that makes men behave badly at sea, but the officers were concerned because the crew on board was seventy-five strong and so the possibility of escalating trouble was a concern.

A consistent picture emerges from comments by the senior men on board *Solglimt* about Anders' character and behaviour. The doctor, Martinsen, related the story about Anders' heroism when salvaging timber from below deck, and he also praised Anders and the first mate for the effort they put into trying to maintain the men's morale after the ship was wrecked.[‡] Martinsen described the incident that occurred as they were leaving Durban in October as a serious incursion into mutiny. He also used the term 'not mother's best children', and said that it did not take much before dissatisfaction and fomentation broke out on board. Martinsen said that, had Anders not been the calm and resolute man that he was, things would have been very ugly. He also confirmed that at the time of the grounding there was panic on board, and it was fortunate that no lives were lost as the men scrambled to board the motorboat.

On 5 December, after all the shipwrecked crew had arrived in Durban, the ship's secretary, Bjørnstad, wrote in his diary: 'Have, thank God, got rid of the crew, except for two escapees who will get the pleasure of spending a month in prison because of their insubordination.'[§] Incidentally, the status differential between the crew and the officers is also evident from

---

[*] *Morgenbladet*, 12 January 1909, p. 1.
[†] *Tunsbergeren*, 13 January 1909, pp. 1–2.
[‡] *Aftenposten*, 13 January 1909, p. 1.
[§] Bjørnstad, 1908, *Diary Excerpts*, 5 December.

Bjørnstad's comments. He wrote: 'The captain, first mate, doctor [and I] are living as kings, five courses for supper, isn't it great! My own room has a veranda and view over the harbour. Both captains dined with us this evening; afterwards we had a pleasant time on the veranda in the moonlight.'* This would not have been anything like the experience of the remainder of the crew.

At least some of the crew members were less complimentary about Anders and happily aired their views to the press. One of the sailors and hunters, Amandus Fævang (not to be confused with the first mate, Henry Fævang), spoke bitterly to the press about Anders' strict adherence to the clause in the contract forbidding shore leave, suggesting that, when some of the men did eventually go on shore their bad behaviour was more pronounced as a result.† He said that this resulted in 'lively' behaviour and led to the arrest of four men. Fævang argued that Anders' refusal to release the men in custody in Durban until *Solglimt* was ready to depart aroused great indignation on board. Fævang's version of the mutiny was that, just as they were leaving Durban, one of the men, 'who was perhaps a little drunk', went up onto the midship deck and had words with Anders. Anders had then picked the man up and hurled him off the deck. Fævang said that this caused great bitterness among the men, because it could have resulted in serious injury. As a result, one of the carpenters, a Finn, was verbally abusive. Fævang claimed that this was the extent of the mutiny, although he said there was another argument on board caused by a man from Anders' home town, whom Anders himself had hired. Interestingly, the crew members who spoke about the mutiny, or incident, did not deny that something had occurred, but they put the blame squarely at Anders' feet, and did not consider what the aggressive, drunken behaviour would have looked like from the officers' point of view.

Fævang's version of events at the time of the grounding, the 'panic' that Anders was so scathing about, differed somewhat from the officers'

---

* Ibid., 4 December.
† *Tunsbergeren*, 13 January 1909, pp. 1–2.

accounts. Fævang pointed out, quite correctly, that many of those on board were young boys. He did not say as much, but he may have been suggesting that, because they were inexperienced, they would not have known what to do. He did point out that many of them were from Anders' home town. This was the second time he made mention of crew being linked to Anders. It is not clear what he was suggesting with these comments. Perhaps he thought Anders should be more considerate of the people who had joined the expedition because of some sort of association with him. Nevertheless, Fævang claimed that there was no panic, and that those who were most rattled were the officers. He claimed that a couple of the officers fled in one of the motorboats. This accusation was not repeated in any of the inquiries or court cases relating to the shipwreck, and there is no evidence to support the claim.

It would not have been surprising if there was indeed some panic on board. It is possible that at least some of the crew could not swim. This was the case with the very similar disaster that befell the Norwegian factory ship *Fridtjof Nansen* in 1906 when she struck an uncharted underwater reef off the east coast of South Georgia while looking for an entrance to Cumberland Bay. The ship almost immediately broke into three parts and nine of the fifty-eight hands on board drowned.* During the inquest it emerged that most of those who drowned could not swim, and, even if they had been able to, they had to be rescued quickly or they risked perishing because of the cold water.

Fævang absolutely refuted Anders' claims about bad behaviour on the island once they were shipwrecked. He said that all the men participated in the salvage work and that it was completed within three days. This is consistent with the first mate's praise of the efforts of the crew in those first few days. Fævang did acknowledge that provisions were stolen, but said that was only reasonable because they had gone three days with only hard bread and coffee. Fævang said that Anders was as keen as anybody to find what they all thought were diamonds (although Anders was not really

---

* Michener, 2015, p. 3.

criticising the men when he wrote about this), and he argued that Anders and the other officers took the lead in shooting birds, to no one's benefit. It is difficult to know, at this distance in time, what motivated these claims and comments from both Anders and the disgruntled crew.

Fævang said that the conditions on *Inyati* were appalling, and that none of the crew had wanted to board her. He said that sixty-two men were placed in one room, that they were supposed to sleep on the floor, the bread was inedible and the meat was rotten and had to be thrown overboard before they reached London. If the number of sixty-two is correct, that means that eleven of *Solglimt's* crew were provided with better accommodation on *Inyati*. This would not have been surprising: all but Anders and the secretary travelled back to England on this ship, so the officers, the doctor and senior crew were presumably given cabins, noting that *Inyati* was a passenger liner. Fævang concluded by saying that Anders was thoroughly disliked by the crew because he was harsh and did not know how to treat people.

Several other crew members speaking to the press gave a view of events that was consistent with Fævang's. One newspaper said that it would not have commented on Anders' relationship with his crew members if he had not made such damning public comments about them.* In the interview in that newspaper it emerged that the drunk man who approached Anders was one of the stokers. Apparently, he was asking for 5 shillings he believed he was owed as a loading for his boiler work. The Finn who decided to tell Anders what he thought about this episode was reported to have told him that he might as well fill his oil tanks with seawater and abandon the expedition, because none of the crew would be prepared to work for him.

The press were quick to point out that Anders had cost the state a lot of money,† and that, in the opinion of a number of experts, the *Cathrine* shipwreck was caused by carelessness and inadequate seamanship,

---

* *Social-Demokraten*, 14 January 1909, p. 2.

† Discussion about the cost of rescue and repatriation started as early as 3 December 1908 (*Aftenposten*, p. 2) and continued for months.

suggesting that the *Solglimt* shipwreck might have been similarly caused.[*]
It was also claimed that the investigation into who was responsible for
Cathrine's shipwreck was discontinued after Anders was awarded the Order
of St Olav, implying that this was cause and effect, which may well have
been the case. At any rate, it was described as great carelessness that a ship
with so many men on board should be travelling in such dangerous and
poorly mapped waters, and that the promotion of Anders as an example
of skilled Norwegian seamanship should therefore be moderated in favour
of genuinely skilled and less arrogant mariners. One left-wing newspaper
editorialised that Anders' claims about the behaviour of the crew were
grossly exaggerated, as evidenced by the crew members' comments and
what emerged during the investigation into the grounding.[†] The newspaper
also suggested that Anders was not mature enough to be master of a ship or
the leader of an expedition.

Anders was incensed by the crew members' comments and put pen
to paper to reinforce and elaborate on the comments he had made earlier.[‡]
He said that he was standing on the bridge and had just signed off the
pilot escorting them out of Durban when one of the stokers came up on
to the bridge wanting a quarrel. Anders had not previously heard anything
about bad bread on board the ship, and he thought that the man just
wanted an argument because he was drunk. The stoker was abusive and
swore at Anders. Anders asked what sort of master would countenance
such behaviour and said that it would certainly not be allowed on board
a ship of his. Anders acknowledged that he had forcibly removed the man
from the bridge, with no attempt to use kid gloves. The crew on the lower
deck took umbrage at this, and the Finn, who was a big man, came rushing
onto the bridge with the intention of attacking him, saying amongst other
things that he would kill him. Anders boasted that it would take more
than one Finn to get the better of him, and he dealt with him as he had
with the stoker. Apparently, the men on the deck were planning another

* *Social-Demokraten*, 14 January 1909, p. 2.
† *Arbeidet*, 18 January 1909, p. 2.
‡ *Kysten*, 18 January 1909, p. 1.

attack, but Anders thought they were too drunk to act on this threat, while at the same time a storm with strong winds and heavy seas broke over the ship, with the result that the men crept away, one by one.

It was then quiet for a while, until the doctor suddenly rushed up to the bridge asking for Anders' revolver. Some of the crew had made their way to the officers' quarters with the intention of helping themselves to brandy. Anders gave the gun to the doctor and called for the second mate to go to the aid of the other officers. Because the storm was growing in intensity, and they were still quite close to land, Anders was unable to leave the helm himself. Shortly afterwards somebody came running up to the bridge to say that the men who had invaded the officers' rooms were refusing to leave and were threatening to strangle the second mate. On hearing this Anders called the first mate up to the helm and hurried down to the cabin, where he saw what he described as 'a beautiful sight'. Two of the men demanded that they be given brandy or they would have fun with Anders. One had the second mate by the throat, while they demanded that the other was to be given the brandy. Anders later wrote that he did not know how he got the men out of the cabin without being killed. He said that the claim that he had given the men brandy was an outrageous and abominable falsehood, saying, 'Thank God I have other ways of brokering peace on board my ship without buying it with brandy.' He surmised that the bottle might have already been stolen by the men before he went down to the cabin, which in itself did not speak well of the crew members involved. He said that it was only thanks to the storm that there was not an even bigger mutiny on board that night, and that all of the ship's officers agreed with this. Anders acknowledged that there were many good people on board *Solglimt*, but said the fact that a police force of sixty had been necessary to keep the crew on board in Durban gave an indication of the extent of trouble on board, and he also said there were a number of other incidents on the voyage that he would not mention since there would be little to gain from that.

Without doubt there was bad blood between Anders and at least some of his crew, and the trouble that occurred in, and while leaving, Durban was quite serious in nature. While not resulting in a full mutiny, it was certainly inappropriate and insubordinate behaviour. The phrase used by the doctor, 'incursions towards mutiny', seems apt. It is interesting to reflect on the fact that Anders could have avoided a great deal of negative publicity if he had simply refrained from criticising the crew in the newspapers.

After *Cathrine* was wrecked, Anders had written the long article bemoaning the poor state of Norwegian stewards, clearly referring to the steward he had hired for that expedition and, after *Solglimt* was wrecked, he again publicly attacked those he considered the worst of the men in his crew. It is hard to avoid interpreting this as displaced anger about the traumatic loss of the two ships of which he was master. He was a young man, full of ambition and a sense of adventure who had a strong belief in his own abilities. At least at this point in his career he seemed to have been more prepared to criticise others than to question his own degree of responsibility for the outcomes of these two expeditions.

This photograph shows a hall decorated in honour of Anders in 1907 when he returned to Norway. The decorations included flags, and in front of each guest's place there was a model of a whaling ship in full sail, with its crew on deck, all made from marzipan. There were many speeches, and a song was composed for the occasion. *Photographer unknown.*

Left Anders with his wife, or wife-to-be, Marie Harboe-Ree (née Skar). This photograph may have been taken on the couple's honeymoon in mid-1909. Marie is the woman Anders hinted at but chose not to name in the *Cathrine* diary, at a time when he was not at all sure that he would survive and be able to return to Norway and his sweetheart. *Photographer unknown.*

Right Anders is on the right in the front, seated. It is possible that this photograph is from his wedding day, which was 24–06–1909. *Photographer unknown.*

This photograph shows a group on a walking tour on either Possession or Marion Island. It is not possible to link this photograph to a specific one of the three voyages Anders took, in 1906, 1907 and 1908. Anders is second from the left.

The graveyard on Possession Island provided a reminder to the castaways that they could also end their days on this remote island. The memorial plaques on the wooden crosses marking two of the graves were still legible in 1906 and identified the men as young whalers who had found their last rest there in the 1860s, one from Prussia and one from Iceland. The man shown here was on the *Cathrine* voyage, and possibly one of the *Solglimt* voyages.

A view of the forbidding coastline of Possession Island, Crozet Islands, 1906 or 1907.

This photograph of wandering albatrosses on Possession Island is from *Solglimt*'s first voyage, in 1907. *Solglimt* can be seen at anchor behind the birds. Surprisingly, there are very few known photographs of *Solglimt*. The photographs of Possession and Marion islands taken on the *Cathrine* and *Solglimt* voyages are almost certainly the first ever taken there.

Rockhopper penguins on Marion Island, 1908. Anders featured this species of penguin in his painting of the *Solglimt* wreck.

King penguins on Marion Island, 1908. The penguins they found on the islands were novel birds to the men, who were fascinated by them. Notwithstanding Anders' declaration to the birds when he first saw them that they came in peace, the penguins became the castaways' main source of food after both shipwrecks.

The crew assembled for the crossing the equator ceremony on board *Solglimt* on the 1908 voyage. 'Neptune' is standing, third from the left, with his 'wife' second from the left and three helpers on either side and behind him. Many of the men are wearing their *Solglimt* caps.

This watercolour by Anders of *Solglimt* lying wrecked on Marion Island is the best image available of the ship. Inscribed in the lower right-hand corner are the words: Solglimts Bay, Marion Island, AHR, 1908. The rock to the right is now informally called Dragon Rock, and the one behind the ship is called Abseil Rock. The left-hand of the two huts shown is the kitchen. There are rockhopper penguins in the foreground. The painting, which is 31cm x 23cm, is the property of the author.

The wreck of *Solglimt*, Marion Island, 1908, lying in Ship's Cove, which Anders called Solglimts Bay. This photograph, which appeared in the *Newcastle Daily Chronicle*, was attributed to the ship's secretary, Asbjørn Bjørnstad.

The opposite view of the wreck of *Solglimt*, in a heavy swell. This photograph is dated 26–10–1908. On the following night a tremendous storm snapped the vessel in two.

A male southern elephant seal on the beach in Ship's Cove, Marion Island. As there is no evidence of the wreck, this photograph must have been taken on 15–10–1908, the first day's hunting for *Solglimt*'s crew and the day before the wreck occurred.

One of the eleven huts built on Marion Island by *Solglimt*'s castaways in 1908. There are fourteen men in the photograph, and the distinctive Abseil Rock is in the background. The caption to this photograph in a private album says: 'Everything that was saved came in handy.'

This is the kitchen hut, which was built in a central position within the *Solglimt* 'village' and has steps leading up to another level on its right. The men found it very difficult to find suitable building sites for their huts, as this photograph attests. This is another of the photographs that appeared in the *Newcastle Daily Chronicle*, attributed to the ship's secretary, Asbjørn Bjørnstad.

Another of the *Solglimt* huts. This one has fifteen men standing outside it. It was originally intended that each hut built would house four men, but only eleven huts were built, including the kitchen. It is possible that this and other photographs show all of the men living in a particular hut. The caption to this photograph in a private album says, cryptically: 'Something has to be done'. This may refer to the urgent need to get the men off the island and away from the living conditions they were experiencing.

This hut was called Olastua, or Ole's cabin. There are only four men standing outside the cabin, which, if the full complement, would have been quite luxurious. Where possible, the huts were built under an overhang or abutting a rock wall to improve the shelter and reduce the amount of building materials required.

This hut appears to be situated on the beach, but it is more likely to have been on a rise above it. The chaos of barrels and other material from the wreck on the beach indicates that this photo was taken after the storm of 27–10–1908.

This photograph shows a number of the *Solglimt* men in a hut on Marion Island, in 1908. Anders is seated to the left of the table. The document he is holding is the newspaper they created while they were trapped on the island. The title, SKRAVLA, translates as 'gossip', or 'idle chatter'. The illustration is almost identical to the watercolour Anders painted of *Solglimt*. The caption of this photograph in a private album is: 'Evening atmosphere. Björnne's hut.'

Remains of one the *Solglimt* huts, which was built to take advantage of the shelter provided by an overhang. Photograph by Allan Crawford, who was the Officer-in-Charge of the first overwintering South African expedition, which was undertaken in 1948. *Courtesy of Antarctic Legacy of South Africa.*

Another photograph by Allan Crawford showing the remains of one of the *Solglimt* huts in 1948. *Courtesy of Antarctic Legacy of South Africa.*

A stove in the ruins of the *Solglimt* 'village' kitchen hut on Marion Island. The photograph is from either 1948 or the early 1950s. *Photographer unknown. Courtesy of Antarctic Legacy of South Africa.*

South African researcher Jaco Boshoff diving on the *Solglimt* wreck in 2011. Diving is difficult and dangerous in these extremely cold waters with temperatures between 4°C and 10°C. Photograph by Andre Botha. *Courtesy of Iziko Museums, South Africa.*

Archaeology of the *Solglimt* village site underway in 2013 by the Iziko Museums research team comprising Jaco Boshoff, Tara Van Niekerk and Sven Ouzman. Photograph by Sven Ouzman. *Courtesy of Iziko Museums, South Africa.*

In 1917 Anders formed and led a company to commission and acquire ocean-going, concrete-hulled vessels. This was a pioneering venture, and in 1919 the company took possession of the ship shown here, which it named *Concrete*. This was one of the largest of its kind ever built in Europe. *Image courtesy of Dag Bakka.*

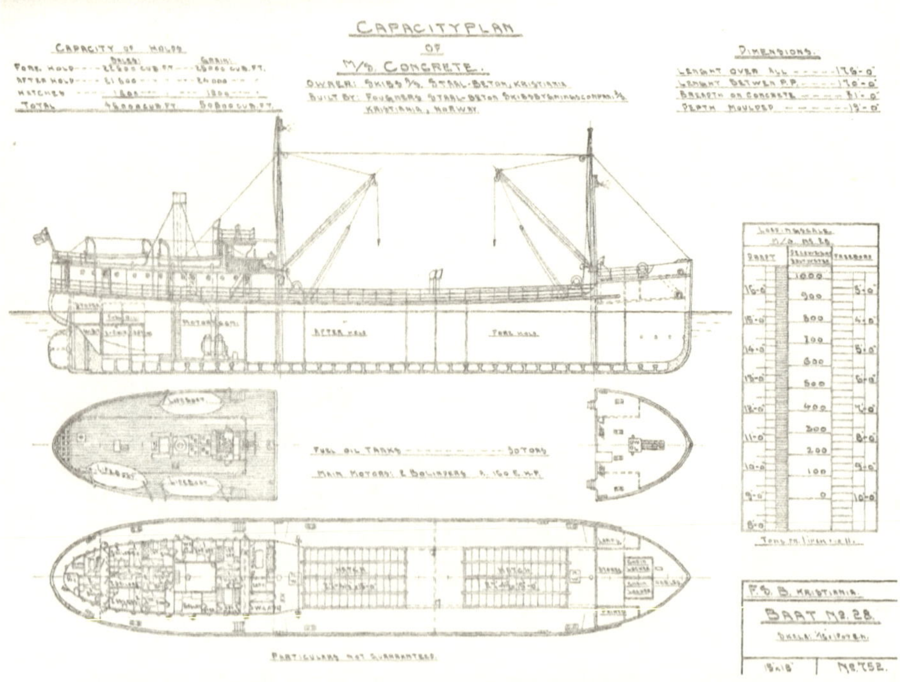

This drawing showing *Concrete*'s specifications appeared as Attachment 10 in the Norwegian journal *Ship Building*, number 7, 1919. *Image courtesy of Dag Bakka.*

Anders was an accomplished and prolific woodcarver, an artform that is highly valued in Norway. These two images show a mirror (left) and a cabinet (right). When he retired, Anders produced a huge number of carved and painted items and held several exhibitions in Norway. *Photographers unknown.*

Oil painting of Anders Harboe-Ree by John Paulsen (1892–1972), dated 1950. It measures 31cm x 41cm. Anders would have been 69 years old when this portrait was painted. Smoking a pipe was clearly a life-long habit. *Painting property of the author.*

CHAPTER 11

THE END OF HIS TRIUMPH

Everyone forgets that Icarus also flew …
I believe Icarus was not failing as he fell,
but just coming to the end of his triumph.

Jack Gilbert, *Failing and Flying*[*]

CATHRINE

In late 1907 and early 1908, while Anders and Bull were in the Southern Ocean on the first *Solglimt* expedition, the legal and reputational fallout from the loss of *Cathrine* started playing out in official inquiries and the court of public opinion. The first hint of this came in response to a sharply critical reaction by the Tønsberg Shipowners Association to the naming, in the Maritime Office's Yearbook pertaining to 1906, of shipowners and captains who owned or were masters of ships that suffered damage or loss.[†] The Association claimed that those named suffered reputational damage, without the Maritime Office looking into the cause of the damage or loss, which might have been completely accidental. The Association argued that, even in cases where only minor damage had occurred, those named would have doubts hovering over them for years to come, which it could be said incurred a penalty much greater than that intended by the law. The loss of *Cathrine* was cited as an example of the injustice of the Maritime Office's practice of naming people before investigations had been concluded. In this

---

* Gilbert, 2005.
† *Morgenbladet*, 24 January 1908, p. 1.

instance the Yearbook stated that the wreck was caused by poor navigation. The Association commented that the references in the Yearbook as they related to *Cathrine* were 'childish in the extreme in their lack of logic', and went on to point out that Anders had been awarded the Order of St Olav in recognition of his seamanship. To highlight their concerns, the Association resolved to publicise their criticism of the practice and urge other Norwegian shipowners associations to do likewise.

Although the Tønsberg Shipowners Association no doubt thought it was being supportive of Anders when it made its complaint about what appeared in the Yearbook, their use of *Cathrine* as an example to help its argument actually made matters worse for him. For a start, it was not true that the Maritime Office had published information about the cause of the loss of *Cathrine* before its investigation had been completed. The Maritime Office's investigator had received the report from the Norwegian Consul General in Melbourne, Gundersen, on the circumstances surrounding *Cathrine*'s loss and, in the absence of any further information from government sources, had made his findings on the basis of that report and recommended that the case should be dismissed, thereby concluding the investigation.

Gundersen's report included criticism of Ander's decisions leading up to the wrecking. The Maritime Office had based its comments in the Yearbook on this report, and it decided to make it public in its defence once the Shipowners Association had publicly criticised the comments made in the Yearbook.* However this dispute is considered, Anders was caught in the cross-fire at a time when he was out of the country and could not respond or defend himself. Extraordinarily, and to make matters worse, it emerged that Anders had not been given a copy of the final report and its findings, or provided with the opportunity to respond to it.

Gundersen's report included the excerpts from *Cathrine*'s logbook that Anders had provided. These contained a record of the events leading up to the shipwreck, including the speed with which the weather had

---

* *Kysten*, 28 January 1908, p. 1, and 29 January 1908, p. 4.

deteriorated and the difficulty of taking action when the wind and sea rose, and the fact that the engine was incapable of getting the ship out of the bay. The excerpts also explained the initial decision not to cut the rigging, since to do so would risk disabling or breaking the propeller or shaft if the rigging got caught up in them. The consultation of the ship's council to make the major decisions was noted.

An issue that later proved contentious was the decision not to leave the bay when the wind abated after 24 hours, after which it had come back with renewed force later in the day. Bull and a number of *Cathrine*'s crew members commented that the sea remained very high after the first period of the storm and so they were unable to leave the bay, but the excerpts do not stress this point.[*] In fact, they say that the men were able to rest after a sleepless night when the weather calmed down, but they fail to mention that the situation was still difficult.

In addition to the inclusion of such excerpts in his report, Gundersen provided a record of his interviews with both of the men who had accompanied Anders in *Hope*. Antonsen said that *Cathrine* was anchored at the Crozet Islands with a much stronger anchor than would normally have been used and, in his view, nothing could have been done to prevent her drift towards the shore once the gale force winds started. Setting sail and trying to get clear of the bay in which they were anchored would not have been feasible. He confirmed that the ship's council had met twice. On the first night of the storm, they were aware that the ship had drifted towards the reefs, and they measured a depth of 15 metres. After the first boat with six of the men had left *Cathrine,* the wind increased, the sea rose even higher, and eventually the decision was made to cut the rigging. However, before this could be done the stern struck a reef and the ship was abandoned as quickly as possible, without the chance of taking anything other than what they were wearing, or any of the food on board. Within half an hour of the crew leaving *Cathrine,* she shattered on the reef. Johansen said that he was in complete agreement with Antonsen's version of the events.

---

[*] *New York Times*, 15 December 1907, p. 50.

The Maritime Office's investigator who reviewed Gundersen's report made several adverse findings. He concluded that there were two main causes of the loss. First and foremost, he found that Anders had been careless in allowing *Cathrine* to be anchored in American Bay, which is exposed to the east, with only a 20-horsepower engine to provide assistance to the sails. Secondly, he characterised as inexperienced the decision to allow the men to rest after the worst of the storm had abated, rather than attempt to leave the bay. He asserted that the vessel could have been moved out of the bay if the chain had been provided with a buoy rope and an associated buoy, and then the chain could have been let go when the ship was in 13 metres of water. At this point, he claimed, they would have been able to motor out of the bay against the high eastern sea and find a sheltered anchorage site on the leeward side of the island. He concluded that, because Anders did not take either of these actions, he must have been relying on luck and the heavy chain they had deployed.

The investigator acknowledged that the rescue mission by Anders and the two crew members should be characterised as brave and bold. However, he qualified this by saying that this was especially true of the two crew members, because the captain, while having a strong desire to help his crew, was the one who had, by his actions, brought the crew to the position they were in. As an honourable sailor he was obliged to risk his life to try to get help for his men, any other hope of rescue being unlikely. The investigator noted the loss of the valuable vessel and its load and the great cost to the government resulting from the rescue of the crew, and concluded by recommending that the case be dismissed, as mentioned above.

SOLGLIMT

The Maritime Office's investigation into *Solglimt*'s loss began in earnest in Kristiania in the middle of January 1909.* This was a standard investigation following the loss of a vessel, not a judicial hearing. Anders presented a

* *Norges Sjøfartstidende*, 13 January 1909, pp. 1, 4, *Tunsbergeren*, 14 January, p. 2, and other newspapers.

copy of the declaration he had made in Durban and drew on excerpts from the ship's logbook to describe the sequence of events. He said that they had not been sounding because they had been in the same area the day before, when they had sounded regularly, and the *Admiralty Charts* included no hazards on that stretch of the coast. He said that he had sent the helmsman away from the bridge on an errand and had taken over the helm himself before the grounding occurred. He also reiterated his criticisms of the behaviour of the crew during and after the grounding, although it is not clear exactly what bearing that would have on the investigation.

In response to a question from the investigator as to whether *Solglimt* was lying with her port or starboard side towards the land, Anders replied that it was her starboard, but the shipping inspector demonstrated that this was impossible, to which Anders responded that he could not say, nor could he recall, whether he had turned the ship to starboard or port. Much was made of this exchange by some of the crew and several newspapers, who argued that it was an indication of Anders' poor seamanship, just as he had been accused of the poor seamanship that resulted in *Cathrine* being wrecked. When examining the details of *Solglimt's* grounding, however, it is difficult to see how the direction the ship was turned could have had a bearing on what occurred.

Anders presented a map of Marion Island showing where he believed the grounding had occurred, although it was stated on the map itself that it was unreliable, and Anders could not say with certainty where the underwater reef lay. It was noted in the proceedings that the reef was not visible to anybody prior to the incident.

The question of whether or not soundings had been carried out on the morning of the grounding became a major line of inquiry throughout the investigation. Anders said he thought that soundings had been taken every half minute the day before, with no significant change in the depth of the water on the route they had taken, and they had not touched bottom with 46 metres of line out. The route they had been on the day before was the same route they had just started to retrace when the grounding occurred.

Anders pointed out that, after *Solglimt* was wrecked, they were rarely able to see any breakers in the vicinity, even from high observation points on the island. Every witness was asked about soundings and possible visibility of the reef, but the only possibility of sightings mentioned were the claims that some of the crew had seen what they thought was a whale spouting. The third engineer was in a motorboat checking its engine when the incident occurred. He was circling *Solglimt*, had passed right over the spot and had seen nothing untoward.

Another issue pursued in the investigation was whether or not there were adequate lookouts. Anders said that he had a clear view right around the horizon from his position at the helm, and the first mate said that he was not ordered to keep a lookout while he was hauling in the anchor, but had done so anyway out of 'old sailor's instinct'.

Eleven witnesses were interviewed during the Maritime Office's investigation, and at the end of the process the shipping inspector asked that legal proceedings be initiated, although at this point nobody had been charged.[*] The resulting judicial hearing commenced immediately.[†]

The state's first witness, the Finn, August Sjøblom, was a ship's carpenter and one of the people involved in the mutinous incident when *Solglimt* was leaving Durban on her way south. Sjøblom said that he was hauling in the chains with the first mate when the grounding occurred, and he could not say whether or not the mate had been keeping a lookout. Sjøblom claimed that he and two of the Swedish men and another crew member had seen the sea breaking over an underwater reef on the port side of the ship and had told the second mate this, who replied that it was probably the whale spout that other crew members had already spoken about. Sjøblom said they saw the sea breaking every few minutes. He also said that he saw the spray from the shore, and he was convinced that this was the same underwater reef that *Solglimt* had struck. Sjøblom did not know that the motorboat had circled the ship a couple of times and could

---

[*] *Morgenbladet*, 11 February 1909, p. 2.
[†] *Tunsbergeren*, 12 February 1909, p. 2.

not say whether or not the shipwreck was due to negligence on the part of the ship's officers. He did, however, say that in the two months' journey from Norway to Marion Island there had been no lifeboat exercises carried out. When questioned by the shipping inspector, Sjøblom said that there were bad relations between Anders and the majority of the crew, including himself, due to the fact that Anders treated them harshly and offhandedly. This witness was later recalled to be asked if Anders had been at the helm when the ship struck the reef. He replied that Anders was walking backwards and forwards and that nobody was at the helm.

The second witness, the sailor and boilerman Ingard Hansen, had been on the first *Solglimt* voyage a year earlier. He confirmed that sounding had been done on the previous day but not on the day of the grounding, and that he had seen something of the reef that *Solglimt* struck, but he had thought it was a whale spouting. He claimed that the first mate knew about the reef because, when they were on shore after the grounding, he had pointed to the break and said that that was the whale spout they had seen. Hansen had been at work at the boilers on deck when *Solglimt* struck.* He said that there was only one person on the bridge – Anders – at the time, and no lookout had been posted. He also claimed, contrary to the statement by the engineer driving the motorboat, that it had not passed over the reef. He agreed that there was no option but to beach *Solglimt*, and repeated the statement made by the first witness that there had been no lifeboat exercises carried out during the voyage, although the whaleboats had been put on the water in Shields while they were taking on coal, and again once they had arrived at Marion Island. He was unable to comment on whether or not crew members had obtained spirits once they were marooned, and said he had not seen any drunkenness. He said that he had a good relationship with Anders, but there were a few who were on a less good footing with him. Finally, he said that, in his opinion, there had indeed been negligence because no soundings had been taken on the day of the grounding, and there were no lookouts.

---

* The boilers referred to here were those used to process the seal blubber.

The third witness, Amandus Fævang, who had had a great deal to say to the press, said that he was in his berth when the grounding occurred and so could explain little about the catastrophe, but he testified that soundings had been taken the previous day and that he had heard talk of a whale spout having been seen. He also said that the crew did not like Anders.

The fourth witness, Thorvald Johansen, shed some interesting light on the relationship between Anders and members of his crew.* Johansen had been the bosun on *Cathrine*, and had set off with Anders in the whaleboat *Hope* to seek rescue for those remaining on the Crozet Islands. This was an extraordinary experience to share, and Anders had been full of praise for him at the time. Johansen was in the motorboat circling *Solglimt*, testing its motor, when the grounding occurred, and had not realised there was anything amiss until he saw the ship proceeding awkwardly to shore. He had not seen any disturbance in the water but had heard talk of the whale spout, and he said that there were no lookouts. He agreed that no lifeboat exercises had been done, and he did not know if they had been inspected, however all the whaleboats had been on the water multiple times. With regard to the relationships between Anders and his crew, he said that these were strained, and that among sealers there were different kinds of people and that did not always go well with a 'big shot' like Anders. Johansen said that he could not recognise Anders as being the same man from two years earlier. And perhaps he wasn't. He was shouldering significantly more responsibility on this voyage than had been the case on the earlier voyage, and it is altogether possible that the huge jump in crew numbers took him beyond his management ability.

The fifth witness, seaman and hunter Emil Eriksen, was working on shore when the incident occurred so he could not comment on what happened at sea, but he said that he had seen the whale spout and had told the second mate and a number of the stokers, and he said that he was sure that the second mate had heard him. His comment about the relationship between Anders and the crew was that it was as bad as it could get.

---

* *Tunsbergeren*, 13 February 1909, p. 2.

The sixth witness, sailor and boilerman, Olaf Maritvold, said that he had been involved in sounding every few minutes the day before the incident. He confirmed the positions of Anders, the first mate and Sjøblom at the time of the incident, as well as the statement made by others that there had been no lifeboat exercises during the voyage. He said that the lifeboats were not in good order and some equipment was missing. Several other witnesses were called, and these backed up the claims and statements made by the earlier witnesses.

Only two of the witnesses, the second witness, Hansen, and the machinist Hans Christian Jensen, said that they had no complaints against Anders. Jensen said that he did not know what reasons others might have had for criticising him.

Responding to witnesses' claims about whether or when a whale spout was seen, the manager of the company that owned *Solglimt*, Sverre, wrote to the press saying that the comments were misleading and contradicted earlier statements.[*] Sverre, who was obviously worried that what was being said in court could have a bearing on insurance claims, said that nobody had told the captain about having seen a whale spout, and that it was not until after the shipwreck had occurred that the opinion was established among some of the witnesses that what they saw might have been waves breaking on a reef. Sverre also asserted that nothing had emerged in the maritime inquiry or court hearing that had any bearing on the relationship between the shipping company and the insurance companies.

The second mate, Henrik Hansen, also wrote to the press to say that he was not present in court when statements were made referring to him.[†] He said that on the morning of 16 October he had gone ashore with the other men who were hunting that day and had seen nothing resembling breaking waves or a whale spout before leaving the ship. Nor did he recall any crew member reporting this. By this time, a number of the crew had accused Anders in the press of having caused the shipwreck through incompetence,

---

[*] *Norges Sjøfartstidende*, 20 February 1909, p. 1.
[†] *Kysten*, 23 February 1909, p. 1.

and the testimonies given in the court consistently included information that would encourage a jury to think likewise. Hansen's response suggests that at least some of the information provided by the crew was skewed to give an unfavourable impression of the ship's officers, especially Anders.

After a delay of several months with the judicial hearing, Anders was called to appear at the court to respond to the accusation that he had negligently caused *Solglimt*'s grounding by not having taken soundings on the day of the grounding, not having posted a lookout and not having ordered lifeboat exercises. A number of newspapers stated that Anders had been charged with negligence, and he speedily denied that he had been charged.* Further, he said that there had been no investigation into him personally on the part of the prosecution and, as he was not aware that he had shown any negligence, he awaited the judgment of the jury with confidence. For legal representation he had engaged the Supreme Court Attorney Lauritz Hofgaard[†].

Anders then announced several days later that, through Hofgaard, he had petitioned the public prosecutor to have his responsibility for *Cathrine*'s wrecking investigated at the same time, saying that he had been unfairly criticised for this without his knowledge and without having been given an opportunity to defend himself.[‡] The newspaper that had been most critical of Anders when it heard about *Solglimt*'s loss supported his desire to have the matter properly investigated.[§] Whether this was because it felt that its own criticism of Anders would have greater validity as a result of what would be revealed in an investigation, or because it felt that Anders had not been treated fairly, it is not possible to say. Other newspapers also supported Anders' bid to have *Cathrine*'s shipwreck further investigated, noting that the questions about Anders' culpability risked tarnishing the reputation of the Order of St Olav he had received relating to the same incident.

---

* *Arbeidet*, 29 April 1909, p. 2, *Trondhjems Adresseavis*, 29 April 1909, p. 2 and other newspapers.
† *Kysten*, 3 May 1909, p. 2.
‡ *Morgenbladet*, 6 May 1909, p. 2.
§ *Kysten*, 11 May 1909, p. 2.

On 10 May Anders was questioned for over four hours and, on the following day, for a further two and a half. He defended his decision not to take soundings on the day in question and said that he was in a good position to act as lookout himself. He said that he assumed that *Solglimt* had struck an underwater peak rather than a shoal, and that sounding would not have revealed this until it was too late. He said that he did not see a whale spout or breaking waves but, later from shore when the sea was lower, he was able to see where the peak might have been.

On 18 June 1909, even though the judicial hearing had not been completed, the prosecutors issued an indictment against Anders under section 151 of the Criminal Code.[*] If found guilty, Anders could have been facing a gaol sentence of up to three years.

On 24 June, with the judicial hearing still unresolved and the indictment trial yet to commence, Anders married Marie Skar. One assumes that he and his bride would have preferred less stressful circumstances in which to celebrate the beginning of their life together.

The judicial hearing that had commenced in February dragged on, largely because a number of the witnesses were proving difficult to locate. In late July another sailor appeared in court to testify about the grounding.[†] He said that he had not seen a whale spout or waves breaking in the vicinity of the ship and had only heard about it several days later. He said that the relations between Anders and his crew were good, although a number of the hunters were on the whole quite impossible, always grumbling and

---

* Det Kongelige Justis-og Politidepartement [Ministry of Justice and the Police], 1902. Section 151 states that if any maritime damage as is referred to in section 148 is caused by negligence, the offender will be liable to fines or imprisonment for a term not exceeding three years; Section 148 states that any person who causes any maritime damage that may easily result in loss of human life or extensive destruction of another person's property, or who aids or abets thereto, will be liable to imprisonment for a term of not less than two years and not exceeding 21 years, but not less than five years if as a result of the felony any person dies or is seriously injured in body or health; Note that the website providing the English translation of the relevant Criminal Code states that it is an unofficial translation.

† *Morgenbladet*, 27 July 1909, p. 1.

complaining about something.

In mid-September the trial dealing with Anders' indictment began in the Kristiania Court of Appeal.* The indictment alleged that Anders, through negligence, caused the damage to *Solglimt* that resulted in the loss of property and could easily have resulted in the loss of life. In addition, the prosecution alleged that insufficient sounding had been done and that the required lifeboat exercises had not been carried out. Anders pleaded not guilty to the charges. The prosecutor reprised the details and arguments that had been revealed in the earlier hearings and said that, although it was now impossible to gather witnesses because they had spread all over the world, there was no reason that the case could not proceed. The bad relations between Anders and his crew were noted, but the prosecutor also said that there were undoubtedly a number of trouble-makers on board. It is intriguing that the topic of the relations between Anders and the crew was dealt with so prominently in the various hearings. At no stage was it explicitly stated that this had caused, or had an impact on, the loss of *Solglimt.* However, the prosecutors may have been building the argument that bad morale on the ship could have led to more calamitous outcomes.

Only two of the crew appeared as witnesses for the prosecution. One said that he had not seen any sign of a whale spout or breakers, while the other said that he had, although he was working on shore at the time *Solglimt* struck ground. A shipowner who was called as an expert witness said that under the circumstances as stated the lack of sounding could not be considered negligent and, although a lookout in the rigging might have been helpful, it was also arguable that that would not have been the case, because underwater peaks can be very difficult to see. He noted that the motorboat that was on the water at the time had seen nothing of a reef or breaking waters. Regarding the lack of lifeboat exercises, the shipowner said that, as a practical sailor, he did not think this was something to make a fuss about, but he recognised that, in order to comply with the regulations, they should have been carried out.

____

* *Kysten*, 16 September 1909, p. 1.

A second expert witness, a shipowner, thought that because of the poor maps they were working with the greater caution of having a boat in front of the ship to undertake soundings would have been desirable. Regarding the lack of a specific lookout, he thought that having a man in the rig was unnecessary, and he said that the issue of lifeboat exercises had no practical significance, only legal.

On 17 September Anders was found not guilty of causing *Solglimt*'s grounding, but was found guilty of the minor misdemeanour of not having carried out lifeboat exercises. The majority found the offence so trivial that it considered no fine should be imposed, but settled on the law's minimum penalty, 1 kroner (A$11). The chairman of the court voted for a fine of 50 kroner (A$560), but the majority prevailed.*

The prosecution immediately announced that it would appeal to the Supreme Court of Norway to have the decision overturned.† This incensed Anders. He was distressed by the degree to which *Solglimt*'s loss had already been investigated, the personal attacks on him in the press (notwithstanding the fact that he had drawn fire to himself to some degree), and the rejection by the courts of his request to deal with *Cathrine*'s shipwreck in the same proceedings. At this point Anders decided to argue his case in public.‡

He said that, although there had been 'legal investigations, interrogations and similar things' carried out by the Maritime Office in connection with the loss of *Solglimt* for over a year, the Office had not succeeded in convicting him of having caused the shipwreck. He thought that to many of the people who knew him and who had followed this matter in the newspapers it must have looked as if he was a terrible person, and it was painful for himself, as a man of honour, to read the things that had been said about him.

Given this, he thought it no more than reasonable that people should also hear from him about how the Maritime Office had behaved towards him. He said that he willingly admitted that he had been extremely

---

* *Arbeidet*, 29 September 1909, p. 2.
† *Norges Sjøfartstidende*, 22 September 1909, p. 3.
‡ Ibid., Tuesday 19 October 1909, p. 1.

unlucky, and that he had involuntarily cost the state large sums of money in the form of rescue expeditions, repatriation of crews and so on, and for this reason the Maritime Office had had just cause to proceed stringently. However, he argued that for one to be pursued and sought to be made a criminal by the institution that should be one's support and help, that was hardly just. Although it is understandable that Anders was very unhappy about the inquiries and legal proceedings, it is less obvious why the Maritime Office should be criticised for doing what it was required to do under the law. This probably highlights an inherent conflict in its multiple roles: that of creating an environment in which shipping could thrive, and having to investigate possible breaches of the law.

Anders asserted that it was neither in his power nor the power of any human being to prevent the disaster that had befallen *Cathrine*. In defence of this claim he said that his innocence was apparent from the inquiry held at the Consulate General in Melbourne and from the ship's journal, there being no other facts available. Anders pointed out that, after the shipwreck, he had returned to Norway and remained there for many months, during which he heard not a word suggesting that he had done anything wrong. No further testimonies had been required and no allegations had been made against him. On the contrary, he said, he received from His Majesty King Haakon an acknowledgment that he had acquitted himself honourably when *Cathrine* was wrecked. This suggests that Anders himself equated the honours he received with exoneration from any responsibility for the shipwreck. Surely he was not at fault in assuming this when no further action was taken by the Maritime Office.

This made news of the damning report in the Office's Yearbook – that he had been held responsible for the shipwreck through poor seamanship – even more galling. He argued, quite rightly, that this had taken place behind his back, and without being given the slightest chance to defend himself. He allowed himself to ask: 'Is this "fair play"?', and said that, had he suspected that something like this was going on, he would have immediately demanded a new maritime investigation with all men interviewed as soon as they had arrived in Norway. He repeated his question as to why the Maritime Office did not interview any of the crew when it suspected that something was wrong with regard to the shipwreck, and why it did not give him occasion to defend himself, even though there was ample time for that.

Anders said in his letter that he had written to the Maritime Office requesting that the criticism referred to be changed, but this request had been denied. Further, he said that to sue the Maritime Office would give rise to significant expenses that he could not afford at the time, thus he would forever and always be unjustifiably condemned to appear in the Maritime Office's black book as guilty of things about which he claimed innocence. He used the letter to state that he did not accept the situation, and that he was thereby allowing himself to publicly inform the author of the Maritime Office's Yearbook for 1906 that the criticisms relating to the shipwreck of the schooner *Cathrine* contained therein were incorrect in their most significant points, and were therefore considered by him to be invalid as long as it had not been proved before the courts of the country that he was actually guilty.

Moving on to consideration of the *Solglimt* shipwreck, Anders asserted that he had again been subjected to similar treatment. He pointed out that it had been stated in the court judgment that the Maritime Office had worked behind his back without providing him with what was his right, namely that he should have been informed that he could have been in court either personally or represented through a lawyer when witnesses were interviewed. He also wryly noted that the Maritime Office had succeeded in calling those of the crew whom Anders himself would least have liked to have on board, the vast majority of whom had committed crimes against him either on land or at sea. He had had to reprimand these men, with the result that they detested him. Even taking into account Anders' clearly aggrieved state, it does appear that the injustices he pointed out in this letter had some validity. Certainly, no officers were called as witnesses, which seems strikingly odd.

Anders concluded his letter by saying that hundreds of masters around the country agreed with him that both individual members and the entire industry had been ruthlessly treated by the current management of the Maritime Office and, although it was possible that other masters may have been treated in a similar way, he thought that none could have been treated worse than him.

In late October the Supreme Court rejected the Maritime Office's appeal against the decision to find Anders not guilty of negligently causing the *Solglimt*'s shipwreck, and his year-long battle with the Office ended.[*] Presumably the Maritime Office believed it had a strong case against Anders, which would explain why it pursued Anders in the courts. Further, the company of which he was a major shareholder would have had to repay the rescue and repatriation costs if Anders had been found to be responsible for wrecking the ship.

The end of the Maritime Office's legal case was not, however, the end of Anders' financial worries concerning *Solglimt*. In February the ship's company manager, Sverre, had anticipated trouble with the companies *Solglimt* had been insured with. He pointed out 'that nothing [had] emerged during the maritime declarations or subsequent investigations that [had] any bearing on the relationship between the shipping company and the insurance companies.'[†] By June, however, it was clear that Sverre had been right to be concerned and he was forced to initiate proceedings against two of the companies that had insured *Solglimt*'s hull and were now refusing to pay out the ship company's claims.[‡] Other shipping company managers were very concerned about this and asked for the names of the insurance companies that were refusing payment to be released publicly, in tandem with the reasons they were giving for the refusal. Sverre obliged by publishing the names of all the companies *Solglimt* had been insured with,

---

[*] *Norges Sjøfartstidende*, 1 November 1909, p. 2
[†] Ibid., 20 February 1909, p. 1.
[‡] *Morgenbladet*, 3 June 1909, p. 1.

including those who were refusing to pay.[*][†]

Four insurance contracts had been taken out for *Solglimt*'s expedition, covering the hull, equipment, cargo and interest. The dispute arose because the wording in two of the contracts, those for cargo and interest, stated that *Solglimt* was going to the Crozet Islands to hunt. The contracts for the hull and equipment included the phrase 'and other islands', but the other two did not and, on this basis, the insurance companies rejected the claims, because *Solglimt* was lost at the Prince Edward Islands, not the Crozets. It was generally accepted at the time that 'Crozet Islands' meant all of the islands in the southern Indian Ocean, but the insurance companies defended their decision on the basis of a literal reading of the contracts. In July 1910, the Norwegian Maritime Court, while noting the wording of the contracts, found against the insurance companies and ordered them to pay the sums sought.[‡]

The insurance companies appealed, and the case was heard two years later by Norway's Supreme Court.[§] This time the court, although it agreed that 'Crozet Islands' had a broad meaning, found in favour of the insurance companies, arguing that the wording of the contracts could not be overridden. The value of Anders' shares in the company that owned *Solglimt* was immediately and disastrously reduced.

To put the loss of *Solglimt* in a broader context, she was not the only Norwegian ship lost at that time, although she certainly attracted the most attention. The official record for the last quarter of 1908 identified a total of twenty-six vessels lost. Of these, twelve had been stranded and wrecked, six, including *Solglimt*, had grounded, three had been condemned as unseaworthy, two had disappeared, one had had a collision, one had sunk

---

[*] *Kysten*, 26 June 1909, p. 1.

[†] Sverre continued his career as a ship's manager, specialising in southern hemisphere voyages. His next ship after *Solglimt* was a sealing vessel, *Eclipse*, which was a more simply equipped vessel than the very expensive *Solglimt*, so it carried less risk for the company, and was presumably covered by very precisely written insurance clauses.

[‡] *Kysten*, 11 July 1910, p. 1.

[§] *Norges Handels og Sjøfartstidende*, 28 June 1912, p. 3.

and one had been abandoned. Regarding the loss of Norwegian ships in the Southern Ocean, in addition to *Cathrine* and *Fridtjof Nansen* in 1906 and *Solglimt* in 1908, in 1910 the 1,480-ton steamship *Wennipeg* was wrecked on Kerguelen Islands. With echoes of *Cathrine*'s loss, *Wennipeg* was dragged onto the beach in a violent storm, despite having both anchors out.[*]

COST OF RESCUE AND REPATRIATION

The day that news of *Solglimt*'s loss became known in Norway, debate began about whether or not the state should meet the costs of rescuing and repatriating sailors home to Norway who had been marooned because of a shipwreck, a vessel being condemned, or as the result of piracy.[†] The policy then in place reflected Norway's commitment to its maritime industry, which was highly important to its financial security, but the costs that the state had been accustomed to meet had, to that date, been mainly for sailors in the northern hemisphere, or for sailors who were unable to find a working passage home from other ports, so involved relatively low numbers of people and relatively low costs. However, this was unlikely to be the case when hunting vessels were wrecked or disabled in the southern hemisphere, and the costs associated with bringing *Solglimt*'s men home gave both the state and the general public pause for thought. The early estimates put this at a minimum of 300 kroner (A$3,400) per man, or 22,500 kroner (A$254,000) for the whole crew. With sums of this magnitude involved, there were immediate suggestions that the state should only have to meet some of the rescue and repatriation costs, not all. It is worth noting that Norway's provisions at that time were very generous. In America, for example, the state made no contribution towards the rescue of shipwrecked crews or their repatriation.

The argument made in Norway was that successful hunting expeditions yielded huge profits to the companies and individuals involved, with some,

---

[*] Globally, in the fifty-year period after large steam-powered sealing vessels were introduced, 400 were lost and nearly 1,000 men perished. See Crockett, 2015.
[†] *Norges Handels og Sjøfartstidende*, 1 December 1908, p. 2.

though not commensurate, benefit to the state, while the state was meeting the full costs of rescue and repatriation when things went wrong. It was suggested that the shipping companies should take out insurance to meet at least half of these costs, just as they had to have insurance for the loss of their vessels, equipment or cargo. *Solglimt*, including her equipment, was insured for approximately 400,000 kroner (A$4,380,000). In response to questions about this, the Minister for Maritime Affairs, Lars Abrahamsen, said that he thought it unreasonable to expect the state to meet the full cost of rescue and repatriation when expeditions were hunting in little-known, partially charted waters.[*]

Of the four shipwrecks used as recent examples of the state's rescue and repatriation costs associated with whaling and sealing expeditions, Anders was master of two, *Cathrine* and *Solglimt*. The rescue and repatriation of *Cathrine*'s crew had cost the state 25,000 kroner (A$273,000).[†] The state's expenses in connection with the *Fridtjof Nansen* shipwreck off South Georgia were a more modest 7,000 kroner (A$76,000). The state's expenses in connection with the fourth ship, *Frigard*, are not known, although they were reported as being quite large. She was, however, wrecked in the North Sea, so the costs could be expected to be somewhat lower than those associated with expeditions to the southern seas. Thus, the lion's share of the state's rescue and repatriation costs at that time was attributable to the expeditions Anders was associated with.

The Maritime Office's 1907 yearbook listed the annual rescue and repatriation budget for the period 1 May 1907 to 1 May 1908 as 147,000 kroner (A$1,600,000). This was distributed among 126 wrecked or condemned ships. If an average of twelve men per ship is assumed, then each man would have cost the state approximately 100 kroner (A$1,100). The amount allocated for the following year, 1 May 1908 to 1 May 1909,

---

[*] *Aftenposten*, 3 December 1908, p. 2.

[†] This was made up of 18,000 kroner (A$197,000) for the rescue attempts, 3,000 (A$33,000) for repatriation of the crew from Melbourne and 3,600 kroner (A$39,000) to the English shipping company whose ship *Turakina* had succeeded in rescuing the crew.

was 200,000 kroner (A$2,200,000), of which 37,500 (A$410,000) was to be repaid by shipping companies. These repayments would occur where it was determined that somebody on board was responsible for disabling or wrecking the ship. Repatriation of *Solglimt*'s crew was expected to be approximately 200 kroner (A$2,200) for each man, or twice the average for other vessels, plus any claims that would be made by the two vessels that rescued the men or for accommodation and provisions in Durban.

The argument was by no means one-sided. A Norwegian newspaper with a focus on maritime affairs criticised the minister,* saying that it was highly inappropriate of him to react to what he perceived as a slight advantage to the shipping industry by immediately attempting to snuff out the advantage. The newspaper pointed out that the same minister showed no signs of remorse over the fact that the industry comprising shipping, fishing, whaling and sealing enjoyed very little benefit from the state but was taxed heavily and unfairly. Moreover, it brought an enormous amount of money into the country and the Norwegian treasury, in the order of 150,000 kroner (A$1,650,000) a year.† Against this, the state paid out a pittance to meet the costs of rescue and repatriation of ships' crews, while providing millions of kroner in protection to other industries of far less importance to the country. In addition, the shipping industry did not diminish the natural wealth of the nation, but brought in riches from faraway lands. Finally, the newspaper argued that in other countries the shipping industry enjoyed tax benefits, while in Norway special tax burdens were applied, and it challenged the minister to justify the benefits that much smaller industries enjoyed in the form of tariff protection.

Several days later the same newspaper doubled down on its criticism of the minister, saying that it was as mean an act as one could imagine, and quite indicative of the support and sympathy the maritime industry could

---

* *Kysten*, 4 December 1908, p. 1.

† This does not seem to be a significant amount in comparison with the state's budgeted costs, but that is the figure cited in the article. It is likely that the figure is missing a zero, which would make it 1,500,000 kroner (A$16,500,000).

expect from the man who was supposed to be its foremost spokesperson in government but who, immediately on taking up his role, was ready to burden the industry with increased expenses.* He was criticised for making public statements before careful consideration could be given to the issue, and it was argued that the result of what he was suggesting would be the abandoning of shipwrecked or marooned Norwegian sailors to their fate in foreign ports. Further, the timing of the increased expense to the industry could not be worse, because of the prolonged downturn in the viability of the freight industry. With this in mind, the newspaper suggested that the focus of any inquiry should be on just the whaling and sealing parts of the industry, noting that these expeditions carried greater risks and had started to cost the government a significant amount. After cutting this section of the industry adrift with this argument, the newspaper then backtracked and said that, even so, the costs to the nation of repatriating whaling and sealing crews should not be an overall deterrent to the industry.

The newspaper then isolated Anders, saying that he was responsible for the greater part of the costs in recent years, and since *Solglimt* had been wrecked the matter had been drawn to everybody's attention, but it would be unfair to burden the entire industry just because of Anders, particularly when the state had chosen to single him out for distinction.

This was a very complex conjunction of several opposing ideas. Presumably the newspaper was offering the minister a range of arguments, hoping that one or more would be persuasive. Was Anders to be damned or let off the hook? It is difficult to know what the newspaper's position was. However, it ended the article singing the praises of the whaling and sealing industry, commenting on how important it was to a capital-poor country, and asserting that those determined enough to go into this glorious business should be supported.

Seven weeks later, no doubt prompted by the knowledge that the minister intended to raise in parliament the matter of who should pay for rescue and repatriation costs, the same newspaper had lost its

---

* *Kysten*, 8 December 1908, p. 1.

ambivalence about Anders and his role in raising the prospect of increased costs being incurred by the maritime industry, and proceeded to launch an all-out attack on him.* It argued that because Anders' shipwrecks had possible significant ramifications for the industry, it was appropriate to consider whether or not he was a typical representative of the industry and, therefore, whether his misadventures could be considered sufficient grounds for altering the state's attitude towards all fishing, whaling and sealing companies in Norway. The newspaper pointed out that the government had in recent years expelled whalers from Norway's waters, which had caused a number of enterprising industry leaders to investigate foreign shores, build whaling stations far from Norway and send fishing boats and floating factories to distant hunting grounds. These ships sailed in waters that were only partially mapped, and then returned with valuable cargo. Despite the fact that these ships were operating in dangerous waters, there had been very few shipwrecks, with only the sinking of *Fridtjof Nansen* resulting in significant cost to the state. The fact that numerous expeditions had succeeded despite the risks proved that they had been well-planned, well-equipped and excellently led by wise men in difficult conditions, resulting in the addition of great wealth to Norway and livelihoods for many families. These shipping companies, captains and crews had undoubtedly earned the respect of the nation with their energy and skill and should unreservedly be trusted. However, they had worked in silence without broadcasting their activities and without publicity, and neither had anybody thought of giving them St Olav orders or medals, although they were, in all honesty, deserving of them.

The newspaper then turned its attention to Anders, saying he was a man who had received a great deal of attention from the press, as if the nation had just been waiting for his deeds in order to praise them. The waves of publicity and the ensuing fame that occurred immediately after news of the heroic boat trip in *Hope* by Anders, Johansen and Antonsen were so overwhelming as to drown out any thoughts of why the boat trip

---

* *Kysten*, 27 January 1909. p. 1.

was needed in the first place, or before any guilt could be apportioned for the wrecking through an inquiry. The newspaper repeated the information previously published that the shipping inspector had determined that *Cathrine* was wrecked because of carelessness and poor seamanship on Anders' part (notwithstanding the fact that he had been given no opportunity to defend himself against such claims). It also repeated comments made previously by a number of newspapers that Anders had had an obligation to risk his own life in an attempt to bring rescue to his men because he had caused the disaster in the first place. Instead of dealing with possible poor seamanship, the state had awarded Anders the highest honour in the land and held him up as a heroic sailor of whom the nation could be proud. If the government had allowed the shipping inspector to complete his task without interference, the nation might well have moderated its opinion of Anders, and his prospects of mounting a new expedition would have been diminished. As it was, Bull and Anders had no trouble raising the funds for *Solglimt's* first expedition, and the newspaper credited what was effectively state sponsorship for this success, noting that, with this support, it appeared that Anders was a leader who could be trusted. In fact, Bull was the expedition leader for *Solglimt's* first voyage, but the newspaper chose not to include that information, and it was certainly the case that all the publicity surrounding Anders would have attracted investors to the expedition.

The newspaper's next line of attack was that, although *Solglimt's* first expedition returned before it had a full catch because it had inadequate provisions to continue, and despite the fact that experienced observers then pulled back from the general praise afforded to Anders, confidence in him was so well-established that he was nevertheless able to mount another expedition, with the result being his second shipwreck. It is not at all clear why the newspaper made the claim that *Solglimt* returned from its first expedition without a full load. There is nothing to suggest that this was true. Anders and Bull were thrilled with the expedition, and all of the reports refer to a full load. Anders had commented that they could have caught more but they did not have any more storage capacity. He also said that their supplies were starting to run low and the seals had begun their annual migration and so hunting would have become progressively less efficient, so all in all it was time to head for home. Perhaps it was these comments that had been reinterpreted as meaning that they had returned without a full load, but that does not appear to have been the case.

Having traduced Anders, the newspaper argued that the state could only blame itself if the man that it held in such high esteem, thereby enabling him to undertake his voyages, should then cost it dearly, and it should not complain. Nor should it consider that Anders was a typical whaler hunter, or that the burdens resulting from his misadventures should be passed on to other whale hunters. The newspaper suggested that the state should insure itself against any repatriation costs if its own preferred captain, Anders, was to go out for a fourth time, but serious whale hunters had not given the slightest cause for new cost arrangements to be introduced. The modern phrase for this is 'hanging the man out to dry', and the newspaper's position does seem to have been cruelly harsh. Regardless of whether or not Anders was responsible for *Cathrine*'s wreck, he was not responsible for the extraordinary fame that followed, nor for being awarded the Order of St Olav. He and Bull certainly capitalised on the situation they found themselves in, but they were determined to try to mount another expedition before they had any inkling of the publicity that was ultimately to aid them in their efforts to raise the necessary funds.

The claim made by the newspaper that numerous expeditions had succeeded despite the risks is also worth interrogating. Most of the Norwegian vessels operating in the Southern Ocean at the time were whale catchers or floating factories processing whales, and it was these that had succeeded, not sealing vessels. Sealing was an inherently dangerous sailing venture, even in better known hunting fields.

Sealing around the partially charted islands of the subantarctic added a serious degree of danger, because the ships had to approach land to hunt the seals in the bays, whereas whaling ships were hunting their prey in open waters. The newspaper was prosecuting an argument in an attempt to try to persuade the government not to reduce its commitment to meeting rescue and repatriation costs and appears, by that stage of the debate, to have been in no mood to complicate its case by providing any commentary that would soften its criticism of Anders.

In early February 1909 the Norwegian Government considered the issue of repatriation costs. It allocated 170,000 kroner (A$1,900,000) in the budget for the coming year, which was 30,000 kroner (A$340,000) less than the previous year. By this stage the estimated cost of repatriating *Solglimt*'s crew had risen to 55,000 kroner (A$620,000).[*]

One member of parliament argued against any change to the current Act, for the reasons already outlined. Minister Abrahamsen argued in favour of changing the Act and recommended that there should be a distinction between costs associated with the ship's crew and costs associated with men who were engaged in the hunting activity, such as whalers, floating factories and so on, with the costs of the latter being met by the shipping company involved. This recommendation was approved, meaning that Anders' unfortunate experiences had a direct impact on Norwegian policies regarding the whaling and sealing industry in ways that would not have endeared him to companies and expedition leaders operating in those industries. There was, of course, pushback on this change to the cost allocations. Some newspapers pointed out that in England a seafarer was legally defined as 'any person employed or engaged in any position on board a ship', while others queried whether the distinction would always be clear.[†] For example, at least twenty people on *Solglimt* were engaged to

---

[*] This included payments of €1,000 (A$160,000) each to *Agnes G. Donahoe* and *Beatrice L. Corkum* for loss of earnings, comprising €350 (A$57,000) for each company and €150 (A$24,400) for each member of the ships' crews. In addition, the two captains were each awarded a sterling silver vase. In contrast, the crew of *Solglimt* arrived home poorer than when they had left several months earlier and some, fifteen in all, whose contracts did not cover time on shore, did not receive any wages for the time they were stranded on the island. *Social-Demokraten*, 24 March 1909, p. 2.

[†] *Kysten*, 15 February 1909, p. 1.

undertake both sailing and hunting duties.

In the same sitting of parliament 75,000 kroner (A$845,000) was allocated to Roald Amundsen's expedition with the vessel *Fram*.* Three members of parliament voted against it, but the recommendation was carried. The expedition Amundsen had sought support for was to be a second attempt, following Fridtjof Nansen's earlier attempt in *Fram* on his 1893–96 Arctic expedition, to try to reach the North Pole by allowing the vessel to drift in the ice. When Amundsen learnt that the American explorer Robert E. Peary claimed to have reached the North Pole in 1909 he secretly changed his plans and sailed south to race Robert Scott to the South Pole. It is ironic that the Norwegian parliament allocated a considerable sum of money to a hazardous non-commercial sailing voyage in the same sitting that they determined to carry less of the risk associated with whaling and sealing.

---

* *Morgenbladet*, 6 February 1909, p. 1.

CHAPTER 12

SUCH STUFF AS DREAMS ARE MADE ON

Yea, all of which I inherit, shall dissolve;
And, like this insubstantial pageant faded,
Leave not a rack behind. We are such stuff
As dreams are made on, and our little life
Is rounded with a sleep.

Prospero in Shakespeare's *The Tempest**

Unlike the majority of wrecks in the Southern Ocean and on the subantarctic islands, *Solglimt* and her story have not been left to dissolve completely with the passing of time, even though the wild winds and incessant rain, sleet and snow have done their best to achieve this end. This is because *Solglimt* has been the focus of extensive archaeological investigation by teams of South African researchers. The Prince Edward Islands, including Marion Island, were claimed by South Africa immediately after the Second World War, and Marion Island has been continuously occupied by South Africa since 1948. Since 1965 there has been an unbroken research presence on the Island, investigating meteorology, geology, fauna and flora and, more recently, *Solglimt* and her 'village', or camp. The first scientific activity was conducted by meteorologists, who relieved the men in the initial naval party in 1948 and who were, by all accounts, pleased to leave the island after a stay of less than two months. It seems that they felt the same way about Marion Island as its first known resident, the sealer William Dane Phelps, who

---

* Shakespeare, 1990, IV.i.148–158.

stayed on the island from 1818 to 1820 and who referred to it when he was leaving as a 'treeless, verdureless, desolate island of the ocean!'*

After *Solglimt*'s unhappy visit to the Prince Edward Islands in 1908, mariners generally avoided them out of respect for their inherent dangers. Most people who had actually heard of these islands associated them with storms, disaster and death. It was as if nature was making a great effort to maintain the exile of these orphan islands,[†] which had been 'discovered' on three separate occasions. The first, in 1663, was by the Dutchman Barent Barentszoon Lam of the Dutch East India Company. He named what is now known as Prince Edward Island 'Dena' and Marion Island 'Maerseveen',[‡] but he erroneously recorded their location, and they were not found again until the Frenchman Marc-Joseph du Fresne visited them in 1772. At first he thought he had discovered the fabled great southern land mass, Antarctica, naming the Prince Edward Islands 'Terre de l'Esperance' (this is now Marion Island) and 'Île de la Caverne' (now Prince Edward Island). He realised his error, spent five days attempting to land and narrowly avoided complete disaster when both of his ships scraped rocks along the shoreline.[§]

The islands' next visitor was James Cook, in 1776, who named them Prince Edward Islands after the fourth son of King George III. Cook was also unable to land, but he and other early explorers brought back glowing reports about the vast wealth of seals and birds to be found on the islands, and sealing commenced just a few years after Cook had been there. The first landings on the islands are not known. The American sealer *Catherine* had landed there in 1803, and several names and the year 1806 are engraved on a rock next to Hope Stream on Prince Edward Island. Seals on the islands were heavily hunted from this time. The sealing era is said to have lasted from 1799 to 1913, although very little sealing had occurred in the decades prior to *Solglimt*'s visit in 1908. From 1799 to 1913, 103 vessels

---

* Terauds, 2010, p. 52.

† Marsh, 1948, p. 21.

‡ Terauds, 2010, p. 52.

§ Marsh, 1948, pp. 22–23.

are recorded as having visited the Prince Edward Islands.

There are eighteen sites on Marion Island alone that contain evidence of sealing activity. In 1989 Tom Graham, an honours student from the University of Cape Town, found that there had been seven known shipwrecks around the Prince Edward Islands, not including other shipwrecks that had probably occurred but had not been recorded.[*] This figure was revised in 1998 to eight known wrecks:[†] five on Prince Edward Island and three on Marion Island. One of the earliest and most dramatic wrecks was the British brig *Richard Dart*, which ran aground on Prince Edward Island in 1849. Fifty-two people, including all five women and the ten children on board, drowned. The survivors spent a gruelling seventy-two days on the island, losing another of their number before being rescued by the South African sealer *Courier*, which reported seeing evidence of three other wrecks. *Courier*'s owner, John Jearey, lost one of his own ships, *Maria*, on the Prince Edward Islands in 1857. This was another wrecking like that of *Cathrine*, with a southeasterly gale springing up suddenly, parting the vessel from her anchors and driving her onto the shore.[‡]

There is some debate about another possible shipwreck in the same bay where *Solglimt* beached. An American sealing vessel, *Uxor*, which had visited the Prince Edward Islands a number of times, was wrecked 'on the Crozettes' in 1841, and the survivors, including the captain, were rescued by another of Jearey's vessels and taken to Cape Town. The term 'Crozet Islands', as mentioned earlier, was often used to refer to all of the subantarctic islands in the southern Indian Ocean, including the Crozet Islands, Prince Edward Islands and Kerguelen Islands. The description of the bay in which *Uxor* was wrecked matches that of the bay in which *Solglimt* lies, so the wreck is attributed to Marion Island, rather than one of the islands in the Crozet group.[§]

---

* Graham, 1989.
† Hänel and Chown, 1998.
‡ Marsh, 1948, pp. 28–38.
§ Van Niekerk, 2016, pp. 30–31.

After *Solglimt* was wrecked in 1908 there was only intermittent sealing on the island for several decades, mainly by South African companies. In 1910 the islands were unsuccessfully searched for any sign of survivors from the lost liner *Waratah,* which was thought to have disappeared in the vicinity with 200 people on board.[*] Crew from the search vessel, *Wakefield,* landed in Ship's Cove,[†] which they found to be almost blocked by *Solglimt's* submerged hull. On the beach they found three boats, hauled up out of reach of the sea, just as Anders had described, three iron try pots and a quantity of timber.[‡] Then, in October 1912, the Norwegian sealing schooner *Seabird,* operating out of South Africa, was wrecked in exactly the same way that *Maria* had been wrecked very close by, fifty-five years earlier. *Seabird's* crew, split between Marion and Prince Edward islands, spent six miserable months enduring almost constant gales and near freezing temperatures. The men on Prince Edward Island struggled to survive on elephant seals, birds and eggs. Those on Marion Island fared better, because they had *Solglimt's* huts to help protect them, as well as some supplies, mainly flour and margarine, although this was in poor condition. The men on Prince Edward Island made the hazardous five-hour journey between the islands several times to replenish their supplies and, with two of their number now dead, they eventually all relocated to Marion Island. Even though the cache of supplies there was also running out, they at least had the huts for protection. With winter approaching, *Seabird's* captain, T.G. Hystad, decided to fit out one of *Solglimt's* whaleboats in order to make a desperate bid to reach Cape Town. The boat he chose was probably the one that Anders and *Solglimt's* crew had been preparing four years earlier for their rescue attempt. Hystad made primitive tools out of pieces

---

[*] It is now thought that *Waratah* was wrecked much closer to the South African coastline.

[†] The bay *Solglimt* was beached in is now officially called Ship's Cove, in recognition of its association with shipwrecks. Anders named it Solglimt Bay, or Cove, and this name was used for a time, intermittently. It is also referred to as Ship Cove, or Ships Cove.

[‡] Try pots were large pots used to remove and render the oil from seal (or whale) blubber.

of metal from the *Solglimt* wreck and for timber he broke down portions of the huts. Anders would have left all of the tools from *Solglimt* on the island, so presumably they had been taken by other sealing vessels in the intervening years. As had transpired for the crew of *Solglimt*, *Seabird*'s men were rescued while the work of preparing the whaleboat was underway, and so the journey away from the island in the whaleboat to seek help was not required.[*]

After this, the Prince Edward Islands were largely left in peace, until in 1929 when they were visited by the British steamer *Deucalion* looking for survivors of *Kobenhavn*, the world's biggest windjammer, which had vanished en route from the River Plate in South America to Australia with nearly ninety Danes on board. *Deucalion*, taking heed of the warning in the *Admiralty Sailing Directions* not to rely too heavily on the charts, did not approach land but circled the islands at a distance and saw no signs of life.[†] The last record of men landing on either island prior to the Second Word War was of a South African crew in 1930 investigating the possibility of resuming sealing. The sealer, *Kildalkey*, spent a month working the east coast of Marion Island, but was so harried by the incessant gales that she gave up and returned to South Africa with her tanks unfilled.[‡]

The landing party that secured the annexation of the Prince Edward Islands on behalf of South Africa late in 1948 had its own experience of the dangers of approaching the islands. Their efforts were hampered by kelp unlike anything they had seen before. The men gave up trying to row through the kelp and used their oars to 'lever' their way across the barrier instead. This was the same type of kelp that had caused so much trouble for Anders and the men in his boat when they were striving to reach land while *Cathrine* was being wrecked in the storm.[§] The South African landing party, after getting ashore, not without difficulty, and raising the South African flag, was forced to beat a hasty retreat because

---

[*] Marsh, 1948, pp. 48–52.

[†] Ibid., p. 52.

[‡] Ibid., p. 52.

[§] See Chapter 3.

their boat, which was in difficulties in the surf, had struck rocks and been holed. As they rushed to the boat they saw evidence of previous visits by people, including half-bricks and some steel plates.* When they were able to land again and establish a camp, they also experienced the alarming dangers of the mires and, as had been the case for *Cathrine*'s crew forty years earlier, the men in the party were instructed not to leave the camp unaccompanied.[†]

Early the following year, two South African ships visiting the island saw a sea break about two kilometres east-northeast of the point where the flagstaff had been planted. They carefully observed it and saw that it was breaking every few minutes, and it continued to do so for only a few hours. This was the first time in three weeks of occupation of Marion Island that the break had been observed, and a check showed that one of the ships had taken a sounding, measuring 115 metres, just 100 metres from the break. Had she sailed closer she would almost certainly have struck the reef. Subsequent observation of the break revealed that it was rarely visible, and then only during a certain combination of wind, sea and current. Marsh investigated reports of *Solglimt*'s loss and said that there is little doubt that this was the pinnacle of rock on which she came to grief. Two of the South African ships had narrowly avoided the same fate as *Solglimt*.[‡]

These early South African visitors also discovered a plague of mice on Marion Island and wondered if this was one of *Solglimt*'s legacies, as hers was the only known shipwreck on the island at that time. It is possible that there had been mice on the island since the sealing activity in the early 1800s, however there was no mention of them in any of the reports about the *Solglimt* crew's time on the island, so they may well have been a legacy of *Solglimt*.[§]

A later landing party also experienced tragedy when four men assisting with the transfer of prefabricated segments for huts were thrown into the

---

* Marsh, 1948, pp. 73–77.
† Ibid., pp. 88–89.
‡ Ibid., pp. 130–131.
§ Ibid., pp. 135–136.

icy water when their boat capsized. Several men waded and swam out into the bay to help those who had been dumped, and all the men were dragged back onto the shore. They had been in the water for barely five minutes, but all were semi-conscious from the cold and shock by the time they were pulled out of the water. A fifth man, who appeared to have been struck on the head during the incident, was pulled lifeless from the water, and the man who had attempted to rescue him was numb and blue with the cold and had to receive treatment before he revived. This tragedy supports *Solglimt*'s doctor's description of Anders and the first mate's effort to salvage timber from *Solglimt*'s holds while standing naked in the icy water as a heroic undertaking.

The largest of the wrecks on the Prince Edward Islands, and the only one with a known location, is *Solglimt*, whose hull remains lying partially submerged where it was beached in Ship's Cove on Marion Island. Ship's Cove is a small bay on the northeast side of the island. It is one of the few bays around the island that forms a natural harbour and where landing is possible. It is overlooked by towering 60-metre cliffs, has a beach approximately 200 metres long of black sand and loose boulders, and is protected on the north side by a distinctive island of rock 50 metres high. There is a valley leading into the bay from the north that is sheltered to a certain extent from the strong winds that blow over the island from the west. The valley comprises steep hills covered in grass and ferns, waterlogged gullies, irregular level areas, boulders and rock overhangs. The beach and valley are home to various wildlife populations, including elephant seals and various penguin species, and the cliffs are used by nesting birds such as the wandering albatross. The grass-covered embankments above the beach are subject to significant erosion due to the constant runoff from the cliffs above.

The valley and the beach are scattered with remains of *Solglimt*'s village and wreck. In 1948, when the wreck was sighted by the South African landing parties, her bow, looking like a killer whale's fin, could be seen protruding from the water, and two large black shapes, the portions of her hull, could be seen underwater in the bay. On the northern side of the cove in which she lay the explorers found the remains of the village, including ladderways, steps and floors that, while rotten, were still in position. The walls and roofs of the huts had fallen in or been blown away. Pots and pans and other cooking paraphernalia were lying around, and six bottles labelled 'Worcester Sauce' were found where they had apparently fallen through the decaying floor of one of the huts. Although the bottles had been on the island for 40 years, the taste of the sauce had not deteriorated.[*]

In 1989, because the *Solglimt* wreck could still be investigated, and because some remains of the village were also still there, the first steps towards serious archaeology of the site began. This first foray was carried out under the auspices of the South African Cultural History Museum, which would become part of Iziko Museums in 2000. Iziko Museums then established the Archaeologies of Antarctica Project in 2012, which in turn gave rise to the Antarctic Legacy of South Africa Project.[†] The research teams involved believe that the archaeological investigation into the *Solglimt* wreck and her village is the first of its kind in the subantarctic. Their work is intended to provide information about sealing in the first part of the twentieth century, survivor dynamics and strategies, and the impact of the wreck on the natural environment, amongst other things. Archaeology of the site is challenging due to the difficulty of reaching the site and the inherent dangers of investigating a submerged wreck in bitterly cold water that surges into the bay. The site in Ship Cove's is a difficult 4-kilometre walk from the South African base camp on Marion Island. The researchers have found that the most efficient way to operate is to drop a small container of equipment by helicopter several hundred metres from the shoreline, taking care to avoid the penguin and seal colonies. Even this strategy requires careful transport of equipment over swampy ground and slippery rocks to where it is needed, and sensitive equipment such as magnetometers, gradiometers, GPS units and cameras have to be carried on foot.

---

[*] Ibid., pp. 182–183.
[†] Cooper, Boshoff, Harboe-Ree and Van Niekerk, 2018, pp. 4–12.

Prior to the establishment of the Archaeologies of Antarctica project, and following the publication of Marsh's book (1948), the site was exposed to unsupervised access by people curious about the wreck and village. This resulted in some disturbance of the site, including the souveniring of artefacts. The village, although difficult to access, was easier to investigate than the submerged wreck. Even so, the wreck was explored by several divers before the Archaeologies of Antarctica project assumed management of the site.

While there may have been other unrecorded dives, in 1988 and 1989 marine biologists dived on the wreck to look at fish populations, but from an archaeological perspective this had little or no impact on the site. Also, in the late 1980s, a group of South African Military Special Forces divers recovered some of *Solglimt*'s copper pipes and fittings, some of which were displayed at the base camp on the island. Partially successful dives were carried out in 2011, hampered by compressor problems, but in 2014 a more successful investigation was carried out, yielding a great deal of information about the wreck, and a number of photographs were taken.[*] These photographs have been examined by marine biologists, and it is intended to investigate the biota being supported by or degrading the wreck over time.

The main part of the wreck lies on a sandy bottom, about half a metre below the surface, in shallow water a maximum of 6 metres deep. The stern is not visible at all, and may be some distance from the main wreck site. The divers did not see much evidence of the reported 900 tons of coal *Solglimt* was carrying. However it would be difficult to see against the black sand, and the long swells that surge into the bay mean that the seabed is in a dynamic state. Neither was there any evidence of timber. However, numerous engine parts, boilers and fittings were visible at the time. *Solglimt*'s boilers were positioned on the decks resting on brick beds., which probably explains the source of bricks that have been found during excavations of the village.

---

* Boshoff, Van Niekerk and Wares, 2015.

In 1989, when Graham conducted the first archaeological work on the village, he had limited time on the island. He carried out a small pilot excavation in one of the huts formed around a rock shelter. This hut, or shelter, was also recorded in 1948,* when some of the structure was still standing. By 1998 much of the structure had been flattened and timber was scattered and embedded further down the slope. By 2015 very little of it remained, indicating that the site has been affected by marine animals, natural erosion and souveniring. Graham found that this hut may have been built on the site of an older structure. It is possible that *Uxor*'s survivors had previously built a shelter there.

The remains of the village have been the subject of further investigation by a University of Cape Town masters student, Tara Van Niekerk, in 2013 and 2014.† Van Niekerk's aims were to add to the knowledge and understanding of the archaeological remains on Marion Island, as well as to analyse them in the context of current survivor theory, thereby adding to the existing body of knowledge about shipwreck survivor camps. The village the *Solglimt* castaways constructed was evidently built in the only areas accessible to them, these being the areas above the reach of the ocean, where they made use of rock shelters and flat areas where possible, with some protection from the wind afforded in the valley. In two of the shelters they found square nails in the rock face, which they concluded were likely to have been used to secure sailcloth that provided some cover.

The area chosen by the shipwrecked men for the site of their village had several advantages. Its proximity to the wreck made salvage work, while this could still be undertaken, easier. In addition, they had a constant source of fresh water and were as near as possible to their food sources: seals, birds and fish. The site also featured a number of caves and rock overhangs that could form part of some of the shelters, and they had access to good vantage points where they were able to keep a lookout for passing ships.

---

* Crawford, 1982.
† Van Niekerk, 2016.

Survivor theory suggests that there are four main activities that take place in survivor camps: subsistence, habitation, escape and defence.* The *Solglimt* village was organised for the first three of these activities, and it would not have required the fourth, defence, at least not against external aggressors. Nevertheless, given the presence of large numbers of weapons and the insurrection that had occurred on *Solglimt* as she left Durban on her way south, it is not beyond the realms of possibility that defence against each other might have become necessary had they stayed on the island for a long period, especially if supplies had been running low. As has already been noted, very quickly after *Solglimt* was beached it became necessary to lock up provisions to avoid looting, and the relationships between Anders and some of the crew were strained.

Ship's Cove is one of the areas on the Prince Edward Islands that lies in a protected zone because of its penguin, albatross and seal colonies. The islands are now managed and protected by various South African jurisdictions and acts.† In order to carry out her work, Van Niekerk required archaeological permits from several organisations and agencies. In 2007 the Prince Edward Islands were also designated as Ramsar Wetlands of International Importance Especially as Waterfowl Habitat.‡

In the time available to her, Van Niekerk examined six sites associated with huts or shelters, as well as the beach. Although much of the village has disappeared over time, Van Niekerk found that the wet environment had preserved some artefacts and materials. Items found included cartridges, wrought iron hooks, metal straps, timber, nails, glass fragments, clay brick

---

* Clark and de Biran, 2010.

† The relevant agencies include Heritage Western Cape and the South African Heritage Resources Agency. South Africa has declared the Prince Edward Islands to be a special nature reserve and they are managed and protected under the Environmental Conservation Act (no. 73 of 1989), the National Environment Management Act (no. 107 of 1998), the National Environment Management: Protected Areas Act (No.57 of 2003) and the National Environment Management: Biodiversity Act (No.10 of 2004).

‡ The Ramsar Convention on Wetlands is an international treaty for the conservation and sustainable use of wetlands. It is named after the Iranian city Ramsar, where the convention was signed in 1971.

remains, coal remnants, a cast iron stove, an earthenware jug, a bilge pump, a trypot and a barrel stave. In terms of quantity, timber was the most prevalent, followed by coal fragments and then pieces of metal. The cookhouse, which was centrally located, revealed no coal fragments, but this may have been because it was erected on the most exposed site. The third largest category of remnants was of cartridges and bullets, some of which could be clearly linked to the *Solglimt* sites. Other cartridges found were for use with rifles not thought to have been used by *Solglimt's* crew, which probably indicates the presence of other visitors to the bay, but the four sites where cartridges have been linked to *Solglimt* suggests that the guns were not all under the control of the senior officers. If this was the case, this could have been a serious problem if relationships between the survivors had broken down.

The artefacts collected by Van Niekerk and her team provide only a limited amount of information about the use of the cove by *Solglimt's* crew, although dating of some of the items gives a good indication of when the site was used and the locations of at least six of the eleven huts they built. Van Niekerk laments the looting of the site over several decades and its use by both humans and animals. The protections and controls that now apply to the site will slow down, but not prevent further losses. The seals in particular are unlikely to respect the conservation protocols and protections that have been put in place!

Of interest to Van Niekerk is the psychology of the shipwrecked crew and, drawing on a study of other ships' survivor camps and stories and comparing these with the information available in articles and reports about *Solglimt*, she attempts an analysis of crew behaviour during and after the grounding. She notes the significant age, skill, occupation and status range of the crew, from the lowly ranks of the deckhands and kitchen boys to Anders himself. Through this prism and analysis of the documentary record, Van Niekerk concluded that some individuals performed well in terms of survival throughout the ordeal, while others initially panicked. Notwithstanding Anders' comments to the contrary, it appears that all or most of the crew cooperated with the salvage operation at first, but, after the immediate danger had passed, some started looking after themselves rather than working cooperatively in the interest of the whole group.

This phase seems to have been short-lived, with a degree of social cohesion and stability returning once routines were put in place. This is fortunate, given the high proportion of young people in the group and the claims Anders had made (not verified) about the older men being a bad influence on the younger. Even so, many of the crew were accustomed to the rigours of a life at sea and between them they had the skills, as well as the materials and provisions, that enabled them to house and feed themselves with relative ease. This is in contrast to the traumatised survivor groups discussed elsewhere who, in many cases, were stranded without any means of constructing adequate shelter or of sustaining themselves in this harsh environment.

CHAPTER 13

TWISTS AND TURNS

*Sing to me of the man, Muse, the man of twists and turns
driven time and again off course ...*

Homer, *The Odyssey*[*]

On 20 October 1909 Anders turned 28. Still a very young man, he had a lifetime's worth of experiences behind him and the rest of his working life to consider. Recently married, he also had to plan for family life.

It would not have been surprising if he had turned away from the sea. Nor would it have been surprising if he had had difficulty obtaining a position as captain. This latter possibility was flagged by Bull following *Cathrine*'s loss, when he said: 'the young captain was entertaining a certain fear that any blot should be attached to his reputation as a seaman in case of stranding [on] his first voyage as captain.'[†] By 1909 two of his first three voyages as captain had ended in disaster, and a great deal of effort by the press and the state had gone into attaching a blot to his reputation. Nonetheless, immediately following his wedding in June, Anders was employed as the captain of a ship, *Oddfrid*, carrying freight around northern Europe, and he continued in this role for a year.[‡] In October 1911 he was the commander of an operation to refloat the same vessel when she was stranded in fog, with a different captain at the helm.[§]

---

[*] Homer, 1996, 1.1–2, p. 77.

[†] *New York Times*, 15 December 1907, p. 50.

[‡] *Morgenbladet*, 9 July 1909, p. 4.

[§] *Morgenbladet*, 21 October 1911, p. 2.

This was the extent of Anders' maritime activity from 1909 to 1915. In November 1909, while still an active captain, he made what appears, from this distance, to be an out of character decision when he acquired an old family farm from his younger brother. His three children were all born at the farm, which was called Hosmestad, and the family lived there until 1915, when the farm was sold and they moved to Kristiania. Hosmestad, which was close to the farm Store Ree where Anders was born, was a traditional – albeit large by Norwegian standards – mixed produce farm with a white, four-storey timber dwelling and extensive barns and sheds.

While farming may not have been Anders' first choice of career, he had some success in agricultural shows with his produce and threw himself into local and rural politics, quickly assuming a leadership role. In 1912, for example, he became the spokesperson for his farming community when there was a suggestion that local government might take on ownership of the communally owned Almenning lands,[*] and in 1914 he organised a meeting to discuss the implications of the impending war on Norwegian farmers.[†] The Norwegian Government had predicted that war would not be declared in Europe. This view, together with its fundamental philosophy of neutrality, had left the country ill-prepared for war. When war was declared, there was a scramble to organise troops to protect Norway's neutrality and to ensure that its population was fed. To this end, the government established a Food Commission, banned the export of grain and horses, put in place policies designed to stimulate the production of food, prohibited the use of grain or potatoes for the production of alcohol and banned the sale of alcohol. Anders was sharply critical of many of these policies and took particular aim at the introduction of prohibition.[‡]

Whether because of the war or because he was unable to make a

---

[*] Norway has had a unique system of communal land ownership and management, called Almenning, for over 1,200 years. Almenning refers to collective ownership, usually by farms in a defined area, of forest and grazing areas and/or related businesses like hunting, grazing or sawmilling.

[†] *Oplandenes Avis*, 3 November 1914, p. 2.

[‡] Larsen, 1950, p. 506.

success of farming through of lack of experience or skill, or a combination of these factors, in 1915 Anders sold Hosmestad and declared that it was his intention to become a ship's captain once more. Immediately after the sale Anders took command of a ship, *Sjøgutten.*[*] However, it was quickly apparent that simply becoming a captain again was not going to satisfy him, and his broader ambitions were revealed with the announcement of the formation of a shipping company and the issuing of a share offer in January 1916.[†] The stated intention was to acquire three ships, but the company appears not to have raised sufficient capital and there is no further mention of it in the press. The sale of Hosmestad raised 135,000 kroner (A$1.1 million),[‡] but this was presumably not all profit for Anders. The share capital aspiration for the company was 850,000 kroner (A$7 million), so clearly Anders would not have been able to acquire even one ship in his own right at that time.

The company was to have been called Neutral, which was a clear reference to Norway's position in relation to the war underway, as well as to its broader foreign relations stance. When Norway gained independence from Sweden in 1905 its neutrality, in concert with an active trade policy, were founding principles. In 1914, at the outbreak of the war, Norway was heavily reliant on its shipping industry. It had the fourth largest merchant fleet in the world and the largest on a per capita basis. For the first eighteen months the war provided excellent opportunities for the Norwegian merchant navy, which was known for its willingness to undertake dangerous voyages when others would not. Trade increased during this period, and the Norwegian Government was committed to supporting this critical industry.

This is the immediate background to the period when Anders sold the farm and attempted to establish the company Neutral. Given his actions to this point in his life, it is not really surprising to find that he was tempted by a high-risk venture with the potential to yield significant profits. As

---

[*] *Lillehammer Tilskuer*, 8 December 1915, p. 2.
[†] *Norsk Kundgjørelsestidende*, 13 January 1916, p. 6.
[‡] *Trondhjems Folkeblad*, 27 November 1915, p. 1.

hostilities between Britain, Germany and their allies played out over the course of the war, Norway found its neutrality challenged, the inherent dangers took their toll and the Norwegian fleet was savaged. Overall, it lost 889 ships, approximately half of its tonnage, and 2,000 sailors died at sea. It was not until March 1917, after which all Norwegian ships travelled in convoys protected by the British Royal Navy, that the loss of ships and lives was stemmed.* With this in mind, from a financial perspective Anders was probably fortunate not to have been able to get his company Neutral up and running in 1916, even though as a captain in command of other people's ships during these years he was in great physical danger.

Although he may in time have had cause to wish it was not, Anders' second attempt to establish a shipping company was successful. In September 1917 he founded and was appointed the manager of a new company, Staalbeton.† This was no ordinary shipping company. 'Beton' is the French word for concrete, and 'staalbeton' translates literally as 'steel and concrete', that is to say, reinforced concrete. Staalbeton, which had fully subscribed share capital of 850,000 kroner (A$4.8 million), had a contract for the construction of one, and possibly two, experimental 1,000 -ton concrete vessels at a shipping yard in the Norwegian coastal city of Moss.

At the time of the First World War Norway was a dominant and inventive shipping nation, and Norwegian technical ingenuity was evident as this small nation took the lead in the construction of ocean-going concrete ships.‡ This was due almost entirely to the drive of 33-year-old Nikolay Knudzton Fougner, with whose shipyard Anders' company Staalbeton had contracted. Fougner was a man of the world. Born and

---

* Larsen (1948), p. 510.

† *Trondhjems Adresseavis*, 17 September 1917, p. 4 and other newspapers.

‡ Prior to the First World War there had been little interest in, or development of, concrete vessels anywhere in the world. The first known concrete ship was a dinghy built by Joseph Louis Lambot in southern France in 1848. In the 1890s an Italian engineer named Carlo Gabellini built barges and small ships out of concrete, and several other countries had modest concrete shipbuilding industries, mainly with a focus on barges and small boats.

educated in Norway, by 1917 he had already worked as an engineer in England, America, China, India, Malaysia, Japan, the Philippines, the Netherlands and Argentina, as well as in Norway itself.[*] [†]

Due to the combination of the urgent need to rebuild Norway's fleet and the crippling shortage of steel, there was huge interest in Fougner's concrete shipbuilding business. He had returned to his home country in April 1916, and by August 1916 the first vessel, a lighter, or flat-bottomed barge, had been launched. In August 1917, just six weeks before Anders' company Staalbeton was formed, Fougner's shipyard launched the world's first ocean-going concrete ship, a 25.6-metre vessel named *Namsenfjord*. It was said that from the beginning everything was moving at 'American speed'.[‡] Indeed, the Americans were also very interested in the potential of concrete ships, and Fougner formed an American sister company just a year after establishing his Norwegian shipyard.[§]

As an indication of the high level of interest in this new field of ship-building, when *Namsenfjord* had a trial run from Moss to Kristiania, attracting great media interest, on board were a number of maritime experts and other dignitaries.[¶] Another concrete ship, *Stier*, which was launched in May 1918, was graced on its trial run by the presence of the Prime Minister and other high-ranked politicians.

A decade earlier Anders had been one of the first Norwegians to lead expeditions to the Southern Ocean to re-open seal and whale hunting fields. Now he was attracted to another pioneering venture, the construction of concrete ships.

---

[*] https://www-strindahistorielag.no.translate.goog/wiki/index.php/Nikolay_Knudtzon_Fougner?_x_tr_sl=no&_x_tr_tl=en&_x_tr_hl=en&_x_tr_pto=sc, accessed 19 January 2023.

[†] Of interest to Australians is the fact that in 1910, when Fougner was chief engineer of the Trussed Concrete Steel Co of Westminster, he did the engineering drawings for the construction of the State Library of Victoria's dome, and was presumably responsible for some of the novel engineering solutions that were incorporated into its construction. Lewis, 2003, p. 43.

[‡] *Moss Avis*, 12 April 1938, p. 3.

[§] *Nordisk Tidende*, 6 September 1917, p. 4.

[¶] *Trondhjems Folkeblad*, 28 August 1917, p. 2.

By June 1919 the company Staalbeton had taken possession of the first of the two concrete ships it had planned to acquire, and had commenced trading.* The ship was named in English – descriptively, and no doubt proudly – *Concrete*. As well as being one of the first significant ocean-going concrete ships ever built, she was also one of the largest, at least in Europe. At 950 tons, with a two-stroke, crude-oil engine, she was quite an imposing vessel.†

Anders had an association in various capacities with *Concrete* from June 1919 to September 1922, and perhaps longer. Although the ship was initially owned by the company Staalbeton, of which Anders was the manager, he is listed from the outset as its owner. He is referred to in the media as a shipowner, and he joined the Norwegian Shipowners' Association in 1918 in that capacity.

Concrete traded consistently for her first twelve months, but was then affected by a severe downturn in world trade.‡ In mid-1921 the company Staalbeton was declared bankrupt, and in August Anders was involved in the creation of another company to raise capital to buy the ship.§ One of the possible uses of the ship, as advised in the prospectus, was as an expedition vessel, so Anders may have been considering using *Concrete* for whale hunting or sealing. If this had occurred, it would have been the only time a concrete vessel was used for that purpose. The new company, which was also called Concrete, allowed the ship to operate for several more months, with Anders as the captain, before it also was declared bankrupt.¶ Somehow *Concrete* continued trading, still with Anders at the helm, until

---

* Although the company name was Staalbeton, all listings of *Concrete*'s movements are under the company name Beton.

† The largest European concrete ship built in Norway by Fougner, at 1050 tons, was *Askelade*, although the Americans built a limited number of very large concrete ships around the same time. *Selma*, for example, built by Fougner's American company, was 6,826 tons.

‡ For an indication of the severity of the downturn see: https://www. researchgate.net/figure/NDEXES-OF-WORLD-TRADE-1913-100_ fig3_331779115, accessed 27 February 2023.

§ *Norges Handels of Sjøfartstidende*, 25 August 1921, p. 2.

¶ *Aftenposten*, 12 November 1921, p. 8.

June 1922, when she was sold to a Kristiania-based company that owned two other concrete ships.*

The post-war period was difficult for shipping generally, but the problems experienced by Staalbeton were exacerbated by contractual problems that were not resolved until 1923, when an English court found in its favour in a dispute with the Dutch company that had contracted to use *Concrete* as a chartered freight vessel. The contract was 'subject to approval of the deck', and the Dutch company withdrew from the contract when the ship was delivered, saying that it had not given final approval for the deck. The Dutch company challenged the court's decision, but their appeal was dismissed. Staalbeton was awarded £8,050 (A$660,000), which presumably offset debts, but by then *Concrete* had her new owner.[†] *Concrete* was not destined to have a boring life. In 1926 she was sold to a group of Norwegian idealists wanting to emigrate to the Galapagos Islands. She was renamed *Albemarle* after one of the Galapagos Islands and arrived at her destination safely. *Albemarle* was then sold to the Buenaventura Harbour Authority in Columbia and fell out of sight in 1931.[‡]

When *Concrete* was sold, Anders was employed as the captain of one of the new company's concrete ships, *Fjeldknaus*, for several months, until September 1922, when he took over as the master of a 4,100-ton steamship, *Solborg*, which was owned by another company.[§] He was captain of *Solborg* for over two years, to the end of 1924, carrying freight, especially coal, to and from Norway. In January 1924 *Solborg* ran aground off the Norwegian coast and sprang a leak.[¶] A rescue ship was dispatched to provide assistance, but *Solborg* floated free at high tide and was able to get to shore under her own steam. Fortunately, this was a misadventure rather than a disaster, but it would be interesting to know if the incident brought back nightmares

---

* The company was Halle & Peterson. *Norges Handels of Sjøfartstidende*, 6 June 1922, p. 8.
† *Aftenposten*, 30 October 1923, p. 5.
‡ *Norges Handels og Sjøfartstidende*, 31 July 1926, p. 8.
§ *Solborg* was owned by Borch & Sons.
¶ *Bergens Aftenblad*, 18 January 1924, p. 5.

for Anders from the time when *Solglimt* was shipwrecked.

In August 1921, when the company Staalbeton was declared bankrupt and the new company was being formed, the apartment where Anders and his family had been living in Kristiania was advertised as being available for immediate possession. The family moved to Lillehammer at this time,* and it became Anders' home town for the rest of his life. Family lore tells that Marie was at pains to stress that she and Anders worked until they had paid off all the debts owing when Staalbeton was made bankrupt.

Like Anders' earlier ventures, his foray into concrete ships must have been prompted by dreams of acquiring wealth beyond the prospects of a captain-for-hire. Unfortunately, as with his earlier ventures, this one was not lucky.

There was a belief in the family that the bankruptcy was the result of the concrete ship that Anders had commissioned turning upside down and sinking into the Oslofjord as it was released from the slipway on launching. To add colourful detail to the story, it was claimed that in calm weather the hull could still be seen from above. This story is not correct. It appears that four true elements have been collapsed into one inaccurate story. The first element is the knowledge that Anders had an interest in concrete ships. The fact that his ship was actually named *Concrete* may have caused some of the confusion. The second element is that in 1925 a concrete ship named *Silvestre* sank near Tønsberg, and its hull can sometimes be seen from above. It did not sink on being launched, but as the result of a shipping accident.† The third element is that Anders was bankrupted as a result of his investment in concrete ships. The fourth element is that several shipping yards, including Fougner's, launched their concrete ships by releasing them sideways down the slipway before using a maritime crane to lift them onto the water. Anders' foray into concrete ship ownership was not in the end successful, but it provided him with a better experience than this tale would suggest.

---

* Lillehammer is 160 kilometres north of Oslo.

† *Norges Handels og Sjøfartstidende*, 15 September 1925, p. 6.

Before the end of his involvement with *Concrete*, Anders was an active and influential member of several maritime associations. In June 1918 he was elected to the board of the Norwegian Shipowners Association and in October 1919 he was one of the initiators of the Motorship Owners Group of the Norwegian Shipowners Association and was elected onto its board,[*] and then in September 1920 he was elected as its Vice-President.[†] In November 1920, as a member of the Kristiania Shipowners Association, he successfully argued against new arbitration clauses relating to unloading of coal imports, on the grounds that they would be disadvantageous to shipowners,[‡] and in early 1921 he was part of a committee formed by the Kristiania Seamen's Association to examine new regulations applying to rescue gear.[§]

Evidently, Anders was a man of strong opinions. In February and March 1921, in his capacity as a member of the Seamen's Association, he was leading a group opposed to a proposed mural for the Seamen's School by the up-and-coming artist Per Krohg.[¶] Not beating about the bush, Anders argued that the proposals were ridiculous and completely unsuitable for the school. In an apparent absence of the laws of defamation, he named the chair of the selection committee, Director Jens Thiis, stating that other more serious artists declined to submit proposals in the knowledge that Thiis would not look on them favourably. Heated discussion ranged over two meetings of the Association, at the end of which the proposals for the mural by Krohg were rejected.

Largely as a result of Anders' strongly held conservative views, the Seamen's School was deprived of an important artwork. Per Krohg went on to become a major figure in the renaissance of mural painting in Norway. He is most famous as one of three artists whose work features prominently

---

[*] *Haugesunds Dagblad*, 17 June 1918, p. 4.

[†] *Norges Handels og Sjøfartstidende*, 23 September 1920, p. 4.

[‡] Ibid, 25 November 1920, p. 3.

[§] Ibid, 18 March 1921, p. 5.

[¶] Ibid, 24 February 1921, p. 3, 3 March 1921, p. 3

in the Oslo Town Hall. He studied under Henri Matisse and went on to become a professor at the State Art Academy in Oslo. For various reasons construction of the Town Hall was significantly delayed. It was eventually completed, including with its remarkable murals, by 1950. It is possible that Anders, who died in 1959, saw the murals, and it would be fascinating to know what he thought of them, 30 years after the Seamen's School brouhaha.

While the company Staalbeton and its ship *Concrete* were obviously Anders' main focus in the period 1918–1922, he had other irons in the fire. After he had established Staalbeton in September 1917, but before he received the ship *Concrete*, he was involved with the establishment of another shipping company, Bryns Rederi.* This company was registered in July 1918 with a stated intent to provide capital and operating expenses for three ships that had already been acquired. Like many shipping companies in Norway in this period, Bryns Rederi went into liquidation in November 1921,† with the business finally being wound up in December 1924.‡ These were tough times.

In 1918 Anders was also on the board of a newly established reinsurance company,§ and he was the deputy chairman of a company, Portland, which operated a ship named *Portland*. As an indication that this company was also experiencing difficulties, in 1919 its board resolved to write-down the share capital by twenty-five per cent and not to pay a dividend to its shareholders.¶ In May 1919 Anders applied, unsuccessfully, for the position of director of Saltens Steamship Company.** It is possible that in this period before Staalbeton had taken possession of *Concrete*, which it did in June 1919, Anders found himself with costs and insufficient income,

---

* Ibid, 26 April 1918, p. 5.
† *Aftenposten*, 12 November 1921, p. 8.
‡ *Norges Handels og Sjøfartstidende*, 10 June 1924, p. 10.
§ *Dagdladet*, 8 August 1918, p. 1.
¶ *Aftenposten*, 15 April 1919, p. 4.
***Bergens Aftenblad*, 4 May 1919, p. 7.

hence the application for this position, however, the timing is odd unless the position could be held concurrently with his other commitments.

This was indeed a period of twists and turns for Anders. In a period just shy of a decade he had left, or been forced to leave, a career as a farmer and had become involved with, and then been bankrupted by, the pioneering industry of ocean-going concrete ships. In addition, he had an association with a number of shipping companies, none of which thrived. It cannot have been easy for him to have his ambitions and dreams shattered and his capital lost, yet again, in unsuccessful, unlucky ventures. Although many shipping companies failed in the post-war period, it may also have been the case that Anders' optimism and entrepreneurial drive outstripped his abilities.

Anders had been both unlucky and unsuccessful in his career to this point, but in many ways he had also been lucky. He was well-born, had many opportunities that others less fortunate did not, no lives – including his own – had been lost in the shipping disasters he had been central to and he had suffered no serious legal consequences.

CHAPTER 14

SKILLED IN GAMES

Homer, *The Odyssey*[*]

This brings us to the final, and most perplexing, twist in this fraught period for Anders. To set the scene for what happened next, it is necessary to know that in the decade from 1917 to 1927 Norway had a strictly enforced prohibition against alcohol.[†] The prohibition effectively started during the war, when the government was primarily concerned to ensure that the nation's resources were focused on producing essential goods, especially food. Grains and potatoes were only to be used for food, and both the import and production of spirits and fortified wines were banned. A plebiscite held after the war, in 1919, led to an extension of the prohibition that was hotly contested but assiduously enforced. There had been a perceived decline in drunkenness as a result of the prohibition. However, one unintended consequence of the prohibition was ongoing trade problems with the wine-producing countries France, Spain and Portugal, which threatened not to buy Norwegian fish if Norway would not accept their liquor and fortified wine. Another unintended consequence

[*] Homer, 1996, 8.185–190, p. 196.
[†] See Chapter 13.

was a boost in doctors' incomes because they were able to prescribe brandy as medicine. A third was the creation of a thriving smuggling trade.[*]

By the 1920s smuggling alcohol had become quite a business. The prohibition against fortified wine was not lifted until 1923, and the ban on liquor continued until 1927. Perhaps the smartest form of smuggling was to attach it to legitimate trading activity supported by existing forms of transport, warehouse storage and clientele, although the most lucrative involved a number of large supply ships, sometimes in the form of 'floating trading partnerships' that operated from ships lying out from the coast and supplying smaller craft to make the dash to shore. In response to all this, police and customs officers were kept very busy at the ports and in the courts, and customs were equipped with faster cruisers armed with cannons and machine guns. From 1924 to 1927 four smuggling ships were sunk after being attacked by customs vessels. Smuggling, then, was not for the faint-hearted.

In mid-February 1925, Norwegian newspapers were agog with the news that Hendrik G. Melsom,[†] the distinguished captain of the whaling ship *Lancing*, had been arrested by the police and charged with smuggling under a law that said captains would be charged if contraband was found on their ships and the culprit was not known.[‡] The mainstream newspapers, which tended to be anti-prohibition, were aghast that a man of such high standing should run the risk of a 50,000 kroner (A$200,000) fine and six months in gaol for a crime he did not commit. Apparently, it was the first time that this particular law had been applied so strictly.

Anders was on *Lancing* as the second officer. Melsom was eleven years older than him, but was a man cut from the same cloth. He came from a farming and seafaring family and went to sea at 15, seeking adventure and advancement. By 21 he had his master's certificate and at 24, the same age Anders was when he departed in *Cathrine* for the Southern Ocean, he was a harpoonist on Svend Foyn's ship *Providentia*, shooting exploding

---

[*] Johansen, 2013, pp. 46–63.
[†] Hendrik G. Melsom (1870–1946).
[‡] *Aftenposten*, 19 February 1925, p. 2.

grenades into whales. In 1897 he went to the east and was employed there for the next fifteen years as a ship's captain, mainly in whaling. During the Russo-Japanese war he evaded Japanese warships by sneaking past them into the safe haven of Shanghai harbour in the middle of the night, without lanterns or lights.[*] He is best known, however, for his involvement with the ship *Lancing*, which was owned by Melsom & Melsom, a company he formed with his brother.

Public opinion across party lines was very divided on the merits of the prohibition, which made it difficult to manage politically. However, there were strongly held views in the community. Chief among the opponents to prohibition were shipowners and the newspapers that generally represented their views. Within hours of the news that Melsom had been arrested, one maritime newspaper was railing against the law,[†] saying that the fanaticism for prohibition was not only costing Norway huge sums of money, but it was also dragging Norway back into the Middle Ages, with innocent people being punished because the guilty party could not be identified. The newspaper made the point that the law provided the opportunity for people with malicious intent to bring liquor on board a ship, then inform the police with the specific intention of harming the captain. The article concluded with the statement: 'This ungrateful nation rewards the people, who less than ten years ago risked their lives and rendered invaluable service and attracted honour to the country, with a law under which they can be imprisoned for crimes they have not committed. This is how far we have come under governments that allow themselves to be ruled by a foolish psychiatrist and other fanatics.'[‡]

The fact that Melsom was a well-known and highly-regarded captain may have been a factor in the speedy response his arrest elicited. The arrest

---

[*] https://skipshistorie.net/Larvik/LVK200Melsom%20Melsom/Rederne/ LVK20000000000003%20H%20G%20MELSOM.htm, accessed 19 January 2023.

[†] *Norges Handels og Sjøfartstidende*, 19 February 1925, p. 3.

[‡] This refers to Dr Johan Scharffenberg (1869–1965), a Norwegian psychiatrist and vocal proponent of the abstinence movement.

was announced on 19 February and just the next day, 20 February, the newspapers carried a letter from the Norwegian Shipowners Association to the Prime Minister urging him to intercede to ensure that Melsom would not be imprisoned without a special reason to think that he was implicated in the smuggling.* The Association also recommended that the law be changed so that it would be the authorities who bore the burden of proof that the master had not shown due diligence.

As more information about the smuggling affair began to emerge, however, the maritime newspapers and the Shipowners Association found that they had jumped into the fray a little too early. Just hours after this material first appeared in the newspapers Anders had declared himself to be the guilty party, and he was duly charged.† Then the Norwegian left-wing newspapers, which were in favour of the prohibition, and were presumably not unhappy to focus on a scandal involving shipowners and senior officers, carried out their own investigation that revealed much that the first reports did not.

One of these newspapers sarcastically expressed sympathy for the captain, saying 'Poor captain! One could even feel the urge to shed a tear over the terrible injustice he has suffered!'‡ Instead, they claimed that the captain, senior officers and a prominent lawyer and businessman who was on board as a passenger were all involved in the smuggling. They stated that the crew had brought fifty-one cases of liquor on board under customs seal while the ship was in Antwerp and stored it under instruction in an empty cabin near the captain's cabin. From there, it was claimed, the captain and his collaborators carried the consignment to his cabin with the clear intent of smuggling it into Norway.

When the ship had arrived in Norway the crew members were detained for several hours before they could disembark because the mustering office was not ready to clear them for entry into the country.

---

* *Haugesunds Dagblad*, 20 February 1925, p. 1, and other newspapers.
† *Nordlandsposten*, 19 February 1925, p. 2, and other newspapers.
‡ The left-wing newspaper, *Norges Kommunistblad* took the lead in questioning what had happened. This quote is from 20 February 1925, p. 1.

One young crew member, a cook, asked for compensation for this extra time, and threatened to go to the police if he was not paid. The captain attempted to call his bluff, and then quickly capitulated, but it was too late. The police had already been informed and they arrived on board a short time later. They did not find all of the liquor, but enough to determine that smuggling had occurred. The businessman, Anders Jahre,* tried to argue that the liquor that was found was his for personal use. Curiously, customs officers had already searched the ship and failed to find any liquor on board. It is not unreasonable to assume that they had been bribed, because such a supplementary source of income to customs officers was another unintended consequence of the prohibition. Finally, the left-wing newspapers reported that Jahre drove Anders to the police station himself and, therefore, must surely be implicated.

The version of events reported by the left-wing press appears to be consistent with the version reported by the police. When interviewed, the Assistant Chief of Police, Rolf Olsen, said that Melsom had not been arrested under the section of the law that allowed them to arrest a captain if the guilty party could not be determined.† Olsen said that law had not, to date, led to any arrests, and that on the few occasions he had had cause to use the section he had contented himself with giving the ship's master a warning. According to Olsen, Melsom had been reported to the police by the crew for smuggling. That is, for smuggling liquor that he and Jahre had brought on board. The police were aware that there should have been fifty-one cases of brandy on board, although the customs officers had not found anything when they inspected the ship. Neither had any customs-sealed alcohol been declared. The police found forty-eight bottles of brandy in an air duct in the wall of the captain's cabin, an open bottle of brandy on a table in the cabin, a case of liquor in the captain's wardrobe, and eleven cases of brandy in one of the lifeboats. When they arrested Melsom it was not because of his responsibility as a captain if no guilty party was

---

* Anders Jahre (1891–1982) was at the time a lawyer and businessman.
† *Dagposten: Trønderen*, 20 February 1925, p. 2.

identified, but because there was reason to suspect him of smuggling and the police did not want him to be able to tamper with the evidence. In response to a question about how the captain explained the presence of the alcohol in his cabin, Olsen replied that Melsom claimed not to have the slightest knowledge of it.

With their tails somewhat between their legs, the maritime newspapers tried to extract some credibility by pointing out that at least the '*Lancing*-affair', as it became known, provided an illustration of what the law they had complained about could be used for.[*] They said that it should be noticed that an attempt to resolve a dispute about whether a crew member should have overtime pay by threatening to report a captain for smuggling under the offending legal clause amounted to extortion. At the very least a report of this nature, regardless of its merits, would result in a review, causing great inconvenience to the shipping company and senior officers. In this instance the newspapers suggested that, given the young age of the crew member who reported Melsom to the police, he probably did not understand what he had done, therefore it would not be appropriate to investigate his behaviour to determine if he was guilty of extortion. The Shipowners Association withdrew into a dignified silence.

The left-wing newspapers kept the scandal alive in the public arena, pointing out that Melsom must have been both blind and deaf if he was not aware that the liquor had been taken into his cabin, as he claimed. They also acknowledged that Anders had acted honourably by coming forward as the owner of the liquor, but queried why no crew members had been questioned by the police. Regarding the argument put forward in the press that the contribution made by sea captains during the war should be taken into account, the left-wing press countered by saying that it was wrong to speak so admiringly of 'well-known, highly-regarded captains', with the affair of *Sagatind* fresh in the country's memory. *Sagatind* was one of several Norwegian vessels used to smuggle liquor into the USA at the time, and those involved had recently been caught. In 1924 the same ship

---

[*] *Norges Handels og Sjøfartstidende*, 20 February 1925, p. 2.

had been used to smuggle about a million bottles of liquor into the USA, in two trips. In this case the Norwegian Shipowners Association had also defended its members, arguing that it was not easy being a Norwegian shipowner in such difficult times, and Norwegian shipowners should not be excluded from such a lucrative trade when those from other countries were making the most of the opportunities provided by countries that had prohibitions in place.[*]

Perhaps in response to the encouragement given to it by the left-wing press, the Norwegian Sailors' and Firemen's Union wrote to the Prime Minister unequivocally rejecting the argument made by the Shipowners Association that their members would maliciously expose captains to the law.[†] The Union asserted that crew members were at least as honourable as the ships' officers, but then undercut its own argument by claiming that it had evidence of countless numbers of times when officers had tried to cheat sailors of their rights. It would also not be so strange, in the opinion of the Union, if seafarers occasionally resorted to informing on captains if all other avenues were closed to them. However, if seafarers were the kind of people that the Shipowners Association suggested, such cases as the one with *Lancing* would probably have occurred more often. This was quite a complicated and contradictory set of arguments to put forward!

Melsom and Anders were both interviewed by the police, after which they were released from custody, with Anders required to report to the police weekly until the case was settled. There was then a court hearing in March, during which Melsom argued that Anders' fine character and the Order of St Olav he had been awarded should be taken into account. The magistrate and most of the press, however, thought that, if found guilty, he should be stripped of his award for bringing it into disrepute.[†]

By late May, as preparations for *Lancing*'s departure to the Southern Ocean were underway, the left-wing press claimed that it was a scandal that the smuggling case had not been resolved, that there were forces at

---

[*] Johansen, 2013, p. 13.
[†] *Sverre*, 6 March 1925, p. 5.

work to delay it, and that those involved should not be allowed to leave the country before the case was finalised.* They claimed public opinion had it that Jahre was the actual owner of the liquor, noting again that he had been a passenger and had shared a cabin with the captain. There was a suggestion that the police were waiting for documents from Belgium, but with a consulate in that country that could readily have supplied the documents, it appeared nobody in Norway was interested in a speedy resolution of the case.

Lancing left Norway on 3 June 1925, with both Melsom and Anders on board, on a voyage that was to achieve both fame and infamy, transforming the whaling industry by successfully deploying a slipway at sea to haul carcasses on board for immediate treatment, and, for the first time, hunting without a British licence, following British cancellation of licences and concessions after the war.

Lancing, weighing 7,563 tons, had been built in Glasgow in 1898. When she arrived in Sandefjord in February 1925 she was on her way to a shipyard in Norway where she was to be reconstructed with a new slipway.† *Lancing* was a factory ship, not a whale catcher, and she was accompanied on the expedition by four whale catchers, or chasers, as they were known. These were the direct descendants of the small rowboats that the earlier whalers used, like the one that became *Hope* after *Cathrine* was wrecked. By 1925 many chasers were fast steam- or diesel-driven ships that hunted the whales, killed them and brought them back to the factory ship.‡

Once again Anders was involved with a ground-breaking venture, mixing with like-minded men who were pushing the boundaries of their industry. *Lancing* had a successful, albeit eventful, voyage to the south. The first whale was caught off the Congolese coast and the slipway was deemed a success, although improvements were made during the voyage and later. For *Lancing*, the focus of hunting was in the waters around Antarctica,

---

* *Arbeiderbladet*, 25 May 1925, p. 5.

† The slipway was made to a design patented by a Norwegian engineer, Petter Sørlle, who also accompanied the ship on this expedition.

‡ On the 1925 voyage *Lancing*'s chasers were named *Pol I-IV*.

especially off the South Orkney Islands.* In April 1926 *Lancing* and her four chasers were impounded by the Argentinians, on the grounds that they had been whaling in Argentinian waters. Norwegian Government representatives in Buenos Aires became involved and the ships were released six days later with no conditions attached.[†]

By July 1926, *Lancing* had returned to Europe and the press reported that charges had been filed against four men who had been involved in the smuggling affair. The two named were Melsom and Jahre.[‡] Anders and the first mate, Peder Hansen, would have been the other two charged. *Lancing* left Norway again on 24 August without the case going to court.

She arrived back in Norway on 11 June 1927, prompting the scandalised left-wing press to comment that the smuggling case had still not been resolved, two years after the event. There were accusations of deliberate sabotage of the investigation on behalf of 'certain people'.[§] Anders was questioned on 11 August, but no further action was taken because Jahre had argued that it was essential for the defence that Hansen be interviewed, and that could not occur because he had remained in Montevideo with the chasers. He had not been interviewed the year before, either, because he had been in Gothenburg supervising the repairs. The press said that this had all been very deftly done, but the scandal was just growing larger.

Lancing left Norway several days after Anders had been questioned and returned in March 1928. Hansen had remained in Montevideo, purportedly due to ill health, and once again the left-wing press was up in arms.[¶] Interestingly, after the original flurry of comment in 1925, no other newspapers showed any interest in the case. Again, accusations about improper delaying tactics and attempts to quash the case were made. The

---

* The South Orkney Islands lie in the Scotia Sea, about 600 kilometres northeast of the tip of the Antarctic Peninsula.
† *Aftenposten*, 29 April 1926, p. 1.
‡ *Jarlsberg og Larviks Amtstidende*, 16 August 1926, p. 2.
§ *Nyt Land*, 17 August 1927, p. 2.
¶ *Vestfold Fremtid*, 7 May 1928, p. 1.

Assistant Chief of Police, Olsen, said that he had asked for the case to be brought before a jury, but Jahre's objections had prevented that from occurring. Olsen reported that he had taken the case forward on the basis of Anders' confession. Anders, however, later announced that he would accept neither a fine nor a verdict. Olsen then tried to get a prison sentence handed down on the grounds that Anders was preparing to leave the country again, but the Supreme Court rejected this attempt. When asked if the case would lapse through the passing of time, Olsen replied that it would be open for five years.

In the meantime, *Lancing's* associates were carrying out a charm offensive, which included inviting the Prime Minister and other national and local dignitaries on board for inspections and lunches.[*] Even then, *Lancing* was beset by other dramas. Melsom's younger brother, Gjert Bull Melsom, who was the ship's first engineer, was killed in a terrible accident when a valve exploded, releasing hot steam,[†] and a 20-year-old who was visiting the ship fell overboard and drowned.[‡] In addition, there were attempts, though unsuccessful, to employ strike-breakers to undertake repairs on the ship.[§]

Finally, the smuggling affair came to an end. Just before the case was due to go to court, in 1928, it was reported that the people involved had accepted fines, on the condition that their names and the amounts of the fines were not disclosed. The police said that they were satisfied with the result.[¶] By this stage Norway was no longer prohibiting the import of alcohol, although smuggling continued to be against the law, of course.

When Melsom had brought *Lancing* into Sandefjord in February 1925, he must have had a lot more on his mind than just the contraband on board. He had no guarantee that his planned expedition to the Southern Ocean would be successful, and indeed one industry observer is reputed

---

[*] *Aftenposten*, 2 April 1928, p. 6.
[†] *Morgenavisen*, 30 April 1928, p. 1.
[‡] *Langesunds Blad*, 5 May 1928, p. 2.
[§] *Nybrott*, 9 May 1928, p. 1.
[¶] *Arbeiderbladet*, 11 August 1928, p. 2.

to have commented, when the ship subsequently left in June that year: 'There goes the biggest disaster that ever sailed on the sea.'* The amount of money at risk in that venture must have been stupendous, with five ships and hundreds of crew members involved. Taking into account Melsom's business concerns and the fact that he was a man prepared to tackle all sorts of adversity, it is likely that he regarded the '*Lancing*-affair' much as one would an irritating mosquito.

On the other hand, it is difficult to know why Anders, 44 years old and a father of three with very few resources behind him by this stage in his life, would have accepted the blame. Clearly the plan was to try to avoid the huge fine and possible prison sentence that Melsom faced, but why it was Anders who stepped forward, rather than Jahre or the first mate, is harder to understand. Perhaps he did so because he was the recipient of the Order of St Olav, and he and the other men involved thought that the courts would deal with him leniently. The fact that Anders had strong anti-prohibition views probably also influenced his decision to be a party to the smuggling, and then to cooperate in the attempt to minimise the impact once their plan was discovered. In the event, he was not stripped of his award, but it seems unlikely that he consulted his wife before stepping into the fray.

Jahre, the businessman at the centre of the smuggling case, went on to become a shipping magnate, a major player in the whaling industry, the richest man in Norway and a generous philanthropist. Anders worked for Jahre's whaling company Kosmos in the period from 1928 to the Second World War. Perhaps this was the payoff for offering himself as the guilty party, or perhaps it simply indicates Jahre's loyalty to those batting on his side. After Jahre's death there was controversy about tax fraud and avoidance, and in the 2000s the Norwegian Government succeeded in retrieving some of his fortune from the Cayman Islands.[†]

There is no public record of whether or not the cook who reported

____

* https://skipshistorie-net, drawing on *The whaling company Globus A / S 1925–1950 (Ø. Næss)*.
† https://no.wikipedia.org/wiki/Anders_Jahre, accessed 22 January 2023.

Melsom ever worked on a ship again, but one suspects not. Assuredly, however, his actions must have reinforced Anders' opinion that cooks and stewards could be bothersome individuals.

And *Lancing*? She met her end in 1942 when she was torpedoed by German forces, with the loss of one life.[*]

It is likely that Anders was whaling in the Southern Ocean on a ship named *Kosmos* in 1929–30. That was Jahre's first venture in his own right in the Antarctic, and it was a highly successful voyage that set him up for a long and lucrative career as a whaling company owner. *Kosmos* is known for two significant firsts: at 17,801 tons she was the first purpose-built factory ship, and she was the first to attempt to use a supporting aeroplane. This second innovation, however, was a disaster because the plane vanished, together with its two crew members.[†] Anders was definitely on Jahre's ship *Fraternitas* in 1930–31 and, on that voyage, he went as far as the Antarctic mainland.

Anders had settled into the career that first attracted him when he was a very young sailor: the bloodthirsty pursuit of whales in icy waters, and he earned a reputation as an accomplished whaler.[‡] This was hard and dangerous work. Between 1924 and 1950, fifty-eight Norwegian whale hunters died in accidents, serious injury was commonplace, and frostbite was a constant problem.[§] Anders was on ships that were whaling 'in the ice' and was at times the captain of whale chasers. Their task was to pursue the whales through icebergs and floating ice, harpoon them, hold them tight until they died, then return with them to the factory ship where they were hauled up onto the flensing deck, cut into pieces and boiled down, all of this carried out in temperatures near or below freezing.

In his last few years in the whaling industry Anders was the store manager on Jahre's ships. In this capacity he had control over the provisions on board, and at last he found himself on ships with well-prepared and

---

[*] https://en.wikipedia.org/wiki/SS_Lancing, accessed 22 January 2023.
[†] Tønnessen, Johnsen, op. cit, p. 276.
[‡] *Norsk Handels og Sjøfartstidende*, 17 October 1931, p. 5.
[§] Drivenes and Jølle, 2016, p. 192.

varied food.* He said at a talk he gave when at home in Lillehammer between expeditions that he was served three meals a day with great variety, sometimes French toast for breakfast and fresh pastries with coffee![†]

In the late 1930s, with the prospect of military conflict looming, Anders was approaching his sixtieth year and his maritime career was drawing to a close. He had, however, more dangers to face and adventures to experience before the conclusion of his time at sea.

Earlier in the decade Anders and Marie had become members of the far-right nationalist party Nasjonal Samling, the party started in 1933 by Vidkun Quisling that eventually became the only governing party during the German occupation of Norway. Their interest in some ways seems consistent with Anders' conservative views, although many conservative people had less extreme views about how the country should be run, of course, with Nasjonal Samling only ever attracting just over two per cent of the vote. By 1937, however, he and Marie had resigned from the party in opposition to its increasing militarism and support for German aggression, and Anders would go on to risk his life during the war in support of an independent Norway.

When war was declared, Anders began to work for the company Nortraship, the Norwegian Shipping and Trade Mission, which was established in London in April 1940 following the German invasion of Norway in order to administer the Norwegian merchant fleet outside German-controlled areas. Nortraship, which operated some 1,000 vessels and was the largest shipping company in the world at the time, made a major contribution to the Allied war effort. In July 1940 Anders was first mate on a ship named *Norseland,* and in 1941 he was captain of two ships, *Sado* and *Kongshavn.* In speaking about his war experiences to a journalist late in his life, he said that he had commanded transport ships

---

* https://www.sjohistorie.no/no/sjofolk/442494/utmerkelser, accessed 22 January 2023.
† *Laagen*, 18 July 1927, pp. 1, 3.

between Europe and America in both the First and Second World Wars and that he had stood on the bridge while bombs fell thickly around him, with machine guns peppering the ship so that in the end it was almost like a hollow sieve. People had been killed around him, but he had come through unscathed, which he thought was quite strange.[*]

While Anders was working for Nortraship he was based in London. *Kongshavn* was to be his last ship, although he did not retire from Nortraship until February 1943. Anders spent the remainder of the war, his first years in retirement, based in Scotland, exiled from Norway. On 7 August 1981 he was posthumously awarded the War Medal for his services to Norway during the war.[†]

---

[*] *Dagningen*, 13 October 1956, p. 3.
[†] https://www.sjohistorie.no/no/sjofolk/442494/utmerkelser, accessed 22 January 2023.

CHAPTER 15

FAR FROM THE SEA

And at last your own death will steal upon you …
A gentle, painless death, far from the sea it comes
To take you down, borne down with the years in ripe old age …
Homer, The Odyssey*

When the war ended Anders returned to his home in Lillehammer. He had not seen Marie for over five years, and for the fifteen years prior to that he is likely to have spent at most only a few months each year with her in Norway. His three children were scattered around the globe. His older son Mons was in Australia, his younger son Helge on the Faroe Islands and his daughter Alis in Denmark. It is difficult to imagine how Anders and Marie would have adapted to this colossal change in their routines. The path Anders chose was to throw himself into his woodcarving and artwork, which had been a constant part of his life since his earliest years at sea.

In November 1956, when he was 75 years old, Anders reluctantly accepted a request from a local newspaper to interview him about his creative output.† He told the journalist that there was nothing to write about, that his aim was not to be a great artist, but, as with any hobby, to first and foremost enjoy himself. Indeed, a series of exhibitions of his work from 1948 to 1952 held in various places in Norway were called 'My Hobby' (in English), and in an interview given at that time he said that he

---

* Homer, 1996, 11.153–56, p. 253.
† *Dagningen*, 13 October 1956, p. 3.

213

kept his hobby alive, and it kept him alive.[*]

His output was extraordinary, and even at 75 he was in his workshop from morning to night; the restlessness that had always been part of his nature translating into innumerable works of art and decorative objects. The journalist interviewing him described the experience of entering the fine old timber house in which Anders and Marie lived, saying that one was met with an opulence of carved chandeliers hanging from the ceiling, cabinets on both floors and walls, carved mirrors and frames on all the walls, and up and along the stairs to the second floor of the house beautiful, harmonious statues, all done by the master of the house. When you looked more closely you would see that many of the paintings were also made by Anders, although elsewhere in the house pictures by famous Norwegian artists were hanging between old family portraits, proof that you had arrived in a home where art and tradition had deep roots. Everything created by Anders was proof of creative joy, imagination, a wealth of ideas and a distinctive sense of form. In short, said the journalist, an artist.

The journalist noted that Anders' age was showing on him, but the man he met was a well-built figure with two real clubs for fists, testifying that Anders must have been a powerful man and, inadvertently harking back to the trouble on *Solglimt*, certainly not to be joked with when he stood on the bridge of a ship under his control in a storm. The journalist noted that Anders was not much more than a young boy when he was master of his first ship, had spent most of his life at sea, had carried out several remarkable seafaring deeds, and had been honoured with the Order of St Olav when he was only 26 years old. He had experienced two world wars at sea and been deeply involved in both of them. He had experienced more than can be conceived for many a man in a lifetime, including several dramatic shipwrecks.

The journalist said that, despite his extraordinarily adventurous life, the old captain did not brag about this himself. On the contrary, when he succeeded in getting Anders to reflect on these experiences and events,

---

[*] *Tønsberg Blad*, 10 May 1950, p. 3.

he only touched on them with a few simple dry remarks – as something mundane that was not worth talking about. This is consistent with the views of the grandchildren who spent time with Anders in this period of his life. They remember him as a quiet, kind man who generously encouraged them to make use of his workshop.

Anders said that he had been carving since he was a boy. He had always loved to draw and use a carving knife, but it was a shipping accident on the coast of Argentina that provided the impetus that really resulted in him taking up woodcarving as a hobby in his spare time. He was just a young man at the time, serving as a helmsman on a three-masted schooner. This schooner had an absolutely beautifully carved transom,* which Anders had amused himself by drawing because he thought it was so beautiful. The ship was hit by a hurricane and suffered a great deal of damage. Among other things, the entire transom was smashed to pieces. With great difficulty they got the ship to a city in Argentina, where it had to undergo extensive repairs. While they were there and waiting, the captain asked Anders if he thought he could carve a new transom, similar to the one broken. Because he had the drawings and he thought it might be fun to try, he accepted the challenge. This was the first major woodcarving job he had done, and he thought that it worked out pretty well. Since then, he had been carving in his free time, and only when he had said goodbye to the sea had it become a more serious activity. He said that one must have challenges, something to occupy one's time; being idle was not for him.

The journalist said that he himself had lived most of his life in close contact with excellent woodcarvers,† and had seen many beautiful works made, and thus did not consider himself completely illiterate in this field. He said that several of Anders' wall cabinets were fabulously well made, and that he had also developed his own style.

Some of the objects were filigree work, fine and meticulously done. Particularly beautiful, he thought, were a couple of smaller wall cabinets,

---

* A transom is the vertical section at the back of a boat that reinforces the stern.
† Norway is famous for its many woodcarvers and woodcarvings.

and a carved iron-clad coffin he had just finished, the paint not yet completely dry. He especially noted several beautifully carved armchairs.*

When asked where he got his ideas from, Anders replied that they came to him naturally, which was what made it so pleasurable and interesting. As an example, he showed the journalist a six-sided container with a lid, reminiscent of a soup tureen, richly carved. Anders said that he called it 'Marco Polo', because the inspiration for the carving came from Marco Polo's famous travels.

Anders had included in some of his exhibitions a number of animal figures carved by his younger son, and so he was asked if carving ran in the family. Certainly, said Anders, and he talked about one of his ancestors, Anders Smith,† who was a famous Norwegian church artist. Smith was originally a Scot, but he came to Norway in 1658 and is considered one of the country's foremost artists in this field. Among other things, he carved the magnificent interiors in Stavanger Cathedral and elsewhere in many churches in western Norway.

The journalist commented on the religious nature of many of Anders' works, which led to a discussion about the altarpieces Anders had carved. These included some in Norway, and another that he had made in Scotland during the war. This was a commissioned altarpiece for the Norwegian army, intended to be carried from one place to another so that church services could be distinctively Norwegian. Anders said that this was a big job, and he considered it to be one of the best he had done, although, unfortunately, it was still in Britain. Inside the cabinet on the altar itself he had carved the crucifixion and resurrection and outside on the two doors King Haakon II on one and General Fletcher on the other,‡ surrounded

---

* Just after this interview Anders and Marie travelled by ship to Australia to visit my family. On the voyage Anders carved another of these chairs, which is now in my sister's home.

† Andrew Lawrenceson Smith (1620–1694), also known by the Norwegian form of his name, Anders Lauritzen Smith.

‡ This was probably Carl Gustav Fleischer (1883–1942), who was a Norwegian general and the first land commander to win a major victory against the Germans in the Second World War. Having followed the Norwegian

by Norwegian soldiers at sea and on land. Anders was mixing the colours himself and doing his own painting and gilding. Remarkably, the only machines Anders had in his small workshop were a fine saw, like a jigsaw, and a small drill. He did all the other work by hand.

Over the years Anders held several exhibitions in Lillehammer, and in retirement he held exhibitions in Lillehammer, Hamar and Tønsberg, amongst other places. The exhibitions attracted positive attention and no doubt supplemented his income at a time when there was no such thing as superannuation or a government pension to provide support in retirement. As far back as 1927 he had won a silver medal in Lillehammer's Jubilee exhibition for works that included wood inlaid with whalebone, walking sticks made of whalebone and many other things, all considered unusual.

While he was based in London in 1941, Anders donated a number of carved works to the Norwegian Club there, as a consequence of which he was interviewed by a London-based Norwegian newspaper.[*] The article described him as a man with many irons in the fire – skipper, shipowner, whaler, farmer and artist, who was happiest when he filled his spare time with carving and painting. It was noted that many of his works were to be found in London homes, as well as countless works in the Vestfold and Hedmark regions of Norway.

Writing about the 'My Hobby' exhibition Anders held in Tønsberg in 1950, a journalist said that a highlight of the exhibition was a painting of the movie star Claudette Colbert, for which, Anders confessed, she had personally modelled.[†] Apparently, while he was in New York during the war, Anders had met Colbert and some of her colleagues and been invited to join them on a car trip to Hollywood. The journalist was particularly taken with the characteristic intelligent twinkle in her eye that Anders

Government into exile at the end of the Norwegian Campaign, Fleischer committed suicide after being bypassed for appointment as commander-in-chief of the Norwegian Armed Forces in exile and being sent to the insignificant post as commander of Norwegian forces in Canada.

[*] *Norsk Tidende* (London), 22 October 1941, p. 2.

[†] *Tønsberg Blad*, 10 May 1950, p. 3. Claudette Colbert (1903–1996) was born in France and was considered one of the pre-eminent actors of her time.

had managed to capture. This episode was a far cry from Anders' other recollections of the war, which featured bombs, machine-gun fire and death.

The story of the *Cathrine* shipwreck and the subsequent dangerous bid to get help had clearly struck a chord in the Norwegian national imagination. Over the years there have been multiple accounts, many remarking on the daring deeds of this modern-day Viking. There were articles in 1927 marking the 20th anniversary, in 1932 marking the 25th anniversary, and another in 1935, for no obvious reason. Not one of these articles mentioned the *Solglimt's* wreck, which was in all ways except the remarkable rescue voyage a more significant event. Anders' 50th birthday was noted in the press with mentions of *Cathrine*, his Order of St Olav, his involvement with famous whaling expeditions in the 1920s and 30s and his reputation as a skilled whaler, but, again, not one of the newspapers mentioned *Solglimt*. His 60th birthday, which occurred during the Second World War, attracted little coverage. When he died, the newspapers carried the same information about him that had been published when he turned 50, with the addition of his great passion for carving, painting and furniture-making. This absence of information about some key aspects of his life goes at least some of the way to explaining why, by the time I was conducting my research, nobody in the family knew about the *Solglimt* disaster, and the only information held by a family member about the *Concrete* episode was incorrect.

The man with an urge to communicate his very strong views was rarely in evidence in the latter part of Anders' life, however, he did not disappear entirely. In 1946, Anders had a bit of fun with a letter to the editor responding to a local who had accused him of being disrespectful of the Norwegian flag. Anders replied: 'A reader says he saw the remains of a Danish and a Norwegian flag used as a bird scarer in my garden facing [the street]. I invite him to a lecture on international flag systems and to which alphabet these flags belong. Otherwise, I do not appreciate being accused of insulting my own flag, or those of other nations. Yours sincerely, And. Harboe-Ree, ship's captain.' Then, in 1952, a large public meeting was held in Lillehammer with a government minister in attendance, and Anders was quoted expressing his scepticism about all the talk of saving the world by increasing production, saying that increased production would only lead to over-production and chaos. After that, all that was seen of him in public was a peaceable and creative man.

On 10 December 1959 this uncommonly adventurous sailor, sealer and whaler, unsuccessful entrepreneur and industrious artist died peacefully in Lillehammer, aged 78, far from the oceans that had shaped his life so dramatically. He is buried in the grounds of the church in Lillehammer.

POSTSCRIPT

At the outset I did not embark on my research in order to discover my grandfather. Rather, I had been given a fabulous diary and enough clues about one thrilling event in a man's life to want to learn more, and each new thing I learnt led me inexorably to the next intriguing event, and eventually through to the end of his life.

To discover as much as I could about my grandfather's life, I examined every newspaper reference to him that was available through the National Library of Norway's online digital collections – a treasure trove of information – as well as newspaper records from Australia, Great Britain and, to a lesser extent, South Africa. I supplemented knowledge gained in this way with expert advice and other sources of information where these were available. For a man who is not a household name, he was the subject of an extraordinary number of column inches. I accumulated hundreds of pages of transcripts and associated translations of newspaper articles. The Southern Ocean voyages and two shipwrecks were extensively reported on in the press of the day. In addition, they triggered court trials and generated numerous photographs and paintings.

It was also my great fortune that the Prince Edward Islands are now annexed to South Africa, because one of the most rewarding discoveries I made was the existence of the South African research team that has been investigating the *Solglimt* wreck, generating a huge amount of information. In fact, this 'discovery' was itself a small miracle. A colleague from my university was attending a conference at the Scott Polar Institute at Cambridge University where one of the South African researchers was presenting a paper on *Solglimt*, and she made the connection between us.

This is largely a book about the public iteration of my grandfather.

Although the rich sources of information about the *Cathrine* wreck included a great deal written by him, with his character and personality very much in evidence, most of the information about the rest of his life has by necessity been drawn from newspapers. This includes a number of interviews with him, as well as letters or articles he wrote, but, even so, everything was pitched to an audience, and the ability to see and understand the private man is diminished. There have been many times when I would have loved to have been able to ask him about his life, what a particular situation looked like to him, or why he made the decisions he did. Alternatively, a more rounded view would have been possible if his wife, children or associates could have been interviewed, but that was also out of the question by the time I started my research, and the recollections of my Scandinavian cousins, while very welcome, are sketchy and relate only to the period after he retired.

My father was still quite young when much of what is described in this book occurred, and by the time he reached his teens his father – my grandfather – was away from home for long periods of time. This way of life was not uncommon for seafarers, but it meant that time with family was very restricted. Then my father left home as a young man to go to sea, and ultimately settled in Australia, after which he had almost no regular contact with his own father. This meant that the time they had together, and the opportunities to discuss my grandfather's life when my father was old enough to have understood it, would have amounted to months, not years.

I am a first-generation Australian and, like many a child of migrants, I had little contact with any of my grandparents. In my childhood, travel was a major undertaking and there was no Internet to facilitate communication. All my Norwegian relatives were just names to me. My maternal grandparents never visited Australia, and Anders and Marie only visited once, when I was five and too young to remember them. The geographical barrier also proved to be a barrier to curiosity, and all I can recall hearing about my grandfather was that he was a ship's captain. In fact, both of my grandfathers were ships' captains and, while I thought it was impressive that I had two Norwegian ships' captains in my family, that doubling up seemed to further dampen my curiosity about other aspects of their lives. Anders died before I made my first visit to Norway when I was 21, and he never wrote to me or my parents, so the man I was researching was to all intents and purposes a complete stranger to me.

Another challenge to my research was the fact that, despite having two Norwegian parents, I did not learn Norwegian as a child because, at that time, migrants were encouraged to speak only English at home so that their children would not be disadvantaged when they started school. When I began the research for this book, which has mainly depended on Norwegian-language sources, I had limited verbal skills in Norwegian and could not read or write it. Until 2005 I did, however, have the assistance of a mother with exceptional linguistic ability, and I have a brother who lives in Norway. In addition, many generous people have provided advice about the technical terms relevant to a seafarer's life, and Internet translation services have been a great boon. I now have a very skewed Norwegian vocabulary, and possibly know more nautical terms than many Norwegians!

I have also been handicapped by the distance between where I live and most of the source material, which is in Norway. This problem was exacerbated by COVID-19, which prevented me from travelling just when I had the time to dedicate myself to research. In this regard my brother in Norway has been pivotal to my research, as has the extensive digitising that the National Library of Norway has done. Nonetheless, I am aware of significant gaps in my knowledge and a higher-than-normal risk that this work contains errors, not least because of my reliance on newspaper articles, which are notoriously unreliable.

Over the course of my research I did, of course, learn a great deal about my grandfather's life, and obviously I understand that I have a close biological relationship with him, however, and perhaps surprisingly, even now at the conclusion of my research, I still find it hard to feel an emotional connection with him. I feel closest to him when I can hear his own voice, such as when I read the diary from the *Cathrine* voyage, but it is easier to acknowledge kinship with the young, optimistic, confident and good-humoured man who wrote the diary, rather than with the man who, as he grew older, became harder, more opinionated and conservative, and about whom I had no access to sources that would reveal more of his feelings and private life.

I feel the strongest connection to my grandfather when I look at, or handle, the objects he created that I own, and that connection is certainly stronger now than when I embarked on my research. These objects are tangible to me, not complicated by disturbing thoughts of seal and whale slaughters, or by my bemusement about the very masculine world in which my grandfather lived. Now, when I walk under the chandelier he carved that hangs in my hallway, or admire the carved lampstand in my loungeroom when I turn on the lamp at dusk, or store papers in the wooden chest that he painted in a traditional Norwegian style, I have a much greater appreciation of the man who created them, and he seems more present in my life. Then I look at his portrait and wonder if he would have been pleased that his granddaughter researched and wrote about his life, or if he would have thought it intrusive.

All I can say is, if he is looking on from somewhere and feeling uncomfortable about having his life investigated in such detail, he should not have had such an interesting one!

BIBLIOGRAPHY

WEBSITES

Calculator Soup Online Calculators: https://www.calculatorsoup.com/calculators/time/sunrise_sunset.php.

Encyclopedia Britannica: https://www.britannica.com/technology/whale-oil.

Det Kongelige Justis- og Politidepartement [Ministry of Justice and the Police], Norway: Act No. 10 of 1902, The General Civil Penal Code [Norway], 2 May 1902: https://www.refworld.org/docid/5d4bdc564.html.

Harboe-Ree, Anders. (1906–07). Diary of the *Cathrine* Voyage. Vestfold Archives. A-2160: https://media.digitalarkivet.no/en/view/117212/1.

National Archives of Norway: https://media.digitalarkivet.no/en/view/117212/1.

National Centers for Environmental Information: https://www.ngdc.noaa.gov/geomag/declination.shtml.

Norwegian Historical Shipping Association: https://www.skipet.no/skip/skipsforlis/1906-1/view.

ResearchGate: https://www.researchgate.net/figure/NDEXES-OF-WORLD-TRADE-1913-100_fig3_331779115.

Royal Navy Lifeboats: https://rnli.org/about-us/our-history/timeline/1907-the-suevic-rescue.

Skipshistorie [Shipping History] (Norway): https://skipshistorie.net/Larvik/LVK200Melsom%20Melsom/Rederne/LVK20000000000003%20H%20G%20MELSOM.htm.

Sjohistorie [Maritime History] (Norway): https://www.sjohistorie.no/no/sjofolk/442494/utmerkelser.

White Star Line History: https://www.whitestarhistory.com/suevic.

Wikipedia: https://www-strindahistorielag.no.translate.goog/wiki/index.php/Nikolay_Knudtzon_Fougner?_x_tr_sl=no&_x_tr_tl=en&_x_tr_hl=en&_x_tr_pto=sc.

NORWEGIAN NEWSPAPERS

Included here are only the newspapers referred to directly in the manuscript.

Aftenposten

Arbeidet

Asker og Bærums Budstikke

Bergens Aftenblad

Bergens Tidende

Dagbladet

Dagningen

Dagposten: Trønderen

Fredriksstad Tilskuer

Gudbrandsdølen

Haugesunds Dagblad

Jarlsberg og Larviks Amtstidende

Kysten

Laagen

Langesunds Blad

Lillehammer Tilskuer

Morgenavisen

Morgenbladet

Moss Avis

Moss Tilskuer

Nordisk Tidende

Nordlandsposten

Norges Handels og Sjøfartstidende

Norges Kommunistblad

Norges Sjøfartstidende

Norsk Kundgjørelsestidende

Nybrott

Nyt Land

Oplandenes Avis

Ringerikes Blad

Social-Demokraten

Sverre

Tønsberg Blad

Trondhjems Adresseavis

Trondhjems Folkeblad

Tunsbergeren

Verdens Gang

Vestfold Fremtid

AUSTRALIAN AND OTHER NEWSPAPERS

The Age (Melbourne)

The Argus (Melbourne)

Brisbane Courier

The Daily Telegraph (Sydney)

Dundee Evening Telegraph

Hartlepool Northern Daily Mail (England)

Lloyd's List (London)

New York Times

Pearson's Weekly (London)

The Register (Adelaide)

ARTICLES, CHAPTERS, REPORTS AND CORRESPONDENCE

Basberg, Bjorn. (1988). The Floating Factory: Dominant Designs and Technological Development of Twentieth-Century Whaling Factory Ships, *The Northern Mariner*, 1, 21–37.

Bjørnstad, Asbjørn. (1908). Diary Excerpts, 14 November to 5 December, translated from Norwegian by. A. Evensen. Unpublished.

Boshoff, Jaco, Haart, D. & Loock, J. (1997). *Survey of Historical Sites on Marion Island.* Report for the Prince Edward Islands Management Committee, by representatives from the National Monuments Council and the Cu;tural History Museum Division. https://alp.lib.sun.ac.za/bitstream/handle/123456789/2426/marion_island_survey_historical_sites.pdf?sequence=4&isAllowed=y, accessed 3 March 2000.

Boshoff, Jaco, Van Niekerk, Tara Rae & Wares, Heather. (2015). Preliminary

Investigations on the Wreck of the SS *Solglimt*, Marion Island, *Bulletin of the Australasian Institute for Maritime Archaeology*, 39, 53–59.

Bull, Henrik Johan. (1907). Castaways' Christmas on a Desert Island, *New York Times*, 15 December, 51–52.

Bull, Henrik Johan. (1907). *Cathrine*'s Sydhavsfærd [*Cathrine*'s Southern Ocean Voyage], *Verdens Gang*, 27 March, 1; 29 April, 3; 1 May, 1, 2, 3; 3 May, 1, 2; 6 May, 2.

Bull, Henrik Johan. (1907). Christmas House: The Adventures of a Shipwrecked Crew, *Pall Mall Magazine*, 40(176), 698–709.

Clark, Geoffrey & de Biran, Antoine. (2010). Geophysical and Archaeological Investigation of the Survivor-camp of the *Antelope* (1783) in the Palau Islands Western Pacific, *International Journal of Nautical Archaeology*, 39(2), 345–356.

Cooper, John. (2016). The *Solglimt* Rediscovered, *Antarctic Legacy of South Africa blog*. https://blogs.sun.ac.za/antarcticlegacy/2016/11/04/the-solglimt-rediscovered/.

Cooper, John, Boshoff, Jaco, Harboe-Ree, Cathrine & Van Niekerk, Tara Rae. (2018). The Wreck of the Norwegian Sealer *Solglimt* on Sub-Antarctic Marion Island: A Continuing Archaeological and Historical Investigation, *Historical Antarctic Sealing Industry: Proceedings of an International Conference in Cambridge, 16–21 September 2016*, edited by Robert K. Headland. Cambridge: Scott Polar Research Institute Occasional Publication Series, 4–12.

Cooper, John & Headland, Robert K. (1991). A History of South African Involvement in Antarctica and at Prince Edward Islands, *South African Journal of Antarctic Research*, 21, 77–91.

Crockett, Zachary. (2015). *The Business of Seal Clubbing*: https://priceonomics. com/the-business-of-seal-clubbing/.

Harboe-Ree, Anders. (1906–07). Notes and letters. Unpublished.

Harboe-Ree, Anders. (1907). *Cathrine*'s Forlis [*Cathrine*'s Loss], *Moss Aftenblad*, 2 April, 1.

Harboe-Ree, Anders. (1907). Kaptein Ree om Crozet-Øerne og Baadseiladsen [Captain Ree on the Crozet Islands and a Boat Voyage], *Morgenbladet*, 2 May, 1.

Harboe-Ree, Anders. (1907). De Skibbrudne paa Crozet-øerne [Shipwreck on the Crozet Islands], *Morgenbladet*, 31 March, 1, 2.

Harboe-Ree, Anders. (1907). Sjøkontrollens Forsølgelse [Maritime Office Persecution], *Norges Sjøfartstidende*, 9 October, 1, 2.

Harboe-Ree, Anders. (1907). Vore Stuerter og Madlavningen Ombord [Our Stewards and Cooking On Board], *Norges Sjøfartstidende*, 30 July, 1.

Harboe-Ree, Anders & Bull, Henrik Johan. (1995). The Diary of Captain Anders Harboe-Ree, translated from Norwegian by Eva and Cathrine Harboe-Ree, *RePublica: The New Land Lies Before Us*, Sydney: Angus & Robertson, 2, 1–14.

Johansen, Per Ole. (2013). The Norwegian Alcohol Prohibition: A Failure, *Journal of Scandinavian Studies in Criminology and Crime Prevention*, 14(suppl.), 46–63.

Kaalaas, Baard. (1911a). Bryophyten aus den Crozetinseln I [Bryophytes of the Crozet Islands I], *Nyt Magazin for Naturvidenskaberne [New Magazine for Nature Scientists]*, 49(6), 82–98.

Kaalaas, Baard. (1911b). Bryophyten aus den Crozetinseln II [Bryophytes of the Crozet Islands II], *Nyt Magazin for Naturvidenskaberne [New Magazine for Nature Scientists]*, 50, 97–119.

Lewis, Miles. (2003). The Dome, *La Trobe Journal*, 72(Spring), 43.

Mäenpää, Sari. (2016). Sailors and Their Pets: Men and Their Companion Animals Aboard Early Twentieth-century Finnish Sailing Ships, *The International Journal of Maritime History*, 28(3), 480–495.

McConville, Andrew. (2007). Henrik Bull, the Antarctic Committee and the First Confirmed Landing on the Antarctic Continent, *Polar Record*, 43, 143–153. doi: 10.1017/S0032247407006109.

Pearson, Michael, Zarankin, Andres & Salerno, Melisa A. (2020). Exploring and Exploiting Antarctica: The Early Human Interactions, *Past Antarctica: Paleoclimatology and Climate Change*. Cambridge, Massachusetts: Academic Press, 259–278. https://doi.org/10.1016/C2018-0-02237-9, accessed 27-11-2022.

Ring, Theodor, P.A. (1923), The Elephant Seals of Kerguelen Land, *Proceedings of the Zoological Society of London*, 93(2), 431–443.

Rubin, Jeff. (2003). Train Oil and Snotters, *The Journal of Food and Culture*, 3(1), 37.

Sjøfartskontoret, Det Kongelige Departement for Handel, Sjøfart og Industri [Maritime Office, The Royal Ministry of Trade, Shipping and Industry]. (1909). Concerning S/S 'Solglimt' (M.C.T.W) of Kristiania, *Journal*, 841, 1–30.

MONOGRAPHS

Brown, Stephen R. (2012). *The Last Viking: The life of Roald Amundsen*. Boston: Merloyd Lawrence.

Bryhn, Birger J., Schyberg, T., & Oestmoen, O.T. (1953). *Round the World with 'Ho- Ho'*, translated from Norwegian by Joan Wright. London: Geoffrey Bles.

Bull, Henrik Johan. (1896). *The Cruise of the* Antarctic *to the South Polar Regions*. London: Edward Arnold.

Carroll, Lewis. (1986). *Alice Through the Looking Glass and What Alice Found There*. London: Victor Gollancz.

Cavafy, Constantine P. (1975). *C.P. Cavafy: Collected poems*. Princeton, NJ: Princeton University Press.

Church, Ian. (1985). *Survival on the Crozet Islands*. Waikanae, New Zealand: The Heritage Press.

Cooper, John, & Avery, G., eds. (1986). *Historic Sites at the Prince Edward Islands*. South African National Scientific Programmes Report No.128. Pretoria: Foundation for Research Development, Council for Scientific and Industrial Research.

Cooper, John, ed. (2010). *Marion & Prince Edward: Africa's Southern Islands*. Stellenbosch, South Africa: Sun Press.

Crawford, Allan B. (1982). *Tristan Da Cunha and the Roaring Forties*. Cape Town: David Philip.

Drivenes, Einar-Arne & Jølle, Harald Dag, eds. (2006). *Into the Ice: The History of Norway and the Polar Regions*. Oslo: Gyldendal Akademisk.

Evjenth, Håkon. (1938). *Gutten Som Norge Glemt [The Boy Norway Forgot]*. Oslo: Gyldendal Forlag.

Galteland, Odd. (2013). *A/S Kerguelen 1908–1921: The Optimism, the Dreams – and the Dull Working Day*. Commander Chr. Christensen's Whaling Museum, Publication No. 34. Sandefjord: Vestfoldmuseene.

Gilbert, Jack. (2005). *Refusing Heaven*. New York: Alfred A. Knopf.

Goodridge, Charles Medyett. (1838). *Narrative of a Voyage to the South Seas, and the Shipwreck of the Princess of Wales Cutter, with an Account of a Two Years' Residence on an Uninhabited Island, by Charles Medyett Goodridge, One of the Survivors*. Exeter, England: W.C. Featherstone.

Graham, Tom A. (1989). *Cultural Resource Management of the Prince Edward Island*. Honours thesis. University of Cape Town. Unpublished.

Haisman, Sylvie. (2010). *This Barren Rock: 1875 A True Tale of Shipwreck and Survival in the Southern Seas*. Pymble, N.S.W.: Harper Collins Publishers Australia.

Harboe-Ree, Anders & Bull, Henrik Johan. (2023). *Diary of the 1906–1907 Voyage of HNMS* Cathrine *of Tønsberg, Including Descriptions of the Shipwreck and Life as Castaways on the Crozet Islands*, translated from Norwegian and edited by Eva Harboe-Ree, Cathrine Harboe-Ree and Anna Ree Cutler. Melbourne: Australian Scholarly Publishing.

Hänel, Christine & Chown, Steven. (1998). *An Introductory Guide to the Marion and Prince Edward Island Special Nature Reserves: 50 Years After Annexation*. Pretoria: Department of Environmental Affairs and Tourism.

Headland, Robert K. (1989). *Chronological List of Antarctic Expeditions and Related Historical Events*. Cambridge: Cambridge University Press.

Headland, Robert K. (2009). *A Chronology of Antarctic Exploration*. London: Quaritch.

Homer. (1996). *The Odyssey*. Translated by Robert Fagles. New York: Penguin.

Huntford, Roland. (1997). *Nansen: The Explorer as Hero*. London: Abacus.

Huntley, Brian J. (2016). *Exploring a Sub-Antarctic Wilderness: A Personal Narrative of the First Biological & Geological Expedition to Marion and Prince Edward Islands 1965/1966*. Stellenbosch: Antarctic Legacy of South Africa.

Kristensen, Leonard. (1896). Journal of the Right-whaling Cruise of the Norwegian Steamship '*Antarctic*', in South Polar Seas Under the Command of Captain Leonard Kristensen During the Years 1894–5. *Transactions of the Royal Geographical Society of Australasia*, Victorian Branch, 12–13, 74–100.

Lansing, Alfred. (1959). *Endurance: Shackleton's Incredible Voyage*. New York: McGraw-Hill.

Larsen, Karen. (1950). *A History of Norway*. New York: Princeton University Press for the American-Scandinavian Foundation.

Magnusson, Magnus. (2016). *The Vikings*. Stroud, Gloucestershire: The History Press.

Marsh, John H. (1948). *No Pathway Here*. Cape Town: Howard B. Timmins for Hodder Stoughton.

Martin, Stephen. (1996). *A History of Antarctica*. Sydney: State Library of New South Wales Press.

McCann, Joy. (2018). *Wild Sea: A history of the Southern Ocean*. Sydney: NewSouth.

McConville, Andrew. (2022). *In Search of the Last Continent: Australia and Early Antarctic Exploration.* North Melbourne: Australian Scholarly Publishing.

Michener, E. (Ted) A. (2015). *Ice in the Rigging: Ships of the Antarctic, 1699–1937.* Hobart: Maritime Museum of Tasmania.

Nordahl, Bernard. (1898). *Framgutterne: Tre Aar Gjennem Skrugar og Nat [The* Fram *Boys: Three Years Through Ice Ridges and Night].* Kristiania: Edv. Magnussens.

Pearson, Michael, Zarankin, Andres & Salerno, Melisa A. (2023). *Archaeology in Antarctica.* Milton Park, Oxfordshire: Routledge.

The Sagas of the Icelanders: A Selection. (1997). New York: Penguin Books.

Sancton, Julian. (2021). *Madhouse at the End of the World: The* Belgica*'s Journey into the Dark Antarctic Night.* London: WH Allen.

Scot, Elizabeth. (1801). *Alonzo and Cora, with Other Original Poems, Principally Elegaic.* Edinburgh: Bunney and Gold.

Shackleton, Ernest. (1920). *South: The story of Shackleton's Last Expedition 1914–1917.* London: William Heinemann.

Shakespeare, William. (1990). *The Tempest.* London: Oxford University Press.

Speculum Regale Kunungs Skuggsja [The King's Mirror]. (1917). Translated from Old Norse by Laurence Marcellus Larson. New York, The American Scandinavian Foundation. London: Oxford University Press.

Stoddart, Michael. (2017). *Tassie's Whale Boys: Whaling in Antarctic Waters.* Hobart: Forty South Publishing.

Tennyson, Lord Alfred. (1842). *Poems.* London: Edward Moxon.

Terauds, Aleks, et al. (2010). *Marion and Prince Edward Islands: Africa's Southern Island.* Stellenbosch: Sun Press.

Tilman, Harold William. (1961). *Mischief Among the Penguins.* London: Rupert Hart-Davis.

Tønnessen, Johan Nicolay & Johnsen, Arne Odd. (1982). *The History of Modern Whaling,* translated from Norwegian by R.I. Christophersen. London: C. Hurst and Company and Canberra: Australian National University Press.

Van Niekerk, Tara Rae. (2016). *An Archaeological Study of the* Solglimt *Shipwreck Survivor Camp on Sub-Antarctic Marion Island.* Master's thesis. University of South Africa. Unpublished.

ACKNOWLEDGEMENTS

A book that is more than thirty years in the making is helped along the way by many people, too many to identify individually, but all of whom I thank. Nonetheless there are many people I would like to thank individually.

My cousin from the Faeroe Islands, Anders Harboe-Ree, sent the *Cathrine* diary and other original material to Australia, thus starting the journey, and the editor George Papaellinas published excerpts from the diary and first prompted me to consider a book.

From Monash University: Lynette Russell connected me with the South African researchers; Graeme Davison encouraged and supported the creation of this book and settled me down when I struggled; John Crossley applied his eagle eye to the manuscript; the Research Connections history group provided collegial support; the School of Philosophical, Historical and International Studies provided a base for me in the University following my retirement; and, the University's librarians did their best to fast-track my research skills.

The South Africans, led initially by John Cooper and then by Jaco Boshoff, generously shared information about their research. Advisors in Norway, especially Stig Tore Lunde from the Vestfold Museum, and Peter Rutherford, resolved specialist translation queries and provided valuable historical information. In Australia, Rodney Clarke and Michael Pearson clarified nautical and Antarctic terms and facts. My friend Doone Robertson helped with editing and was the book's constant cheer leader, and Peter Dann was both the critic it needed and an invaluable technical maestro.

Closer to home: my father, Mons Harboe-Ree, handed the baton to me and fired my imagination; my mother, Eva Harboe-Ree, spent many enjoyable hours with me translating the *Cathrine* diary and other documents; my brother, Henrik Harboe-Ree, pursued innumerable inquiries and solved translation conundrums; my daughter, Anna Ree Cutler, was a wonderful editor and composed songs about her great grandfather's adventures; and, my daughter, Karolina Ree Cutler, will doubtless add her harmonies.

Nick Walker and the team at Australian Scholarly Publishing brought the project to a very pleasing conclusion.

Finally, my husband, Brian Cutler, has always provided the wind in my sails.

www.ingramcontent.com/pod-product-compliance
Lightning Source LLC
Chambersburg PA
CBHW021243060726
47590CB00005B/1880